ART AND SOCIETY
in ROMAN BRITAIN

ART AND
SOCIETY
in ROMAN
BRITAIN

J E N N I F E R   L A I N G

SUTTON PUBLISHING LIMITED

First published in 1997 by
Sutton Publishing Limited · Phoenix Mill
Thrupp · Stroud · Gloucestershire · GL5 2BU

British Library Cataloguing in Publication Data
A catalogue record for this book is available from the British Library.

ISBN 0-7509-0895-5

 TM ALAN SUTTON™ and SUTTON™ are the
trade marks of Sutton Publishing Limited

Typeset in 11/14 pt Bembo.
Typesetting and origination by
Sutton Publishing Limited.
Printed in Great Britain by
Butler & Tanner, Frome, Somerset.

CONTENTS

LIST OF ILLUSTRATIONS

INTRODUCTION

From the sixteenth century to the present day, Roman Britain has interested antiquaries, classical scholars and the general public. As a result, it is arguably the most extensively studied province of the Roman Empire: more is probably known about the Roman period in the British Isles than about any other time prior to the sixteenth century. Data retrieval methods in the past two decades in particular have made it one of the most exciting and dynamic areas for study in the archaeological repertoire.

Serious scholarly interest in Roman Britain began with William Camden in the sixteenth century, and was continued by eighteenth-century investigators such as Stukeley, Horsley and General Roy into the mainstream of nineteenth- and early twentieth-century historical thinking. Interest in these scholars first attracted me to the subject. The province was attractive to classical scholars in particular because the existence of both written records and standing remains allowed firm conclusions to be drawn about material. Inevitably the viewpoints were entrenchedly classical. It is only during the past twenty years that attention has been focused on the social and economic functioning of the province.

The study of Romano-British art is also relatively new. Its modern attraction lies in its theoretical capacity for enhancing the understanding of society as a whole. Many of the questions and answers it provides are of particular relevance to modern society in which a comparable diversity of cultures are interacting.

Art can show the degree to which the native Celtic peoples reacted to Roman values. In some cases the values were genuinely assimilated, and in others modified. Art can show the extent to which native traditions survived – contemporaneous writings and inscriptions are generally silent on this topic. Romano-British art demonstrates the cosmopolitan character of the population and reflects the way Romano-Britons saw themselves at different periods, in different areas, and on different social levels. The art provides insights into the processes of patronage, into technology and trade, and shows how people felt about their beliefs.

The very reasons that make Romano-British art attractive today brought it the disinterest of early scholars. Roman art has traditionally been regarded as the poor relation of Greek, so the Romano-British version was deemed doubly unworthy of scholarly concern since it was produced in the most far-flung province, and embraced diverse 'impure' influences. With the data retrieval methods open to them, the early antiquaries failed to understand the nature of native provincial cultures and therefore regarded Romano-British art as crude or insipid, and generally dismissed it as a travesty

Iron Age coins showing Roman influence, from Edmund Gibson's edition of Camden's Britannia, *1695.*

of classical ideals.[1] So great was the anti-'barbarian' feeling among early antiquaries that when examples of Anglo-Saxon gold and garnet work were discovered in Kent, they were regarded by most scholars as Roman, since it went without saying that non-Roman cultures could not possibly have attained such feats of artistic and technological achievement. The shock of discovering that barbarians could produce and had produced such superb items took many decades to settle down into scholarly acceptance.[2] Its aftermath is still with us insofar as for practical reasons, curricula tend to focus on either barbarian or classical studies.

Most of the studies of the development of antiquarian thought in Britain have concentrated on prehistoric archaeology, yet the investigation of Roman Britain has been equally important in the growing awareness of the past. It was not happenchance that the Elizabethan William Camden (1551–1623) called his pioneering survey of the antiquities of Britain *Britannia* – his purpose was to describe the antiquities of Britain based on the tribal areas of Britannia, and, in the words of Abraham Ortelius, 'to restore Britain to Antiquity, and Antiquity to Britain'.[3] Along the way Camden saw fit to comment on local family history and more recent monuments supplementary to his main goal.

Among his achievements was a survey of the Romano-British inscriptions that attracted his attention. The edition of his work published in 1607 listed almost eighty from the north, and other remains which caught his eye, including the traces of streets visible in Richborough, the discovery of a statue of Commodus as Hercules in Wensleydale,[4] as well as an account of Romano-British coins. Camden was also a pioneer of archaeological illustration – the 1600 edition of his work contained a plate showing Romano-British altars and a map of Roman Britain. Later editions, such as Gibson's of 1696, were even more lavishly illustrated.

The progress of Romano-British studies is reflected in the rate of recognition of mosaic pavements. In the seventeenth century only a few were known; by the late eighteenth century the total had risen to around a hundred. The mid-nineteenth century saw a flurry of discovery and of the 600 or so now known, more than a half have been found since 1880, and over a hundred of them since the Second World War.[5]

John Aubrey, in his *Monumenta Britannica*, as well as looking at such field monuments as Roman forts, devoted a chapter to 'Roman pavements'. His contemporary Christopher Wren thought that the Romans did not use marble floors in Britain because of the climate, and recorded that one Seth Ward had caught a cold from dining at Ham House, which had a marble floor.[6] Aubrey recorded how a pavement was discovered near Bath:

> In the middle of the Floor was a Blew bird (not well proportioned) and in each of the four Angles . . . a knott.
>
> When a large number of people came to see it, the farmer covered it up, but he could not cover it so soon, but the people had torn-up almost all the work before I came thither to see it but his daughter-in-lawe hath described the whole floor with her needle in . . . stitch.[7]

The work of collecting and recording details of Romano-British remains, and inscriptions in particular, was continued by a series of worthy successors. Three figures in particular stand out, all of whom lived in the eighteenth century. The first was John Horsley, who was born in 1684 in Northumberland and educated there and at Edinburgh University before becoming presbyterian minister of Morpeth. The proximity of his school to Hadrian's Wall probably first prompted his interest in Roman remains, which bore fruit in the form of *Britannia Romana*, first published in 1732 after his death. About this magnificent work R.G. Collingwood, the earlier twentieth-century doyen of Romano-British studies, wrote: 'To John Horsley still belongs the glory of having written the one exhaustive work on Roman Britain.' Sir Frank Haverfield also felt compelled to write in 1907 that it was 'till quite lately the best and most scholarly account of any Roman province that had been written anywhere in Europe'.[8] Of the many achievements of Horsley's work perhaps the most

Roman inscribed slabs from North Britain, from John Horsley's Britannia Romana, *1732.*

enduring was to be found in the second part of his book – a catalogue, with translation and interpretation, of the inscriptions found in Britain. This remained the standard reference work until Collingwood and Wright's *Roman Inscriptions of Britain*, vol. I, appeared in 1965. Horsley illustrated a number of works of Romano-British art, though for him their artistic merit was of secondary importance to their historical interest. He provided a systematic account of Hadrian's Wall, with useful maps of the

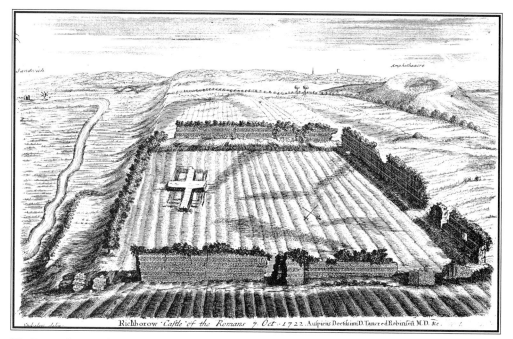

The Roman fort at Richborough, Kent, from William Stukeley's Itinerarium Curiosum, *1726.*

various sections, and his data was plagiarized by Alexander Gordon in his account of the two Roman Walls, *Itinerarium Septentrionale*, which appeared in 1726 before Horsley had completed his own book.[9]

The second great Romano-British scholar was William Stukeley (1687–1765), whose fame perhaps rests more in his work on Stonehenge and Avebury and for the way he established druids in the folklore of British history. But Stukeley was an indefatigable recorder of Roman remains, and his *Itinerarium Curiosum* (1726) was a remarkable series of tours round Roman Britain, following wherever possible the Roman roads. It combined astute observation with personal anecdote.[10] Among Stukeley's early perceptive observations was that the Car Dyke in Lincolnshire was probably a Roman canal used to transport corn from Cambridgeshire northwards.[11] Later in life Stukeley's early reputation for careful scholarship was marred when he was taken in not only by the forged map of Roman Britain supposedly by a medieval monk called Richard of Cirencester,[12] but also by a number of other absurdities concerning British kings and about Oriuna, the supposed wife of Carausius (actually a misreading of FORTUNA on a coin).

In 1722 Stukeley formed a club for the study of the antiquities of Roman Britain, which he called the 'Society of Roman Knights'. Its constitution laid down that it was to include both sexes. The members assumed appropriate names – the Duchess of

Hertford was elected as Bonduca (i.e. Boudicca), while Stukeley's future wife was Cartismandua.[13]

The third eighteenth-century figure was the founder of the Ordnance Survey, General William Roy, who directed the Highland Survey in 1747–55 following the Jacobite rebellions. He prepared accurate plans of Roman forts in North Britain for the *Military Antiquities of the Romans in North Britain*, which was completed in 1773 and published posthumously twenty years later. It remains a model of archaeological survey and draughtsmanship.[14]

The concern shown by the eighteenth-century antiquaries for the military antiquities and history of Roman Britain set the tone for most Romano-British studies down to the later twentieth century. Despite Renaissance appreciation of Roman art, and the efforts of eighteenth-century dilettantes such as Winckelmann[15] to focus on classical art, the artistic remains in Britain were mostly recorded without real evaluation.

In the last years of the eighteenth century and throughout the nineteenth three scholars in particular stimulated the study of Roman Britain – the first was Samuel Lysons, whose meticulous drawings of Romano-British mosaics are still used in preference to photographs, particularly where the original mosaics are now considerably damaged. Lysons drew only what was there, and on the rare occasions when he reconstructed missing parts, he based it on sound evidence and always indicated clearly that which was conjectural. Lysons was responsible for the recording of the mosaics of some of the major villas of Roman Britain – his report on Woodchester was published in 1797. It was followed by *Reliquiae Britannico Romanae* (1813–17) which included Frampton, Horkstow and the villa at Bignor, Sussex, where the mosaics are protected by quaint thatched sheds that date back to the original discovery and are themselves listed buildings. During the nineteenth century Frampton and Bignor attracted considerable attention in Britain, probably because taste for the antique had been fanned by the mid-eighteenth century investigations at Pompeii and Herculaneum in Italy.

The second nineteenth-century antiquary was Charles Roach Smith (1806–90), who started out as a minor retail chemist but whose success in business enabled him to pursue his antiquarian studies. He was an indefatigable collector and publisher of minor antiquities, and began the systematic study of the remains of London, culminating in *Illustrations of Roman London* (1859), which was rich in sensitive observations about Romano-British art. Disappointed by the lack of illustration and prolix discussion in *Archaeologia*, the journal of the Society of Antiquaries, he launched his own publication, *Collectanea Antiqua*, and together with Thomas Wright, the excavator of Wroxeter, instituted the British Archaeological Association in 1843.[16] The first volume of their journal published the bronze head of Hadrian from the Thames (page 126). Roach Smith went a long way to ensure the careful recording and appraisal of Romano-British antiquities, and along with a number of other scholars, such as John Yonge Akerman, whose *Coins of the Romans Relating to Britain* (1844) is still a pioneer work, revived the eighteenth-century tradition of careful scholarship. The third nineenth-century antiquary to make a major contribution to Romano-British studies was John Collingwood Bruce (1805–92), who focused his attention on Hadrian's Wall and on the inscriptions of Roman Britain that Horsley had begun to interpret. Collingwood Bruce's classic work was the *Handbook of the Roman Wall*, first published in 1863, which has the distinction of having been repeatedly reprinted with revisions at regular intervals subsequently, and which is still available today.

In the twentieth century the study of Roman Britain and its art entered a new era, ushered in by Sir George Macdonald, the Curles (Alexander and James), Sir Frank Haverfield and R.G. Collingwood, and continued by equally distinguished scholars such as Eric Birley, S.S. Frere and, as far as Romano-British art was concerned, Jocelyn Toynbee. A scholarly evaluation (predominantly pro-classical) of twentieth-century trends has been provided by Martin Henig.[17]

This book is intended to bring together in outline, as far as possible, the considerable body of material now available on Romano-British art, in a reasonably accessible form for students, teachers and the general reader. I wish to thank, most warmly, J. Blath for unparalleled help with the production of the text. The notes are not meant to suggest that this is an academic work, rather to point the novice in the direction of source material.

CHAPTER ONE

THE DEVELOPMENT OF ROMANO–BRITISH ART

Classical and barbarian art were fundamentally opposed in their aims and, as a result, if each is judged in terms of the other, by definition neither can be successful. This conflict of intention produced some exciting and dynamic artistic results of exceptional interest to modern observers. With the increased focus on Celtic studies, it is possible to view Romano-British art as a seminal lesson in the ability of two totally different and opposing cultures to find a harmony of purpose. As sociological phenomena, even the aesthetically unsatisfactory items have exceptional value.

Classical art was concerned with two key elements: the imitation of nature and the pursuit of the ideal (often expressed in terms of the human form). Symbolism and symmetry were subordinate features to be taken for granted rather than given artistic prominence. The realistic images displayed in Imperial State Art (page 16) are the embodiment of this aim.

In direct contrast, the most prominent feature of barbarian art was symbolism. Pre-Roman Celtic artists were in general not concerned with naturalism, nor had they any concept of the pursuit of a 'classical' ideal. Celtic artists would have regarded their achievements as lying in the almost musical abstraction of the balance and tension of the design. For such barbarian cultures the artist's aim was to express concepts before exact images. Barbarian art used symmetry, but less as mirror imagery and more as a harmonious balance. It was rarely naturalistic or realistic, preferring to express the essence of the subject rather than slavishly copying nature. To confuse the issue further, Roman civilization adopted much from the provinces it enveloped, becoming increasingly different from its Greek and Etruscan origins.

THE ARTISTS

When the two opposing artistic traditions met in Britain, the results in each ranged from the inept to the exquisite. In between lay a huge variety of styles and influences executed by artists, trained and untrained, with a diversity of patrons and an even greater variety of purposes and aspirations. One of the few general statements that can be made is that there was no single, Roman-British art style.

As might be imagined, the purest classical works have been found more often in the most highly-Romanized areas, notably in major towns and in villas. A study of the art from the small towns of Roman Britain has suggested that it was limited in quantity and mostly comprised small portable items such as gemstones.[1] Towns with military origins and walled towns have correspondingly greater quantities of classically-inspired art, whereas unwalled towns have a greater proportion of depictions of native deities.[2]

The dissociation of the Empire with Britannia in the early fifth century meant that new influences came from other barbarian cultures from the Continent (for example, Angles, Saxons, Jutes, Suebians, Frisians) and the purely classical elements were submerged. It is interesting to note that when the classical and barbarian cultures met once more in the late sixth/early seventh century, after the adoption of Christianity by the southern Anglo-Saxon kingdoms, the artists easily assimilated both

Stone head, supposedly of Maponus, from Corbridge, Northumberland. Height: 17.78 cm (Drawing: L. Laing)

barbarian and classical elements. This facility for assimilation was arguably in part the result of the foundations laid in the Roman period.

Although the names of some Roman artists have survived, and the best work was much admired and commanded huge prices, artists were seen as skilled craftspeople. Their task was not to make personal statements, nor statements about the society in which they lived: they executed commissions in line with the requirements and wealth of the patrons. Since much art was symbolic and religious, it is possible that the skill of the artist was of secondary importance to the execution of the former.

The works of good, bad and indifferent artists have survived at random, and in evaluating a work of Romano-British art the scholar must decide whether the appearance of the work was intentional or not. Some surviving naturalistic Celtic sculptures of the human form, for example, appear particularly crude, but they may be unfinished, or perhaps intended to be clothed. The head of a native god from Corbridge, Northumberland, is a good example of the former.

In some cases, artists continued working in the traditional framework, applying the decoration in a traditional manner to new types of artefact. Where the media were new or unfamiliar to native artists (naturalistic bronze figurines, stone sculpture or wall paintings, for example), it is extremely likely that there was no thought in the artist's mind that the interpretation should be other than in line with the Roman models. Rich patrons living in villas or fine town houses would presumably commission such works in order to demonstrate that they were cultured Romans, not natives still proud of their anti-Roman past. Purely classical commissions must therefore be assumed in the first instance to have at least partly a political impetus. Purely Celtic-inspired works, especially in areas known to be hostile (for example the northern border zones) may equally have a political tale to tell. In the Romanized areas the amalgam of styles points to the slow and piecemeal manner in which the province adopted new European outlooks.

The conditions under which artists and craftspeople worked remain elusive. There is comparatively little evidence for the manufacture of even minor works of art in Roman Britain. The wealth of moulds, crucibles and slags that have survived from Dark Age Celtic Britain are generally absent in the Roman period.

Different moulding techniques were employed by the Romans – *ciré perdue* casting (by which a wax model was cased in clay then heated and the molten wax allowed to run out when the metal was poured in) was used for complex castings of statuettes and other items, and had been in use since the Copper Age in the Near East. Piece moulds (usually bivalve) such as were employed at Prestatyn, Clwyd, used a variety of materials to form the original impression on the moulds (page 138).

That sophisticated casting of figurines was carried out in Britain is apparent from the fragments of clay moulds from Gestingthorpe, Essex, which appear to be for a figure of a nude youth, probably Bacchus.[3] The site may have been a temple at which a local smith sold his wares.

The makers of wall paintings and mosaic floors have left virtually no evidence of their lives, although there is more evidence for artistic endeavour from the towns than from the countryside.

CELTIC ART IN BRITAIN

Before the Roman conquest, Celtic art already shared a number of common elements with classical art, even though these were often manifested in what appear at first sight to be diametrically opposed ways. Since its inception in the La Tène Iron Age of Europe, Celtic art had borrowed from classical art without in any way being constrained by it.

In the latter part of the British Iron Age, an insular tradition of art flourished which, while reflecting Continental trends, followed its own lines from the third century BC onwards. This Insular Celtic art was primarily employed in the decoration of the status symbols of Iron Age warrior society (weaponry and armour, items of personal adornment and the like), or items made to honour the gods, but on occasion it was used in simplified form to decorate utilitarian objects such as pots, buckets or even tool handles. The Roman conquest removed the traditional patronage for this art by depriving the Celtic aristocracy of their strength in warfare, and except outside the area of Roman control the production of combat equipment came to an end. The British artists' feel for design did not.

In the early first century AD Roman art increasingly made an impact on Celtic society, simply because decorated objects were often among the first to be traded, after raw materials. Imports from the Roman world were increasing, and Caesar's campaigns emphasized the divide between the Roman-influenced south-east and the periphery. A common cultural province grew up on both sides of the Channel, with similar types of pottery, burial rites and trade goods. There is evidence that many Celtic tribes dealt directly with the Roman world. Writing at the time of the first Roman emperor, Augustus, Strabo records a substantial list of Britain's exports and imports.[4]

After a period of uncertainty around the beginning of the Christian era, the political situation stabilized. Rich burials at Colchester (Essex), and from the Welwyn area (Herts) and outlying districts, show the extent to which the Celtic chiefs were Romanized around the time of the Roman conquest. The graves contained, among other things, imports of silver Augustan cups[5] and bronze statuettes manufactured in Gaul to Roman taste.[6]

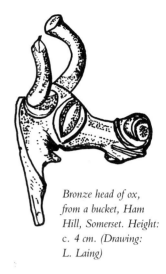

Bronze head of ox, from a bucket, Ham Hill, Somerset. Height: c. 4 cm. (Drawing: L. Laing)

Patterns on Iron Age mirrors: (a) Colchester, Essex; (b) Birdlip, Glos.; (c) Holcombe, Devon. (Drawing: Cilla Wild)

It was probably a growing familiarity with naturalistic Roman art that led around this time to the production of a variety of small votive animals such as the boars from Hounslow, Middlesex and elsewhere.[7] Ox heads also started to be used at this time as decorative escutcheons for buckets[8] and other objects such as firedogs persisted into the Roman period.[9] The full extent to which Roman and native elements were blended in the late first century BC/early first century AD can be seen in the hoard from Crownthorpe, Norfolk, which contains British versions of Augustan two-handled cups, surmounted with enchanting ducks in three-dimensional style.[10]

CELTIC ORNAMENTAL SURVIVALS

Although rich patrons apparently preferred Roman styles after the conquest of AD 43, most of the population still had a taste for Celtic ornamental styles which manifested themselves not on major and expensive items but on smaller items of personal adornment and, on occasion, on objects used about the home. This phenomenon reinforces the view that initially the Roman conquest was essentially a take-over from the top. It also reflects the fact that Celtic art was essentially design used to decorate objects, rather than the production of objects that were works of art *per se*.

Several types of Celtic ornament survived strongly into the Roman period, and probably indicate social continuity on a relatively humble level. The most easily identifiable is Brigantian metalwork of the northern frontier areas (pages 154–5), casket ornament of the south-east, leaf and pellet designs and a kind of 'Art Nouveau'.

Casket Ornament

This art form was very different from the purely classical and survived in south-east England. It shows an interesting amalgam of Roman and Celtic motifs. It is best represented on a series of die-stamped metal mounts for caskets, scabbards, brooches, shields, couches, collars, bracelets, mirrors, tankards, buckets and other objects.[11] Slender-stemmed trumpets (common among the Celts) are a feature of the style, with motifs such as the 'berried rosette' and the 'swash-N' (a motif which is also found on enamelled seal box lids and other typically Romano-British objects). Die-stamping originated in the pre-Roman period – there is a die from North Creake, Norfolk, with a triskele (a three-legged design beloved by the Celts), in the traditions of the Snettisham torc workshops.[12]

Examples of the style come from a diversity of findspots, ranging from the Roman town of Silchester, Hants, to the druidic votive deposit at Llyn Cerrig Bach on Anglesey. It was current in the late first century, as attested by Roman finds from Newstead, Roxburgh, and was still being produced in the fourth century, as witnessed by the finds from Lydney, Glos. The finest example is from Elmswell, South Humberside, and takes the form of a mount with lyre scroll combined with berried

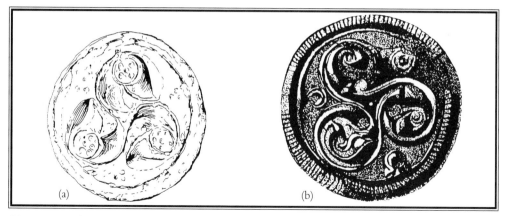

(a) Iron Age die from North Creake, Norfolk; (b) Romano-British disc brooch from Silchester, Hants.
(Drawings: (a) Caroline Bevan; (b) Tasha Guest)

rosettes and palmettes. Juxtaposed is an enamelled panel with Roman ivy scroll probably borrowed from Samian pottery or metalwork.[13]

The lyre scroll (without the rosettes), appears on a strip from Great Tower Street, London,[14] while another from Dowgate Hill in the same city has trumpets.[15] Rosettes appear on a mirror from a hoard from Balmacellan, Kirkcudbright,[16] which also displays slender trumpet patterns. The flat handle is unlike any found on Iron Age mirrors, but is perforated with a simple triskele. Its shape is too close to that of first-century circular-pierced Roman paterae handles of the first century AD to be fortuitous.

From the second century onwards the style is found on disc brooches (page 90). Many of those have triskeles which are also found on another type of disc brooch with a mainly southern distribution in which a triskele is left in reserve against an enamelled ground.[17]

A now-lost plaque from Moel Hirradug, Clwyd, was produced by hammering on to a die made with a wooden model. The style was shallow but angular and the ornament featured a broken-backed triskele in a diamond. The plaque was found with shield mounts in a small hoard buried at the bottom of the ditch of an Iron Age fort, and is likely to have been part of a smith's hoard of the later first (or more probably second) century AD.[18]

The Meyrick helmet is named after a collector in the north of England, and is in the British Museum. It is an important piece in the study of Romano-British art, since it is a Celtic version of a Roman auxiliary helmet, with conical cap and neck-guard. Originally it had side pieces, now very fragmentary, and both side pieces and neck-guard were decorated in relief casket ornament. The Roman numeral II is scratched on

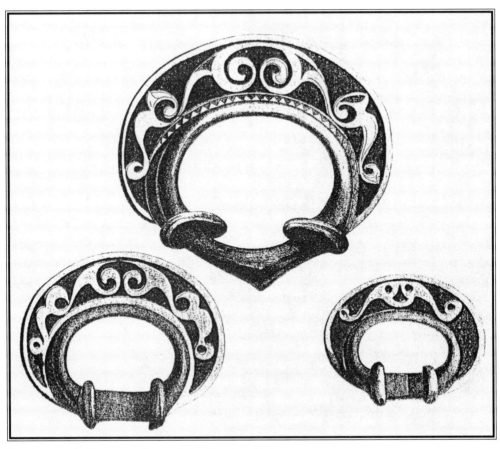

Iron Age enamelled horse terrets, from a nineteenth-century drawing.

the helmet, perhaps suggesting it saw some service on the head of an auxiliary in the Roman army in the later first century AD.[19]

Leaf and Pellet Designs

The leaf-and-pellet (or leaf-and-void) designs that had been used in Iron Age Britain on the eve of the Roman Conquest continued to be used as decorative devices for dress fasteners.[20] It has been pointed out that where they occur in the south, some types of button-and-loop dress fasteners are evidence for surviving native traditions, but, perversely, the same fasteners beyond the frontiers in North Britain appear to represent the impact of Rome.[21]

The same motif was employed on various items of horse gear produced in north Britain, some of which saw service in the Roman army – there are finds from Newstead, Roxburgh, and Corbridge. The related petal-and-boss motif is well

Bronze mount with enamel in 'casket style', from Elmswell, South Humberside. Width: 24 cm. (Drawing: Tasha Guest)

displayed too on a series of bridle bits, the finest examples of which also include enamelling, such as one from Rise, South Humberside.[22]

Art Nouveau

The remaining examples of Romano-Celtic art may be termed 'Art Nouveau'. This tradition employed two ornamental devices – the large stud and the broken-backed scroll – to great effect. The starting point is represented by the Trawsfynydd (Gwynedd) tankard, which is usually, but possibly erroneously, considered to be of pre-Conquest date[23], and which is the finest of a series of such vessels which were certainly being produced from the Iron Age into the Roman period. They are more commonly represented by their handles, though actual tankards such as this one occasionally survive.[24]

The kind of triskele with large central boss that appears in openwork on the Trawsfynydd tankard also appears on a Roman dragonesque brooch from Lakenheath, Suffolk,[25] and on a variety of other objects produced in the Roman period. In the same ornamental tradition is the Mortonhall scabbard from Midlothian,[26] and the Stichill collar from Roxburghshire.[27]

Dragonesque fibula from Lakenheath, Suffolk; second century AD. Enlarged. (Drawing: Cilla Wild)

This magnificent piece has die-stamped swash-N foils with small bosses at the terminals but engraved or tooled decoration on the side and nape sections, displaying running scrolls with bosses. It is closely related to a series of collars from the south-west of England, such as that from Wraxhall, Somerset, which has running scrolls and settings for now-lost glass studs; and one from Portland, Dorset.[28] A related necklet which combines elements of both the beaded torcs and the collars has recently been found at Dinnington, South Yorks.[29]

IMPERIAL STATE ART

Totally different in style and aims from native Celtic art, Imperial State art was contemporaneous classical art at its best. It would therefore have posed the greatest challenge to native artists trying to please pro-Roman patrons. Arguably all produced abroad, relatively few examples survive from Britain, and their most important functions are now perhaps in dating either the contexts in which they are found or other similar pieces. During the Roman period they would have provided the models and inspirations for both patrons and artists.

Before the Roman Conquest of Britain, the Augustan age had developed an art which looked back to classical Greece for its inspiration. Portraits were idealized; figures had flowing draperies; and formal foliage patterns were popular decorative devices. This type of art continued to the time of Claudius and was in essence propagandist – the best talent was used to serve the political end. A good example of this Julio-Claudian style is represented by the magnificent head of (possibly) Germanicus from Bosham Harbour, Chichester,[30] which may, however, be an eighteenth-century loss.

In AD 68, the Emperor Nero broke with tradition to have himself represented as a demigod who gazed upwards with the divinely inspired glance of Alexander the Great. This image (originally adopted by Hellenistic potentates) is projected in the bronze statue of the emperor from Coddenham, Suffolk (page 27).

The Flavian emperors (AD 69–98) started to look back to the 'warts and all' naturalism of the later Republic. The sculpture of Vespasian (AD 70–9) is somewhat transitional in style – although he went bald young, he was depicted with a fine head of hair.[31] Little major art that is distinctively Flavian has come to light in Britain, though one fine bust of a woman with Flavian hairstyle was found in Bath,[32] and there is an incomplete late first-century imported Mediterranean bust of a youth from Fishbourne, Sussex.[33]

Hadrian was an enthusiastic philhellene, and the second century is dominated by the fine commemorative monuments which record Imperial victories. Finely carved sarcophagi, high relief sculpture and scenes of state ceremonial were common, but their appearance in Britain is rare.

Marble bust of a youth, late first century AD, from Fishbourne, Sussex. Tip of chin to where tip of nose should be: 6.5 cm. (Sussex Archaeological Society)

 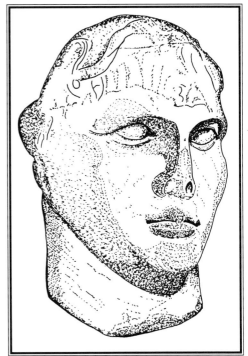

Bust with hairstyle of Salonina, wife of Gallienus, from York, mid-third century AD. Height: 27.94 cm. (Drawing: L. Laing)

Head of Constantine I, early fourth century AD, from York. Height: 45.73 cm. (Drawing: L. Laing)

During the third century, although some art adhered to traditional forms, political insecurity was often reflected in portraiture. Portraits of Philip I, for example, show a man deeply troubled and unsure about the future. Few major works in Britain can be assigned with any certainty to the period; the most characteristic is a bust found at Fishergate, York, which has features reminiscent of Salonina, the wife of Emperor Gallienus (AD 260–8).[34] Her head is slightly to one side, and she looks as though she is pondering some serious problem before commenting.

By the time of the Tetrarchy (AD 293–305), Imperial art had begun to display greater symbolism and an interest in the abstract. It has been argued that a growing concern with spiritualism, mysticism and abstraction were all features of Eastern art and thought. This was making an impact on the Roman world at the time, in particular through Christianity.[35] They were also features of Celtic art and there is no doubt that the trend was apparent in Romano-British art before Christianity became the official religion of the Empire. The changes seem to have grown out of the spiritual uncertainty that affected the Empire in the third century. At this time, there was no tradition of representational art in the Christian community, which felt that image-making was a pagan practice.

The new style is particularly manifest in Christian wallpaintings (page 38) which, although not created as propagandist State art, were none the less expressions of State attitudes from the fourth century on. In early Christian painting, symbolism was used to convey the essential message, and iconography grew increasingly complex in a trend towards conveying coded messages in set pieces.[36] Figures in fourth-century art became stiff and frontal, standing in serried ranks with stylized faces and draperies. Eyes were large to convey the essence of spirituality, and lighting emanated from the figures, rather than fell upon them.

DATING METHODS

Purely classical-style art in Britain has a further appeal to scholars since it can be useful in dating the contexts in which it is found. As a result of the diverse influences in Romano-British art, it is often extremely difficult to date an object in a purely native style unless there are some external clues. A large number of works of art from Roman Britain have been chance finds, without any associated objects that might help assign dates to them. A few, however, have come from archaeological contexts where their deposition, if not manufacture, can be dated. Some objects, for example, have come from hoards which also contained coins, as is the case with the Hoxne Treasure. Others have come from archaeological contexts sealed by other datable archaeological material, as was the case with the finds from the Temple of Mithras at Walbrook, London (pages 33–4). Without firm dates for works of art it is difficult to distinguish trends.

In the case of classically-inspired figure sculpture, female hairstyles in particular can be helpful since styles were subject to fairly frequent change. Usually it was the empress or other members of the Imperial household who set the fashion, and their portraits on coins no doubt helped to spread new styles rapidly through the provinces. By comparing busts with those on coins, female figures can frequently be assigned to a relatively close date bracket.

Men's facial hair can be definitive – for example, in the first century AD men were clean-shaven, but when Hadrian adopted a short Hellenic-style beard, facial hair became the norm for the second century. Hadrianic beards are short, those of the succeeding Antonine period are longer, and in the time of Marcus Aurelius and his successors, very curly. Under Philip I and some of the other emperors of the early third century, clean-shaven faces were again in vogue. Such changes are numerous but helpful in dating and each work of art needs to be considered on individual merit, particularly since, for example, iconographic tradition required that depictions of Jupiter and Neptune were always bearded while Apollo and Bacchus were always clean-shaven, regardless of prevailing fashion.

Details of dress can also help. Jewellery tended to be particularly copious in the fourth century. Thus the figure of Venus in a mosaic from Low Ham wears a type of body-chain fashionable in the fourth century, and represented in the Hoxne Treasure.[37]

If the works contain no such clues as to date, the techniques employed by the artists can help. Roman sculpture was painted, and in the early empire it was left to the painter to provide pupils for eyes, so that early Roman sculptures now appear blind. The introduction of sculpted pupils was a feature of the second century – although it had been tried in other media earlier, it made its appearance in sculpture in the reign of Hadrian (AD 117–38).[38] Portraiture in the time of the succeeding Antonine emperors (AD 138–92) employed techniques of drilling the hair and beard very deeply, creating a contrast with the smooth finish of the skin. Good examples of second-century sculpture are represented in the finds from Lullingstone villa, Kent (page 114).

A final method of arriving at date involves comparison of the work in question with others of known date. Imperial portrait busts are clearly useful for sculpted figures, but in other categories of art details of iconography and style can be compared.

ROMANO-BRITISH ART

The two opposing art-styles were adapted according to the patrons' wishes and needs. Thus very different types of artistic endeavour were produced for different contexts. Romano-British art was concerned with simplification, and with two-dimensional treatment rather than three. Romano-British artists seem to have favoured shallow

Hercules slaying the Hydra, from Corbridge, Northumberland. Second or third century AD. Height: 1.57 m. (Photo: L. Laing)

relief modelling to three-dimensional work.[39] Where classical art paid great attention to the modelling of anatomy in accordance with careful observation from nature, the British artist treated anatomy more as a part of pattern. Thus in a relief of Hercules slaying the Hydra at Corbridge, the hero's pectorals are too high, and little attention has been devoted to the lower half of his body.[40] This simplification is particularly apparent in drapery, which was reduced to linear patterns, and may reflect the fact that Celtic art before the Roman conquest was essentially linear and concerned with abstract pattern. Thus, whereas classical sculpture used draperies to outline the anatomy of the figure underneath, Romano-British art tends to see the lines of the drapery as interesting in terms of pattern in its own right. This is well demonstrated by the funeral relief from Murrell Hill, near Carlisle,[41] or the statue of Juno Regina from Chesters on Hadrian's Wall.[42]

Classical Roman sculpture seems to have been aware of rules of proportion which had originally been formulated by the Greeks and which were familiar to Vitruvius, the Roman writer on architecture and art. In Romano-British art the figures were judged by eye rather than laid out mathematically, though very occasionally there are signs that classical proportions were used for one part of a figure, non-classical ideals for another.[43] In some cases head and neck account for a third of the figure, in others the head seems to have been a quarter of the height. The treatment of the hair was similarly a subject for the creation of pattern, well exemplified by the bronze of a girl from Silkstead, Hants, whose staring, pebble-inlaid eyes perhaps reflect the Celtic pre-occupation with eyes as 'doorways to the soul'.[44]

Bronze head of a girl, with inlaid pebble eyes, first or second century AD, from Silkstead, Hants. Height: 12.7 cm. (Winchester Museum)

Another feature of Romano-British sculpture is the way in which works appear to have been left unfinished, either in whole or in part. Classical tradition required sculptures to be worked over in their entirety at each stage, whereas in Romano-British work once the work was roughed out, sometimes only part appears to have been finished.[45] Even so, Romano-British artists cared about the overall effect of their compositions, and produced balanced results.

Perhaps the most successful amalgam of the two art styles is found on objects which were decorated rather than being works of art in their own right — silverware, pottery, coins, glassware and jewellery for example. Some of these are considered in the following chapters, where the diversity of the art found in Roman Britain is discussed.

CHAPTER TWO

RELIGION

A large proportion of Romano-British art was inspired by religious or philosophical belief. Unlike the modern world, which sometimes appears to regard miracle cures and scientific breakthroughs as so commonplace as to be almost social rights, the Romans did not attempt to sidestep the issues of death, old age or infirmity. Instead they elevated them. The deities were to be appeased to prolong life and health, but in the final analysis there was no point in fighting the inevitable. The celebration of the triumph of life over death often led to some grisly art subjects – comparable with the images of the martyrs or Christ in later times – and the motivations of the artists and patrons should not be confused by twentieth-century, post-Freudian concepts.[1]

Given these basic precepts, art reflected the social aspirations of the patrons and could serve political purposes. The subject matter or decoration was seldom purely secular. Romano-British religious art was not dedicated to a single faith: it was produced to honour a diversity of deities, only some of which belonged to the traditional Roman pantheon. In the pre-Roman period, the native Britons worshipped many divinities and cults, some of which were of purely local significance.

After the conquest, there was a tendency for cults to merge and a number of strands can be distinguished: the native, the imported Roman and the more exotic brought in mostly by the army, though also probably by merchants, from far-flung areas. This merging was relatively simple since Celtic and classical religious belief systems were rooted in the same basic Indo-European tradition in which particular deities presided over specific areas of human experience.[2] Roman policy was to assimilate provincial deities, provided that their worship was not exclusive of the rest of the Roman pantheon, and provided that the cult did not involve human sacrifice and could not be used to stir up anti-Roman feeling.[3]

When the Roman and Celtic pagan religious traditions met, an amalgam of deities was therefore easily established, producing a wide variety of beings in the artistic repertoire. It was not until the rise of certain Eastern cults which demanded exclusivity of belief, that religious differences were expressed in discord. Christianity was the foremost of these. However, towards the end of the Roman period certain attributes of even Christian belief seem to have been identified with the pagan repertoire and subtly included in the iconography. It is interesting to note, from the standpoint of this modern era where choice is paramount, that for the Romano-British, choice was never exercised as often as it was through belief. Whatever the circumstances, whatever the individual's preferences or background, there seems to have been a deity to fit the bill. And if there was not, well, one could be tailor-made. Romano-British religion was, essentially, consumer-led and driven.

The traditional Roman belief system was pantheistic. It was headed by the Capitoline Triad, which was equated with the Roman State, moral values and codes.[4] The extent to which local cults survived in the face of such strong competition is evidence for persistent native traditions in Britain during the centuries of Roman rule.[5]

Of the non-State cults introduced to Britain, the most common were perhaps those from Gaul, and the various mystery cults of Oriental origin. Of these, one group stemmed from Anatolia and another from Syria. Christianity, which became the official religion of fourth-century Britain, was one of these cults.

The diversity of deities produced in the first four centuries after Christ is matched by the variety of cult practices and cult centres. It is notable that very few traditional types of Roman temple are documented in *Britannia*. By the same token, although some monumental sculpture is known (for example, pagan altars), this is particularly associated with the army (page 148). The best surviving religious art in Britain is on a comparatively small scale.

Secular State art and rich domestic art tended to be of a relatively high standard, whereas purely religious art in Roman Britain ranges from the most accomplished and classical to the most crude and rudimentary. Thus there are superbly carved marbles imported probably from Italy, as well as roughly executed images produced for the impoverished faithful by artisans with more enthusiasm than skill or time. The diversity of Romano-British religious art illustrates the cosmopolitan character of the province's population.

EVIDENCE

Romano-British religion manifests itself in the historical and archaeological repertoires in inscriptions, altars, votive offerings, temples and works of art of varying quality. A limited amount of literary material also exists. Congregational worship was not common until the Christian era, so shrines and temples were smaller than, for example, present day mosques or churches. Altars had a votive and commemorative function rather than being the focus of mass ritual.

Celtic religion required shrines and the occasional temple, but the foci were frequently natural phenomena such as springs or rivers. Evidence for such veneration is therefore sparse and generally not structural. In addition to this, a variety of art work was produced and used in a variety of ways. Works of art have survived in various materials, including stone, metalwork, pottery, wall plaster, mosaics and, occasionally, wood.

THE CAPITOLINE TRIAD

Until the formal adoption of Christianity in AD 313, the Capitoline Triad (Jupiter, Juno and Minerva) was fundamental to Roman State Religion. Jupiter, who sometimes appears as Dis Pater or Diespiter (Father of the Gods), and sometimes as

Jovis (Jove), was in origin a sky god. Some of the epithets given him, such as Lucretius (Bringer of Light), Elicius (Bringer of Rain) or Fulgur (Bringer of Thunder), are reminders of this. He was a god of law and order, and of morality, and he was invoked in oath-swearing and in the solemnization of marriage. Although equated with the Greek Zeus, he differed from his Hellenic counterpart in many respects.

The Capitoline Triad represented the core of Roman State Religion and, not surprisingly, images of Jupiter and Juno are often extremely classical. There is a tendency to describe as Jupiter any bearded male head that is not clearly a portrait bust. However, without some defining attribute such as a thunderbolt or eagle, such heads, particularly if they have native characteristics, are more likely to represent native deities.

Jupiter was very popular with Roman soldiers, and his worship was seen as an overt gesture of loyalty to Rome. He was worshipped as Iupiter Optimus Maximus (Jupiter, Best and Greatest), and on 3 January each year army units buried his altar and set up a new one: hence the series of altars dedicated to him at for example, Birdoswald (on Hadrian's Wall) and Maryport (Cumbria). Images of Jupiter (as opposed to dedications) are rarer, but he is often depicted enthroned, as in a bronze from London, or another from West Stoke, Sussex. One bronze, judged to be Jupiter from the treatment of the hair and classical appearance, was found in the Roman fortress at Caerleon, Gwent.[6]

His wife, Juno, was equally formidable, and was more closely associated with women than her Greek counterpart, Hera. Every Roman woman had her *juno* or guardian spirit, the female equivalent of the *genius*. Juno was the protector of the State, and some of her epithets, such as Moneta (The Warning One) reflect this aspect of her character.

Juno does not figure prominently in Romano-British art, though small matronly figurines are often taken to represent her, examples having been found in London and Chester. Her symbol was the peacock, and bronze examples of peacocks from London and Corbridge may be connected with her cult.[7]

Minerva was the equivalent of the Greek Athene, but her cult was notably different and probably derived from that of an Etruscan goddess. Minerva was principally a war deity, but she also presided over the arts, and the craft guilds of the city were located on the Aventine Hill, Rome, where a shrine was dedicated to her.

Minerva was much more popular in religious imagery, often appearing in the guise of a native deity who had conveniently been equated with her to give local custom respectability. She frequently appears helmeted, and can often be identified from her trophy – the head of the Gorgon Medusa, whose glance turned men to stone.[8]

TEMPLES

Virtually no details of temples to classical Roman deities are known in Britain, although they are known to have existed at, for example, York.[9] Roman temples, in contrast to Greek, consisted of a *cella* fronted by a row of columns, and were intended to be viewed from the front instead of from all sides (presumably since they were often built in confined, urban spaces).

Only in the case of the building dedicated to Sul Minerva at Bath is it possible to make any kind of confident deduction about the original appearance of a Romano-British classical temple. This example was tetrastyle: it had four columns supporting a pediment – a particularly pleasing architectural device. The capitals were of composite form and the whole stood on a podium, which always has the effect of adding to grandeur and elegance. At a late stage the temple podium was enlarged, and may have been surrounded by an ambulatory.[10]

The surviving pediment (the triangular carving above the columns) of the temple at Bath is of exceptional interest. In the centre is Minerva's shield, decorated with the head of Medusa. Features of a female head have been conflated with images of

Medusa head from the pediment of the temple of Sul Minerva, Bath, Somerset. Second or third century AD. Diameter: 18.8 m. (Drawing: L. Laing)

Bronze head of Minerva, from Bath, Somerset, second century AD. Height: 24.76 cm. (Drawing: L. Laing)

Oceanus, creating a bearded man. The large, staring eyes look somewhat Celtic, but the overall appearance of the pediment is in the mainstream of classical tradition. Figures of Victory appear to be holding the shield, and there were also flanking tritons (mermen), who further emphasize the aqueous connection of the cult of Sulis Minerva[11] (Sulis was a Celtic water deity). The temple complex at Bath has also produced a magnificently emotionless second-century bronze head of Minerva. Poignant distortions to the neck show that it was forcibly removed from an almost life-size statue in antiquity. It is a masterpiece of bronze casting, perhaps made by a Gaulish artist.[12]

THE IMPERIAL CULT

Closely related to the reverence for the State pantheon was emperor worship. From the time of Augustus, deceased emperors were deified, and depicted being transported heavenwards in a chariot. It is very difficult to establish whether particular Imperial statues were connected with such veneration or were merely reflections of the patrons' generosity or ambition. It is known, however, that there was a temple to the deified Claudius at Colchester (its platform now forms the foundation of the Norman castle). A head which could be of Claudius, clearly torn off a statue in some ancient drama, was found in the River Alde in Suffolk in 1907; it has been suggested that it was looted by Boudicca when she sacked the city of Camulodunum. Toynbee argued that it is too small to have come from the cult statue in the temple, but is more likely to have graced a public place in the city.[13] Less dubiously connected with emperor worship is the magnificent bronze of Nero from Coddenham, near Ipswich, which logic suggests must have come from a temple. Hollow cast and 55.8 cm (22 in)

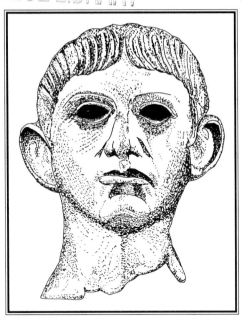

Bronze bust, believed to be of Claudius, first century AD, from the River Alde, Suffolk. Height: 33.02 cm. (Drawing: L. Laing)

high, the statue gazes heavenwards. It is inlaid with silver and niello (a black silver sulphide paste), and is perhaps a Gallic import.[14]

Priests of the cult of the emperor are documented at York and Lincoln, and altars dedicated to the *numen* (spirit) of the emperor are also found.[15]

OTHER CLASSICAL DEITIES

Of the other major deities in the Roman pantheon perhaps the most important, though not always the most commonly represented in Britain, are Apollo, Mars and Venus who were easily equated with native deities.

Apollo, god of light, music, poetry and dance, made people aware of their guilt, and protected herds. Normally he was depicted *au naturel* or with a cloak, and he carried a bow with which to dispense retribution, and sometimes a lyre. He was not particularly popular in Britain, but a cult centre dedicated to his worship (among other deities including Silvanus, Mercury and Diana, and the Celtic deity Rosmerta, who was the equivalent of Fortuna) has been excavated at Nettleton Scrub, Wilts, where the finds included a bronze plaque dedicated to him. Here he was equated with a local god and given the epithet Cunomaglos (Great Hound). Associated with the cult centre was an industrial complex involved in metalworking and a water-powered mill.[16] A purely

Bronze statuette of Nero from Baylham Mill, Coddenham, Suffolk. Height: 49 cm. (British Museum)

classical rendering of Apollo, the product of a Mediterranean workshop, can be seen in a fine bronze from the Thames at London Bridge.[17]

Because Mars could be readily equated with any of the many local warrior gods, he is frequently represented in Romano-British art. Most commonly shown naked, he sometimes appears in full armour. A helmeted statuette from Earith, Huntingdon, is classical in style. It shows the bearded god in a cuirass, his hands gripping a now-missing spear and shield. It is a Continental import dating probably from the later second century.[18] Classical in inspiration but native in treatment is the statue of the god from St Mary's Convent, Micklegate Bar, York, found in 1880. This figure, helmeted and with a cuirass, is simply but forcefully carved out of local gritstone, and dates from the later third or fourth century.[19]

Perhaps the most vibrant rendering of Mars in Roman Britain is the example from Fossdyke, Lincs. Here, classical tradition and local talent merged in the production of a votive bronze on an integral plinth. He wears nothing but his helmet and the inscription on the base explains that the image was made by Celatus for Bruccius and Caratius. Significantly, the

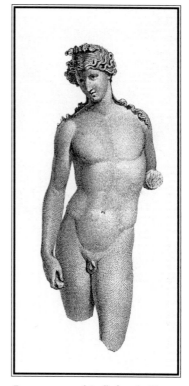

Bronze statuette of Apollo from the Thames at London Bridge. Height 10.75 cm. (From a nineteenth-century engraving.)

artist has a Roman name: the patrons are Celts. The misproportioned, flamboyant helmet could imply the work of a very Romanized native, though a long-standing interpretation would have us believe it to be the work of a visiting Continental artist for local patrons.[20]

Venus was the goddess of beauty and love. She is abundantly represented in Roman Britain, sometimes draped, sometimes without so much as a stitch of clothing. The finest examples are perhaps imported bronzes, such as that from Verulamium (St Albans), found in 1959 on the floor of a cellar which had been filled in during the fourth century.[21] She stands 25.5 cm (8 in) high, and is clad in nothing more substantial than a cloak knotted round the thighs. Although it has been suggested it was the work of an Italian or possibly Gaulish factory, it could equally well be British. The statue holds a pomegranate or apple, symbolic of fertility or to emphasize underworld connections. The latter is an uncommon aspect of the goddess, but one which would have appealed to Celts. In contrast, is a chubby little bronze figurine of the goddess from Bokerley Dyke, Dorset. With a pear-shaped figure, happy smile and double chin, she recalls the mosaic Venus from Rudston, Humberside, and is probably

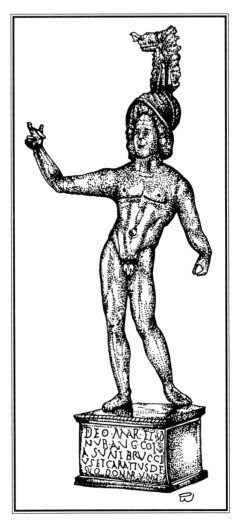

Statuette of Mars from Fossdyke, Lincolnshire, second or third century AD. Height: 27 cm. (Drawing: Cilla Wild)

British-made.[22] Particularly common are pipeclay figurines of Venus, mostly mass-produced by casting in moulds in Gaul. These turn up all over Roman Britain, and some were also probably made there.[23]

Diana, goddess of the hunt, is represented in a marble Mediterranean statue from the Roman villa at Woodchester, Glos. Ceres, goddess of the harvest, is depicted in a bronze from London, mourning her daughter Persephone during the winter months when she had to stay with her husband Pluto, god of the underworld.[24] Mercury, the messenger of the gods, and patron of trade, had a strong native following. He is usually depicted naked apart from his cloak and winged hat, and has a purse and a caduceus (a staff twined with snakes). Bronze statuettes of him were produced in large numbers in the Roman Empire, and are quite commonly represented in Britain where some appear to have been manufactured. The finest Mercury from Britain, however, is an import, found near a temple at Gosbecks Farm, Colchester. An impressive 54.34 cm (21 in) high, it now lacks its arms, and was probably part of a sculpture group imported perhaps from Gaul. His feet are not level, so the statue was intended to be shown at the moment of alighting on some object.[25]

Perhaps the most sophisticated stone rendering of Mercury is a marble from the temple of Mithras in London (page 33).[26] Standing a mere 25.4 cm (10 in) high, and carved from two blocks of Italian marble in the second century AD, it depicts the god as a youth sprawling on a pile of rocks. Originally he held a caduceus, presumably made of metal and now missing, but he still holds a purse. His attendants are a ram and a tortoise, the latter a reminder that he invented the lyre (which had a tortoise-shell for a sounding box), the former that he gave fertility to flocks. Mercury guided the dead through the transition to everlasting bliss, and is associated with other Mithraic cult centres in the Empire.

A temple dedicated to the worship of Mercury has been found at Uley, Glos., where the remains included a superb bust of the god from a larger than life-size stone statue,

Head of Mercury, from his shrine at Uley, Glos. It is nearly life-size. (British Museum)

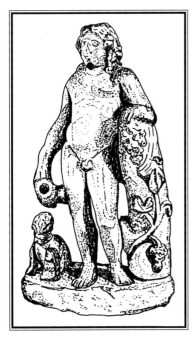

Bacchus with panther, from Spoonley Wood villa, Glos. Height: 39.9 cm. (Drawing: L. Laing)

executed in local material but in very Roman style. It probably dates from the mid-second century.[27] The shrine also produced fragmentary reliefs of Mercury with a goat and cockerel, and a notable collection of curses on lead tablets.

Bacchus sometimes made an appearance in Mithraic contexts. He was also a god of fertility and was therefore associated with a group of wanton female worshippers, the Bacchantes or maenads. Feasting and drinking – one of the features that both Roman and Celtic life had in common – was a prominent element in cult practice. In the later days of the Roman occupation, his cult became particularly popular in Britain, and may have been seen as a rival to Christianity. It is notable that much of the imagery to be found on the magnificent Mildenhall Treasure (page 59) is derived from the cult of Bacchus.

Among the fine sculptures of Bacchus from Roman Britain is a marble from a grave discovered near Spoonley Wood, Glos., a particularly rich fourth-century villa. Here the god, holding a wine cup, leans drunkenly on a vine-coiled tree stump and is attended by a panther.[28] Equally fine is the figure group from the London Mithraeum, with its late Roman inscription HOMINIBUS BAGIS BITAM ('Life to Wandering Men'), which has been interpreted as meaning 'giver of eternal life to wandering mortals'. It dates from around the mid-third century. The god's attendants are Pan, a bald Silenus on the back of an ass, a young nude satyr, and a maenad who holds a *cista mystica* (a sacred casket). Again a panther appears in the group.

Vulcan, the smith god, and Silenus both make occasional appearances in Romano-British art. Also rare, the woodland god Faunus is represented among the dedications in a splendid hoard from Thetford, Norfolk, though he is not depicted. The hoard bore dedications from Celtic followers, and comprised a collection of silver spoons and jewels, as well as a magnificent gold buckle. Two of the spoons displayed Bacchic subjects, and the strainers found in the hoard may have seen Christian usage.[29]

The hero Hercules is occasionally found. A relief of Hercules slaying the hydra, a many-headed monster, has been found at Corbridge, though the victim is now missing.[30] What this piece lacks in artistic finesse it makes up for in vigour. Finally, a fine and chubby Cupid, the god of love, from Cirencester, Glos., probably served as a lamp standard rather than an object of veneration.[31]

EASTERN CULTS[32]

Eastern mystery cults became increasingly popular in later Roman Britain, when political uncertainty increased the attraction of faiths offering personal redemption in the hereafter. A personal relationship was forged between the devotee and the god, and often required elaborate initiation rites and the adherence to strict codes of behaviour. They were mainly the preserve of rich males, notably high-ranking army officers and wealthy town dwellers. The evidence is particularly strong along Hadrian's Wall.

Mithras

Mithras was sent to earth as an ambassador by the Persian sky god Ahuramazda, and was given the task of killing a divine bull, the blood of which released the forces of life. Depictions of the bull sacrifice also show a scorpion and a serpent which tried to prevent the blood reaching the earth. The cult balanced the forces of good and evil – at the entrance to a Mithraeum stood two figures, Cautes and Cautapates, who symbolized the forces of light and of darkness. One held an upright torch, the other carried an inverted torch. The cult was connected with cosmology, and a fine relief from a Mithraeum at Housesteads on Hadrian's Wall shows a rarely depicted episode of Mithraic lore – the birth of the god from an egg (more usually represented by a pile of rocks), surrounded by the signs of the zodiac. Mithraic followers were exclusively male, and initiates suffered a series of rituals which included being buried and having a fire lit on top of the 'coffin'. One such stone-lined burial pit was found in the Mithraeum at Carrawburgh.[33]

The cult of Mithras came under the spotlight of modern public interest when the Walbrook Mithraeum in London was excavated in 1954. [34] A fine Italian marble relief found on the site in the nineteenth century shows the god sacrificing the bull, attended by Cautes and Cautapates.[35] The scene is encircled by the signs of the zodiac, and in the top corners are Luna, the moon goddess and Sol, the sun god, driving his chariot. Below are busts of wind gods. The inscription notes that 'Ulpius Silvanus, veteran

Bust of Mithras, from the temple of Mithras at Walbrook, London. Height: 37.23 cm. (Drawing: Charlotte White)

of Legion II Augusta, paid his vow: he was initiated at Orange'.[36] The piece was probably carved on imported stone in Britain by an immigrant artist. Found with it was a fine marble bust of a swimming river god, presumably in this case intended to represent the River Thames, though it may have been imported ready-made from Italy. It probably dates from the mid-second century.

Bacchus, the Dioscuri, Atargatis, Minerva, Mercury and Bonus Eventus (Good Outcome) were all represented in the Walbrook Mithraeum, and the sculptures also included a composition in British limestone of Mithras slaying the bull; only a portion of an arm and hand has survived. It came from a statue intended to be viewed in the round.[37] Particularly notable is a head of Mithras, wearing his distinctive Phrygian cap, which was intended to be inset into a body of another material, perhaps local limestone or stucco. It is made from Italian marble, but could have been made in Britain.[38] This, and many of the other sculptures from the Walbrook temple seem to have been produced in the second century but deliberately buried in the fourth, perhaps because of the Christian threat. Pottery from the Mithraeum has suggested a construction date no earlier than *c.* AD 240, in which case the sculptures may have been brought from elsewhere.[39]

The Mithraic temple was intended to represent the cave in which the bull was sacrificed, and was suitably dark. The similarity of its plan to that of a church stemmed from the common model of a secular public building, the basilica. Few scientific investigations of Mithraea have been published, but full reports exist for those at Carrawburgh and Caernarvon in Gwynedd. The Carrawburgh Mithraeum displayed three constructional phases with a nave and rectangular apse in its second stage. It had side benches, and an ordeal pit near the entrance.[40] Many Mithraea show evidence of having been destroyed in the latter days of Roman Britain.

Christianity[41]

The destruction of Mithraic temples is usually attributed to Christians, who may, arguably, have seen Mithraism as a particular threat, since it shared a number of features with their own faith, one of which was the concept of redemption. Christianity was different from many previous religious beliefs in that it demanded exclusive worship by its adherents. As time went on, this ideal lessened, and it is notable that many features of other religions were assimilated (and never died out). In particular, many of the images of classical myths were reintroduced through the martyrs.

Christianity may have been introduced in the second century (though folklore would have Joseph of Arimathea bringing the Holy Grail to Glastonbury very much earlier than this). Evidence is comparatively rare and often difficult to evaluate, partly because of the non-pagan habit of interring without grave goods since material possessions were deemed unnecessary in the Christian afterlife. There is also a dearth of Christian Roman cemeteries (which have to be identified by, for example, the uniform orientation of graves). Early Christianity is often seen as the province of women and the poor, but it is unlikely to have gained its later status as the official State religion of the Empire had it not also appealed to rich men. Its value as a method of persuading the indigent and downtrodden to accept their lot has always been considerable.

There is comparatively little direct evidence for ecclesiastical architecture in Roman Britain. Before the Peace of the Church (under Constantine in AD 313), when Christianity became the official religion, most Christian worship took place in private houses, and there are comparatively few early churches in the Roman Empire generally. Early churches were basilican in plan (rectangular with a nave divided by columns into aisles), and are therefore difficult to distinguish from either secular public buildings or the meeting-places of other cults. The building most frequently claimed to be a Christian church in Roman Britain is that excavated in 1892 at Silchester, Hants. It had what has been identified as the site of a font, possibly in a now-vanished baptistry, near the entrance. It was re-excavated in 1961, but without conclusive results. The building had a nave, aisles and narthex, and its apse contained a rectangular mosaic. There were, however, no definite signs of Christian usage, and it did not face east, as might be expected.[42]

At Butt Road, Colchester, Essex, a basilican building in use from c. 320 to the fifth century was set within a cemetery of east–west oriented burials. The 'church' itself was a rectangular building, 7.4 m × 24.8 m (24.3 × 81.4 ft), with an eastern apse. The eastern portion had been partitioned by a screen, and the nave had side aisles.[43]

At Richborough, Kent, two buildings have been postulated as churches, one of timber, the other of stone; the former can only be detected from aerial photography, but the latter was also associated with a baptistry.[44] A baptistry has also been found at Icklingham, Suffolk, where there is a cemetery and a series of lead tanks with Christian symbols.[45]

Continuity of use from the Roman period into the Anglo-Saxon has been argued in a few cases, most notably at Stone-by-Faversham and St Martin's, Canterbury, both in Kent. At the former, a baptistry may have been incorporated into the later church; in the latter, the nature of the Roman building is more problematic. At St Paul-in-the-Bail, Lincoln, a strong case has been advanced for a sequence of churches from the late Roman period through to the Anglo-Saxon, and there is now also evidence for a Roman precursor of Canterbury cathedral.[46] It is notable that in later periods Christian worship has often remained in the same locations, even if villages moved or died out completely. Early churches may well lie under later ones but usually no evidence is available. The proximity of later important country homes to Roman villas is also unlikely to be coincidental.

Despite the recent intensive research on Romano-British Christianity, comparatively little is known about its organization and extent.[47] The limited documentation includes mention of a delegation of three British bishops attending the Council of

Arles in 314 with a priest and a deacon. Another delegation went to the Council of Rimini in 359, when the clerics pleaded poverty and were allowed free travel by way of the Imperial Post. This has frequently been taken as evidence for the poverty of British Christians,[48] but it could equally well denote creative use of the ancient expense account. By 429 the belief was so strong that it was subject to a heresy – Pelagianism – which necessitated a mission led by Germanus of Auxerre from Rome.

Rich Christian Remains

There is some evidence for rich and influential Christians in Roman Britain well before AD 429. The most important comprises silverwork, of which the hoard from Water Newton, Huntingdonshire, is the most significant.[49] The hoard, which came to light in a field near the small pottery-manufacturing Roman town of Durobrivae, comprises twenty-eight items including a silver two-handled chalice, jug, decorated bowl, dish, strainer, part of another jug and a series of silver cups, some with dedicatory inscriptions. In addition, there is a series of votive plaques, one gold, the others silver, with Chi-Rhos on them. (The Chi-Rho was a monogram of the first two letters of Christ's name in Greek, and was often combined with alpha and omega, the first and last letters of the Greek alphabet, in recognition of the text, 'I am Alpha and Omega, the beginning and the ending, saith the Lord' (*Revelation* 1: 8).) Also frequently found is the fish symbol: the Greek word for fish is *ixthus*, which was seen as standing for *Iesous Christos, Theou Uios Soter* – Jesus Christ, Son of God, Saviour. The matter is complicated, however, in that in the fourth century the Chi-Rho also had political overtones. Some of the Water Newton cups have dedicatory inscriptions naming donors, and the whole assemblage seems to constitute church plate with items similar to votive offerings found in pagan shrines. Its deposition is coin-dated to just before the middle of the fourth century.

The tradition of giving fine plate to the Church is reinforced by the lanx from Risley Park, Derbyshire. This large silver dish was found in 1729 then broken up and recast before being lost again and rediscovered in 1991. The subject matter of the lanx is secular (hunting and pastoral scenes), but an inscription on the back records that it was given by Bishop Exuperius to the Bogiensian church (presumably a lost Roman settlement nearby since the lanx is of native British manufacture).[50] Various silver spoons are inscribed with Chi-Rhos, for example from the Mildenhall, Suffolk, treasure;[51] or from Biddulph, Staffs.[52] There is also the silver vessel with the Adoration of the Magi from the Traprain hoard, East Lothian.[53]

Finest and most conclusive of all putatively Christian treasures are the objects in the Hoxne Treasure, discovered in Suffolk in 1992. All twenty-four inscriptions are undoubtedly Christian. A Chi-Rho appears on two spoons, and a monogram cross

Recast silver lanx or plate from Risley Park, Derbyshire. Length: 49.7 cm. (British Museum)

appears on two sets of tableware and on a necklace, while another spoon carries the inscription VIVAS IN DEO (May you live in God).[54] A similar formula appears on a ring from Silchester, Hants., inscribed SENECIANE VIVAS IN DE, and which appears to have been 'converted' from pagan use as it had a bezel adorned with Venus. Another ring from Richborough, Kent, had the inscription *iustine vivas in deo*.[55] The Hoxne hoard was deposited between AD 407 and 450, and is deemed to represent the accumulated wealth of an extremely rich family.

Wealth characterized the owner of the villa at Hinton St Mary, Dorset, where a fine mosaic depicting the head of Christ was found,[56] and the owner of the Frampton villa, where the Chi-Rho was depicted in a mosaic. A Christian must have carved the symbols found at the sumptuous villa at Chedworth, Glos.[57], and a rich Christian owner must have been responsible for the fine paintings in the Christian rooms at Lullingstone, Kent.[58]

The Lullingstone villa contained a house chapel of a type previously known only

Reconstructed Chi Rho fresco, Lullingstone villa, Kent. (Drawing: L. Laing, after Meates)

from Dura Europos on the Euphrates, with scenes of trees, plants and houses and with a line of orantes (praying figures) between columns, their hands raised in the early Christian attitude of prayer. Juxtaposed was a painting of a Chi-Rho in a wreath pecked at by birds. The quality of the paintings was high, and they were executed in the second half of the fourth century.

It is sometimes argued that the occurrence of Christian symbols in art, particularly on portable objects, does not necessarily imply that the owner was a Christian. However, the original owner of the opulent Mildenhall Treasure (page 59), may have been a high-ranking official in the court of Julian the Apostate.[59]

Symbolism

In the late Roman period, art was increasingly symbolic, though most of the works of fourth-century date are essentially personal, and tend to follow traditional subject matter in which pagan themes predominate. It is perhaps in Christian art that the strongest reflection of the trend towards symbolism can be seen. The line of praying figures standing between columns in the Christian wall-paintings at Lullingstone, Kent, are in the mainstream of late Roman Christian art.[60] The arrangement of figures between columns occurs on late Roman sarcophagi, of which the most famous is that of Junius Bassus in Rome. The figures have wide eyes, frontal postures and linear treatment. Colours lack subtlety, and the figures are look-alike dolls, not real people. Their robes are colourful and adorned with pearls, and the idea of sumptuousness is echoed by the Chi-Rho in a jewelled wreath pecked at by doves in the same series of paintings – the composition can be seen on a Christian sarcophagus from the Catacombs of Domitilla in Rome, dated to *c.* 330–340.[61] Similarly unsophisticated is the tantalizing fragment of a fresco, now destroyed, from Comb End, Glos., drawn by Samuel Lysons in 1817. Only the lower portion survives, but it shows what was clearly a complex pictorial composition with roughly drawn figures not unlike the Lullingstone ones.[62]

The same qualities of late Roman art are displayed in other contexts. The head of

Painting of orantes, *Lullingstone villa, Kent, fourth century AD. (British Museum)*

Christ with the Chi-Rho behind, which adorns the centre of the Hinton St Mary mosaic pavement (page 37) is forceful but simplistic. It has been suggested that it was originally intended for a ceiling mosaic, used in the manner of the Pantokrator figures of Christ that appear in Byzantine mosaics, in a tradition which continues to such masterpieces as that at Daphni in Greece.[63] A baptismal scene on a lead font from Walesby, Lincs., has a similarly formal air,[64] and, as Henig has pointed out, the trend to formality extends to the art of mosaics with pagan subject matter.[65]

This tradition of art seems to have continued into the fifth century with the production of the manuscript known as the Vatican Virgil. This book is a text of the Roman poet Virgil, with illustrations in the same general style as those found in mosaics produced by craftsmen operating from Dorchester, Dorset, in the fourth century or possibly the early fifth.[66]

NON-EXCLUSIVE EASTERN CULTS

Some areas assimilated into the Roman world had pantheons of their own which were absorbed, like the Celtic, into the mainstream of Roman provincial faith and then spread through the Empire.

Of great antiquity, the religion of ancient Egypt survived, like its culture, for over three millennia.[67] The Egyptian gods Osiris and Horus were adopted by the Romans under the names of Serapis (a sky and underworld god with healing aspects), and

Head of Serapis from the Temple of Mithras, Walbrook, London. Height: 32.38 cm. (Museum of London)

Harpocrates (a silent, watchful *genius*). Evidence for the Egyptian goddess Isis comes from a graffito on a jug which explains that it belonged to an inn, 'Londini ad fanum Isidis' (of London, near the temple of Isis). Worship of Isis was a mystery cult, involving initiation rituals and holding out the promise of salvation. A rattle shaken by devotees of Isis has been found at Exeter.

From Highworth, Wilts., a fine porphyry bust[68] of Serapis has a socket for a modius (corn measure) on its head. The finest image of Harpocrates from Britain is a silver miniature, 6.5 cm (2.5 in) high, from London Bridge; this is further elaborated with a gold chain and ring. He is depicted as a winged, Cupid-like figure, attended by a dog, a tortoise and a hawk. He has a finger to his mouth, a convention in Egyptian art to indicate that the subject is a child.[69] It could have been made in Alexandria. A number of other figurines of Egyptian deities were imported. Horus, in his original form with a falcon head, was represented in the shrine at Farley Heath, Surrey, while a head of Helioserapis was found at Felminghall Hall, Norfolk.[70]

From Syria came a variety of gods called Baal and goddesses called Astarte.[71] The Baals were sky gods and weather gods, and in the Roman cult the most common fusion was of Jupiter with Doliche (a local Baal worshipped at Commagene who presided over weather and ironworking). His symbols were a double axe and a conical cap, and he is most commonly represented on Hadrian's Wall, though a third-century potsherd with a painting of him was found at Sawtry, Cambridgeshire.

His consort was Juno Regina, and both were depicted on a now fragmentary relief from Croy Hill on the Antonine Wall. This appears to have been set into the wall of a temple or regimental shrine towards the end of the second century AD.[72] A statue from Chesters on Hadrian's Wall depicts Juno Regina standing on the back of a heifer. Virtually life-size, the treatment of the tubular folds of drapery and the running scrolls of the embroidered borders of her tunic suggest an immigrant sculptor familiar with the conventions of his homeland.

The Syrian cult of Sol Invictus (the Invincible Sun) was established in the Empire by Aurelian in the third century. Sol Invictus sometimes appears in temples of Mithras – the most notable depiction is on an altar from Carrawburgh on Hadrian's Wall, where holes have been cut to enable a lamp to represent his rays.[73]. Two fragments of a relief from Corbridge, Northumberland, appear to have come from a temple of Sol which was dismantled in the late third century. It appears to be all that is left of a frieze which ran round the inside of the temple and is a mere 54.61 cm (21.5 in) high. Two further slabs presumably from the same temple show Sol and one of the heavenly twins, Castor and Pollux.[74]

From Anatolia, modern Turkey, came the cult of the mother goddess Cybele and her attendant Atys.[75] Cybele caught Atys being unfaithful to her, and drove him mad so that he castrated himself and bled to death beneath a pine tree. The worship of Cybele involved the celebration of the rebirth of Atys and the start of the new year,

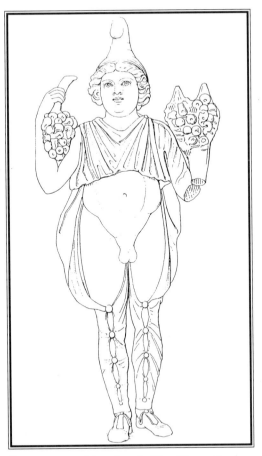

Bronze statuette of Atys, from the River Thames, London. From a nineteenth-century drawing.

Capital with native gods from a Jupiter Column, Cirencester, Glos. Height: 104.14 cm. (Drawing: L. Laing)

attended by bull sacrifice, dancing and, on occasion, self-castration by priests. The cult of Cybele is well represented in London and on Hadrian's Wall. A shrine at Hockwold in Norfolk has yielded a jug decorated with the head of Atys. Like Mithras, Atys is depicted with a soft pointed Phrygian cap, and busts of him are represented at, for example, Mildenhall in Suffolk.[76]

GALLIC CULTS

Some cults were popular in both Gaul and Britain. One version of the cult of Jupiter involved the erection of free-standing columns, presumably the equivalent of a tree in a Celtic grove. The capital from such a Jupiter Column has been found at Cirencester, Glos.; on it the heads of deities emerge from acanthus foliage. The busts show a female with fruit in her hair, a maenad-like woman, a nude male and a similarly sparsely clad Silenus-like man.[77] They are probably Celtic fertility deities. Similar deities in niches adorn the base of another such column from Chesterford, Essex, which was used in the eighteenth century as a horse-trough.[78]

Triple deities were popular in Gallic cults. The most significant were the Tres Matres or Three Mothers, fertility goddesses who appear most frequently in stone sculpture.[79] There are more than fifty dedication inscriptions to them in Roman Britain, where they are generally referred to as Deae Matres. They are shown seated or standing,

Tres Matres, sculpture group from Ashcroft, Cirencester, Glos. Height: 78 cm. (Corinium Museum)

often with plates or trays of bread or fruit, sometimes with children. Ranging from the skilfully portrayed to the schematically crude, several come from the Cirencester area. The finest may have been carved out of local stone by an immigrant Gaulish artist, and shows mothers with children in a charmingly naturalistic manner.[80] Another group from the same town sit stiffly holding their baskets – Haverfield thought them formidable and that their gaze 'would daunt the bravest of men'.[81]

Genii Cucullati, *sculpture from Cirencester, Glos. Height: 78 cm. (Corinium Museum)*

Also in threes are the *Genii Cucullati*, protective godlets who appear in reliefs, again around Cirencester but also clustered in the vicinity of Hadrian's Wall. Their appearance in threes is a British rather than a Gallic trait and, depicted as they frequently are, in hooded cloaks, they evoke some sympathy by their appearance of battling against the British weather.

The Gallic horse goddess Epona is comparatively rare in Britain, but is represented in a small bronze figure from Wiltshire, where she is flanked by ponies.[82]

ROMANO-CELTIC BRITISH CULTS

Nowhere in Roman Britain is the evidence for the survival of Celtic culture more apparent than in religion. Indeed the study of Celtic religion in Britain is generally approached through the remains of the Roman period because Iron Age cult material is relatively sparse.

By far the greatest number of sculptures from Roman Britain comprise native works designed to honour Celtic deities, a tribute to the tenacity of Celtic way of life and beliefs. Stone sculpture was known in the pre-Roman Iron Age, but was generally relatively crude. The chalk idol from Deal, Kent, and the chalk warriors from Garton Slack and Wetwang in Yorkshire are good examples. It should be assumed that much was carved in wood in the manner of the surviving figures of presumed Iron Age date from Ballachulish, Argyll and Dagenham, Essex.

The Iron Age Celts worshipped many deities, often essentially local, such as the spirits that presided over rivers, streams and groves. Other beings seem to have been tribal. Unlike the Greeks and Romans, and as befitted loose-knit tribes with little social adhesion, the Celts did not possess an organized pantheon though some deities seem to have been fairly universal with origins in Indo-European prehistory. Of the 374 names of gods known in Gaul, 305 appear only once, and only four or five of the remainder occur more than twenty times. Roman writers sometimes attempted the uneasy exercise of equating Celtic deities with those of the classical pantheon. Sixty-nine Celtic deities were matched with Mars – which emphasizes the importance of the warrior god in Celtic belief.

Lucan, writing in the first century AD, mentioned human sacrifice and singled out three deities as being of importance in this respect: Esus, Teutatis and Taranis. None of these is prominent in inscriptions, and though attempts have been made to trace them in art, the identifications are not always convincing.

In the pre-Roman Iron Age the druids were the priestly caste responsible for the conducting of religious observance as well as the furtherance of learning. After the capture of Anglesey (AD 77) druidism effectively ended in Britain. The cults of native deities continued, however, often (somewhat surprisingly) furthered by the devotion of Roman soldiers.

Different types of cult site are known in Iron Age Britain and Europe – particularly noteworthy are the Gallo-Belgic examples such as Gournay in France with its ritual enclosures, pits and the grisly evidence of human sacrifice.[83] In Britain human sacrifice is attested, perhaps as late as the Roman period, by the bog burial at Lindow Moss in Cheshire,[84] and the apparently live burial of a young man and woman at Garton Slack, Yorkshire.[85] A British tradition of ritual shafts or pits started in the Bronze Age (for example, the Wilsford Shaft in Wiltshire[86]), and continued into the Roman period.[87] Good examples include the shaft at Dunstable, Beds., which was 35.3 m (116 ft) deep and filled with Roman pottery, human bones, tiles, sandstone slabs and charred wood,[88] or that at Biddenham, Beds., which contained a human skeleton, part of a Roman altar, a mutilated statue, fragments of about fifty Roman pots, pebbles, and bones of horse, dog, ox, fox and pig.[89]

Rectangular timber temples set within rectangular enclosures are attested from the Iron Age onwards. One of the best (and earliest) was excavated at Heathrow, Middlesex,[90] and another good example is documented from South Cadbury, Somerset.[91] There is strong evidence for the continuity of cult sites from the Iron Age into Roman Britain, when Romano-Celtic temples were erected on the sites of earlier shrines.[92] Similarly, there is evidence for the continuing construction and use not only of ritual shafts or wells, but also of the veneration of groves and springs.

Celtic religion was much concerned with cult animals, especially bulls, boars, cocks, ravens, geese, stags, bears, dogs, horses, hares and snakes.[93] This may account for the large number of small bronze figurines of animals from Roman Britain, some of which seem to be associated with shrines.[94] Perhaps the finest are two bronze models of dogs, one of which came from the temple and cult centre of Nodens at Lydney, Glos. It seems likely that dogs were kept in the 'hospital' at Lydney, where they may have licked wounds. One depicts a sitting 'wolfhound', looking back with an alert expression.[95] The little 'mongrel' from Kirkby Thore, Cumbria, has one front paw raised, and seems to be looking up at its owner.[96] An 'Aberdeen terrier' from Carrawburgh on Hadrian's Wall is similarly accomplished,[97], and came from the well of Coventina, where it had been consigned as an offering. Both the latter seem to be of the second century.

Characteristic survivals from the Iron Age are the representations of ox heads which seem to have been used to decorate the escutcheons of buckets from the Iron Age through to the end of the Roman period. A particularly fine later fourth-century example was found on its bucket at Mountsorrel, Leics.[98] Also Romano-British are the many models of boars – again there are good Iron Age examples, including one of the seventh/sixth century BC from Woodingdean, Sussex, and a series from a cult site at Hounslow, Middlesex. Of the Romano-British examples, one from a shrine at Muntham Court, Findon, West Sussex, is

Miniature bronze dog, from Kirkby Thore, Cumbria. Length: 5.91 cm. (Drawing: Charlotte White)

Silver votive plaque of Cocidius, from Bewcastle, Cumbria. Height: 11 cm. (Drawing: L. Laing)

distinctively 'Celtic' with its drawn-up legs and pronounced snout. It appears to represent a dying animal.[99]

Much of the native cult sculpture belongs to particular figure types – a horned god, a warrior god and various goddesses. In the northern military zone of Roman Britain in particular there is abundant evidence for native cults, and

Native goddess Brigantia. Relief from Birrens, Dumfriesshire. Height: 93.98 cm. (Drawing: L. Laing)

inscribed altars (a Roman feature) can help with identifications. Much of this sculpture is of little artistical merit, even though it is informative about Celtic cults in Roman Britain. Of the northern cults, those of Belatucadrus, Cocidius, Mogons, Maponus and Vitiris are prominent.

Maponus, the 'divine youth', is named in five inscriptions in north Britain. His name seems to be preserved in the medieval Scottish burgh of Lochmaben in Dumfriesshire. He is depicted on an altar from Corbridge.[100] Belatucadrus, the 'Bright Beautiful One', was equated with Mars, and appears to have been horned. He is probably represented in a magnificent head from Netherby, Cumbria.[101] Cocidius was also equated with Mars, but in the eastern region of Hadrian's Wall is associated with the woodland god Silvanus. Two of the most famous representations of Cocidius appear on silver votive plaques from Bewcastle, Cumbria, and he also appears as a hunter on an intaglio from South Shields. Vitiris and Mogons were sometimes associated with another one, and the

Sculpture of a native deity from Margidunum, Notts. (Nottingham University Museum)

cult centre of the former was probably Carvoran, on Hadrian's Wall. Vitiris was popular with the Roman army in the north in the third century.[102]

The goddess Coventina was the water deity of Carrawburgh, and presided over a sacred well. She is represented in triplicate, like a Gallic mother goddess, in a relief plaque from her shrine,[103] but she also appears alone, as a classical water nymph.[104] Another deity represented in an inscribed sculpture is Brigantia, the goddess popular in Yorkshire and adjacent areas. She was found at Birrens in Dumfriesshire, in the Roman fort, far from her home territory.[105]

Of the other native deities represented in sculpture, two come from Nottinghamshire. One, from Margidunum, is a small, crude depiction of a warrior god on horseback. The other is a rare depiction of a god and goddess together, from Thorpe-by-Newark. They appear to be the god Sucellos and the goddess Nantosuelta.[106]

Carving of Sucellos and Nantosuelta, from Thorpe-by-Newark, Notts. Height: 27.3 cm. (Nottingham University Museum)

PRIESTLY REGALIA

A number of objects seem to be associated with Romano-Celtic ritual. They include a tin mask, once probably attached to some kind of wooden backing (possibly a pole) from the spring at Bath,[107] an object which has been taken as the binding for a sceptre from Farley Heath, Surrey,[108] and a series of bronze heads, sometimes identified with emperors (which seems most improbable) from rural sites in East Anglia and Northamptonshire.[109]

A priest's diadem was found in the shrine of Nodens at Lydney Park, Glos. It was made of copper alloy and decorated with a scene of the sun god in his chariot flanked by two other male figures and two tritons.[110] A crown from Hockwold-cum-Wilton, Norfolk, was adjustable to the head of the officiating priest, and had repoussé medallions of facing, bearded masks.[111]

Bronze priest's crown, Hockwold, Suffolk. Height: 16.5 cm. (Drawing: L. Laing)

ALTARS AND VOTIVE PLAQUES

Altars are notably absent from Christian contexts (page 36), and differ from modern examples, although they are found associated with most of the other cults found in Roman Britain. They comprise blocks of stone, taller than they were wide, sometimes extremely crudely carved and sometimes executed with great care.[112] Some appear to be blank, possibly because they originally bore painted inscriptions. A few seem to have been portable. The better examples have volutes (scrolls) at the top and a depression (focus) on which an offering could be burnt. They usually have inscriptions to the god or goddess, and a few have an image of the deity as well.

Altars were erected wherever it was deemed appropriate, either in a shrine or outdoors in a place associated with the deity. Some of them commemorate vows taken, others were set up as expressions of thanks for good luck. Few are outstanding as works of art. Some temples or shrines have yielded large numbers.

A somewhat simpler method of giving thanks or commemorating a vow was to offer a votive plaque, usually with a dedication, in the appropriate shrine. Such plaques are well exemplified by the series dedicated to Mars and found at Barkway, Herts. A simpler version with an inscription to the god Nodens from his shrine at Lydney, Glos., notes that the donor, Blandinus, was an armourer. The plaque had been pierced for fixing to a pillar.[113] Sometimes the plaques seem to have been roughly punched out, perhaps in workshops attached to shrines, such as those of the native deity Cocidius from the fort of Bewcastle.

FUNEREAL MONUMENTS

Many of the tombstones from Roman Britain are military in origin (page 149). The civilian examples also shed emotive light on the population of Roman Britain. The tombstone of Regina from South Shields[114] dates from the third century AD, and depicts a seated lady who died at the age of thirty. She originally came from the territory of the Catuvellauni (the tribe whose centre was Verulamium), and married a certain Barates from Palmyra in Syria. This, the legendary Tadmor of the Desert, is famous for its funeral monuments, and the style of the South Shields stone shows that it was carved by a Palmyrene artist, who added an inscription in Palmyrene letters at the bottom of the stone. A larger (not very accurate) Latin inscription explains that Barates was a standard-maker for the Roman army. His tombstone has been discovered at nearby Corbridge: he lived to be sixty-nine. We are fortunate in having another Palmyrene tombstone by the same sculptor (or just possibly the same Palmyrene workshop). Also from South Shields, it shows a funeral banquet and commemorates a certain Victor from Mauretania in North Africa, who was a freedman of a trooper of the First Asturian Horse (from Spain) who had been posted to Benwell on Hadrian's Wall.[115] He died aged twenty.

The quality of these tombstones is very high. Regina sits in a niche on a wicker chair, with a box, and balls of wool in a basket at her feet. She is wearing a necklace and bracelets. The style is completely in keeping with Palmyrene monuments, as is that of Victor's stone, which includes a tiny slave handing him a wine jar, probably filled from the mixing vase next to him. A tree behind symbolized paradise.

An uninscribed tombstone, purely classical in subject-matter but native in style of execution, has been found at Murrell Hill, Cumbria.[116] A lady holds a folding fan (of a type known from an extant example from York), and her child is stretching out its hand to touch a bird on her lap.

A rare glimpse of family life in Roman Britain is provided by a tombstone from

Tombstone of Regina from South Shields. Height: 1.255 m. (South Shields Roman Fort Museum)

York.[117] It was erected by C. Aeresius, a veteran of the sixth legion, to commemorate his family (and subsequently himself), and gives pride of place to Flavia Augustina, his notably tall wife. Of their two children, his son Saenius Augustinus lived for one year and three days, and his daughter, who is not named, lived only a year.

Probably funerary is a fine, very classical relief of a boy charioteer from York.[118] A lion from Corbridge is also probably from a tomb. It was subsequently altered to form a fountain ornament in a house in Corstopitium, its mouth being reworked to take a lead waterpipe. The lion is clearly carved by someone unfamiliar with the living creature, but its aggressive dynamism and the pathetic figure of its victim – a stag with its tongue protruding in death – makes it one of the most dramatic sculptures from Roman Britain.[119]

Tombstone of a woman from Murrell Hill, Carlisle, Cumbria. Height: 1.285 m. (Drawing: L. Laing)

Of very different character are the mausolea in the late Roman cemetery of Poundbury, Dorset. There were a thousand or so graves of the fourth century at this site, mostly oriented east–west and unfurnished, as befitted Christians. But in addition there were some sophisticated mausolea, one with wall-paintings, with what were probably portraits of the deceased in Christian style. [120]

CHAPTER THREE

PERSONAL POSSESSIONS

From the surviving evidence, it appears that most Romano-British art was comparatively small-scale, but it is through considering the everyday articles and personal possessions of the inhabitants of Roman Britain that we are able to see the ways in which Roman art and ideas infiltrated all levels of society. Except perhaps in a few rural areas, the population of Roman Britain was rapidly made familiar with the language and iconography of Roman art through the circulation of coins. The widespread sale of decorated Samian pottery probably meant that all but the poorest became similarly familiar with Roman styles and imagery. Although not perhaps as commonplace, gems, many of them cut in Britain, would have reinforced a widespread acceptance of Roman artistic traditions, while other items of jewellery and small figurines would have been available to a large sector of the community. On a more elevated social level, silver plate and its cheaper alternative, pewter, along with various types of bronze vessel, reinforced the acceptance of Roman ideas. As with religious art, the array of personal possessions betrays how far and how deeply *Romanitas* penetrated society. It also shows the ways in which native tradition responded to the new challenge, sometimes compromising, at other times taking an independent stand.

SILVER

Silver played an important role in Roman society: it lay at the heart of a complex system of economic and social considerations. Because of cost, its possession could be seen as a mark of status, and it could be used politically – gifts of silver could be a method of rewarding supporters, just as swords or torcs were given by barbarian chiefs to their warriors. Silver could also be used to buy off troublesome barbarians, who used it for status and, probably, high-level gift-exchange. In the late Roman Empire silver ingots were used instead of money to buy the loyalty of troops.

Silver plate[1] carried with it additional social overtones. The right equipment for the dinner table demonstrated full integration into the appropriate levels of polite Roman society – the well equipped host would have both the *argentium escarium* (plate for serving food) and the *argentium potorium* (equipment for serving wine, including jugs, drinking cups and strainers).[2]

It is therefore not surprising that a large number of caches of Roman silver plate (in addition to coin hoards) exist in the Roman Empire, a high proportion of which seem to have come to light on the periphery of the Roman world, or even from behind the frontiers. It appears that silver plate was produced in the Roman world in the earlier first century AD, when new sources of silver were probably being mined from provinces such as Spain (and perhaps to a lesser extent, Britain). This was followed by a lull, with a period of renewed vigour among manufacturers in the fourth century. This may be partly explained by the fact that there was sufficient existing plate to meet the requirements of the market in the second and third centuries, but that in the fourth, old silver was melted down and reworked into more fashionable designs. However, this only partly explains the phenomenon, which must also relate to fashionable status symbols in the fourth century.[3]

PRECIOUS METAL PRODUCTION IN BRITAIN

Silver and gold are both obtainable in Britain in modest quantities though it seems that neither was exploited much in Britain before the Roman Conquest. The poor quality of the silver found in Iron Age coins, and the equally poor quality of the gold in coins and ornaments such as the torcs from the Snettisham hoard, are evidence of this. The raw materials for coins and personal adornments probably came from imported currency and perhaps some imported plate, as suggested by the finds of silver Augustan drinking cups from Iron Age burials at Welwyn, and Welwyn Garden City, Herts., and the melted lumps of silver, presumably from plate, from another burial at Verulamium (St Albans).[4] Nonetheless, Strabo's list of Britain's exports before the Conquest includes gold, silver and iron, while at the end of the third century AD a panegyric to the Emperor Constantius Chlorus as Caesar singled out the production of metal ores.[5]

The most common method of obtaining silver in the Roman world was by cupellation from lead. Immediately after the Conquest the Romans were mining lead in the Mendips and in Clwyd.[6] Lead was also mined in Derbyshire. There is some evidence for the production of silver from Silchester, Hants, where, in the late nineteenth century, four sites produced evidence for its extraction from argentiferous copper and lead. In a small house near the south gate, metalworking debris including a furnace was found, and in another craftsman's house furnace bottoms from smelting hearths about 30 cm (12 in) across were found. The hearths would have had to be completely enclosed so that the lead could be totally oxidized leaving only silver. The lead could be reduced to metal again, and such 'reconstituted' lead has been found in pigs found in Britain stamped EX ARG(entariis): 'from the silver works'.[7] The production of silver was on a large enough scale to equip a mint, though there was no mint at Silchester.

HOARDS

Hoards are interesting since they indicate which materials or objects were regarded as important enough to bury in times of danger when banks as such did not exist. The first century AD saw the deposition of some notable caches of silver, both within the Empire and outside (for example, the finds of Augustan vessels from graves in Scandinavia.)[8] The quality of much of this early Imperial silverwork is unsurpassed. The same period saw quantities of Roman silver coin pouring across the frontiers, to wind up in the hoards of barbarians.[9] In Britain it seems that not much silver was imported in the days following the Conquest, though a group of silver cups, once thought to be Augustan but now re-dated to the time of Nero, have been found at Hockwold-cum-Wilton in Norfolk. The cups were found on an otherwise unremarkable Fenland site in 1962, and are believed to be destined for the melting pot. They comprise seven pedestalled and two-handled wine cups, already partly broken apart for melting. Three are decorated: two have incised ornament, mostly of leaves, the third has repoussé relief work of sprays of vine and olive tied together.[10] It has been suggested that the cups were either the property of an Icenian noble, or were looted by the Iceni at the time of the Boudiccan revolt.[11]

Of the later first century there is little silver plate, but the hoards from Backworth and Capheaton, both in Northumberland, can be ascribed to the second century. The

Silver skillet from Backworth, Northumberland; second century AD. Length: 23.49 cm. (British Museum)

Backworth find, which came to light in 1812, comprised a figured vessel and a skillet with a long handle and low foot, along with an assortment of jewellery, coins and spoons, laid in a deep silver pan and covered with an old silver mirror. That it was part of an offering to the local mother goddesses is explained by a dedication on a finger ring and on the skillet handle. The dedicator is named as Fabius Dubitatus. The coins date the deposit to *c.* AD 139. The bowl is plain, but the handle has fine relief ornament of flowers, leaves and swans' heads.[12]

The Capheaton find comprises four decorated skillet handles and a circular medallion, probably from the base of another skillet. (These saucepan-like vessels were used for ritual and votive purposes.)[13] One Capheaton handle and the medallion depict Hercules; Minerva dominates another handle; while the third seems to illustrate rural prosperity. The meaning of the fourth skillet handle is ambiguous. Like the Backworth find, these may all have been imports from Gaul, though Henig has advanced an argument for British manufacture in the late second/early third century for the Capheaton finds.[14]

The superb, round silver mirror from the Roman town of Wroxeter has been assigned to the third century. It has an intricate handle on the back in the form of a Gordian knot and a restrained border of leaves, two panels of oak, two of apple, two of pine, divided by six flowers. Six-petalled flowers also adorn the ends of the handle. It is almost certainly an import.

Most of the silver plate found in Britain belongs to the fourth and early fifth centuries. To the fourth century can be assigned the Water Newton Treasure (page 36), the Mildenhall Treasure, and the Traprain Treasure. To the early fifth belong the Hoxne Treasure and probably the finds from Balline and Coleraine in northern Ireland. A fourth-century date can also be given to the plate found with gems at Thetford and a few individual pieces such as the Corbridge lanx (tray), the Risley Park lanx (page 36), the Walbrook casket and the Mileham dish.

The finest hoard is the Hoxne Treasure, discovered in 1992 in Suffolk. It comprised 14,780 coins and around two hundred gold and silver objects.[15] Several items carry the name Aurelius Ursicinus, but it is probable that the hoard represents the accumulated wealth of a powerful family. It was buried in a wooden box with metal fittings, which contained smaller boxes, some with silver padlocks. Some of the objects seem to have been wrapped in cloth. Buried with the cache was a bone or ivory carved cylindrical casket. The coins were mostly silver, though there were 565 of gold. The latest shows that the hoard must have been deposited after 407. The body of the hoard also comprised items of jewellery and silver plate. The plate comprised 78 silver spoons, 20 ladles, a series of modelled figures and a number of small personal items such as ear cleaners. Four of the modelled 'figures' are pepperpots. One of these takes the form of a silver gilt figure of an empress, possibly Helena, the mother of Constantine the Great; another was in the form of Hercules wrestling Antaeus; the remaining two are in the

Silver spoons from Hoxne Treasure, Suffolk. The short-handled spoon (left centre) bears the name of Aurelius Ursicinus, and is 11.3 cm long. The long-handled spoons (cochlearia) are about 20 cm long. (British Museum)

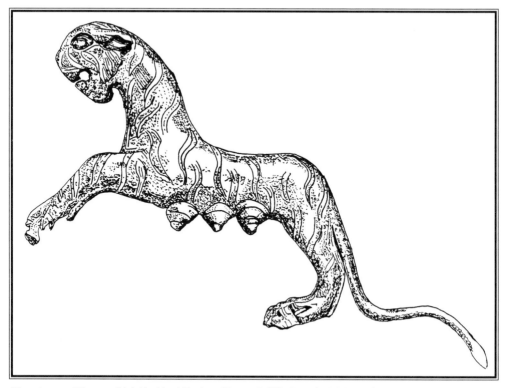

Silver tigress, solid cast and inlaid with niello, from Hoxne, Suffolk. Length: 15.9 cm. (Drawing: L. Laing)

shape of an ibex, and a hound chasing a hare, a popular subject in Roman art. Two silver vases were decorated with leafy patterns, like the vase from the Water Newton Treasure, while five silver bowls were completely plain, and had apparently been stacked with hay between them. Outstanding in the hoard is a figure of a prancing tigress, her stripes inlaid with black niello, that seems to have been the handle of a large vase. It weighs 480 g, and may have been kept long after the vase it came from was lost or destroyed. The spoons include a set of nineteen with gilded figural work depicting dolphins and hippocamps (sea-horses).

After Hoxne, the most sumptuous find is the Mildenhall Treasure.[16] Discovered in the 1940s, it consisted of over thirty pieces of silver plate, mostly with elaborate decoration. The largest item is the Great Dish, 60.5 cm (23.8 in) across, with a central mask of the sea god Oceanus encircled by nereids and fantastic sea monsters. In the outer ring, a

Silver pepperpot, with gilding, in the form of an empress, perhaps Helena, from the Hoxne Treasure, Suffolk. Height: 10.3 cm. (Drawing: L. Laing)

scene includes the figure of Bacchus, with a panther, Hercules, Pan, Silenus, and satyrs and maenads. Next in quality is perhaps a smaller silver platter, 18.8 cm (7.4 in) in diameter, with Pan and a maenad, playing the flute. The back bears an inscription in Greek 'of Eutherius'. A second platter has a dancing satyr and a maenad, and has the same graffito on the back. Figural work also adorns a lid or cover with a zone of centaurs and wild animals divided into groups with human profile masks. Originally it had a knob of some kind, which was replaced with a silver-gilt statuette of a triton blowing a conch. Another bowl also has animals and human heads, with a female profile head in relief in a central medallion. A generally similar bowl with a large flat rim or flange is decorated with animals and trees, separated by profile heads. Its central medallion shows a hunter spearing a bear. Two inscriptions underneath give what seems to be a proverb, and a weight. Two bowls have heads believed to represent Alexander the Great and Olympias, his mother. Other items in the hoard include a fluted bowl with drop handles, a ladle with a dolphin handle, and eight spoons from at least three different sets. The Great Dish and related plates probably had a Bacchic religious significance, and were produced on the Continent, perhaps even in Rome. Other pieces were probably produced in other centres. The Mildenhall Treasure, or at

Oceanus dish from the Mildenhall Treasure, Suffolk; fourth century. Diameter: 60.5 cm. (British Museum)

least the finest pieces, was probably intended for display rather than use as orthodox tableware, even at a grand dinner party. Since its discovery, argument has raged over the identity of its owner. A suggestion has been made that the Eutherius named on the back of the Great Dish was one of the top officials in the court of Julian the Apostate (AD 360-363), the fourth-century emperor famed for trying to restore paganism. This would be in line with the Bacchic symbolism. If so, since Eutherius never came to Britain (as far as is known), it might have been a gift from him to the Christian general Lupicinus.

If the Mildenhall Treasure and the Hoxne Treasure were the personal possessions of

Silver objects from the fourth-century Traprain Treasure, East Lothian. Height of vase: 21.59 cm. (National Museum of Antiquities of Scotland, Edinburgh)

rich individuals or families in later Roman Britain, the best explanation for the Traprain Treasure[17] from East Lothian is that it was a diplomatic gift or bribe to troublesome barbarians on the fringes of the province. Although many of the items in this cache are reminiscent of the Mildenhall find, the pieces are more heterogeneous, and include such oddities as belt fittings from the eastern provinces of the Empire. The hoard came to light at the Celtic fort at Traprain, which had seen intermittent occupation since the Bronze Age. It seems to have continued in use during the time of Roman control of southern Scotland, possibly because of the pro-Roman stance of the local tribe, the Votadini.[18] Most of the pieces in the Traprain find are badly damaged, and were probably on their way to the melting pot, but they include a scalloped dish, six bowls and six goblets which could be inverted and used as pedestalled dishes. One of the goblets bears the graffito CON (perhaps Constantius, an owner's name). The hoard also contains a number of silver spoons and an assortment of coins.

Related to the Traprain find are the hoards of scrap silver from Coleraine and Balline in northern Ireland, presumably again buy-offs for Irish raiders. The silver was also broken up, and the Coleraine hoard is notable for the silver bars it contains, some of them inscribed, which appear to be the official ingots used for making army payments. The associated coins indicate that hoard was deposited after 410, possibly after 420.

SILVER SPOONS, DISHES AND BOXES

A feature of all the late Roman hoards is the presence of various types of spoon. Before the discovery of the Hoxne Treasure, with its 78 spoons and ladles, there were approximately 75 spoons known from Britain. Many of them have religious inscriptions, ownership inscriptions or decoration involving religious subject matter, but although some may have served a religious function (baptismal spoons, for example), their primary function was for eating.

The Corbridge lanx is a large, silver rectangular dish (like the Risley Park lanx), on which the subject matter is connected with the cult of Apollo. It may have been made to commemorate a visit of Julian the Apostate to Delos, the Greek island sacred to

Silver lanx from Corbridge, Northumberland. Length: 48 cm. (British Museum)

Apollo, in 353, and is certainly a Mediterranean product. It came from a hoard of silver vessels found in the eighteenth century in the River Tyne.[19]

A round silver box was found in the Mithraeum at Walbrook, London. It is decorated with relief figures depicting hunts apparently to obtain animals for the arena. The ornamental details compare with scenes in mosaics at Piazza Armerina in Sicily, and thus a Mediterranean origin is likely.[20]

The Mileham Dish is a rectangular plate with engraved plant ornament from Norfolk, which may have been the product of a British factory.[21]

PEWTERWARE

Pewter (an alloy of tin and lead) is less popular now than in Roman times, since it rapidly oxidizes to a dull grey finish. Pewterware was produced in quantity in Roman Britain, partly no doubt because of the availability of the raw materials. The industry is attested by the finds of moulds, but was more popular in Britain than abroad, and British pewter may have been exported to the Continent. It was particularly fashionable in the fourth century when silver was also in demand, and the pewter vessels, which were cast rather than beaten and stamped, may have been cheap substitutes for silver. Most of the pieces found have limited decoration – dishes with fishes engraved on them may have been Christian, but more probably (and prosaically) were for serving fish. The largest collection of pewterware was found in a hoard at Appleshaw, Hants[22], and another find comes from Appleford, Oxon.[23] A large hoard came from Icklingham, Suffolk. Of particular interest is a bowl found near Bath, with a medallion imitating a coin of Constantine the Great, perhaps trying to aspire to the kind of silver plate with medallions of Licinius I that figured in a large hoard of silverwork from Munich.[24]

BRONZE VESSELS

Bronze vessels, especially paterae (effectively saucepans) and jugs, have also been found in Roman Britain, and can be dated to all periods of the occupation. Paterae usually have plain bowls but may have decorated handles. Jugs tend to have ornamental escutcheons where the handle is joined to the body of the vessel.

Bronze vessels were being imported before the Conquest as accoutrements of the high-status pastime, wine-drinking. Imported vessels from Italy were found in the Welwyn burials which produced silver cups (page 55), and doubtless the wine trade lay behind the continued importation of bronze jugs after the Conquest.

Paterae served both secular and religious purposes. As the former, they were used for heating food, but in a religious context they were used for making libations to the gods. As few vessels show any signs of being heated over a fire, it is very likely that the

Silver patera handle, with niello inlay, from Prickwillow, Isle of Ely, Cambridgeshire. Length of handle: c. 14 cm. (British Museum)

more ornate were decorative status symbols. They were probably first introduced to Britain as the mess-tins of the Claudian army, and such examples have round, perforated handles but little other ornament. Another early type has a fluted handle ending in an animal head, usually a ram, though in the case of one from Canterbury, a dog.

The most elaborately decorated probably served a religious function, and many seem to have ended up in graves, for example in the series of Roman barrow mounds at Bartlow in Essex. One now lost from this site had what appeared to be a mask of Bacchus and a series of religious subjects on the stem of the handle; instead of a ram's head terminal it has a ram's head at the opposite end of the handle, where it joins the bowl, the front legs being indicated and extending to grip the bowl.[25] A hoard from Welshpool, in south Wales, produced two paterae, one of which was probably a first-century Italian import and had the head of Bacchus, with eyes originally inlaid with silver, on the handle. A satyr graced the junction with the bowl.[26]

Apart from the silver paterae from Capheaton and Backworth (page 57) perhaps the finest example in Britain intended for religious use is that from Prickwillow, Isle of Ely. It bears an inscription explaining that 'Bodvogenus made it'. This is a Celtic, perhaps British, name but, significantly, the artist had a clear understanding of Roman art. At the end are a pair of dolphins, with intertwining tails and a scallop shell. Beneath are vine-scrolls, and at the junction with the bowl is a winged Cupid emerging from waves, flanked by sea creatures.[27] Niello is used as an inlay.

Like the paterae, the bronze jugs may sometimes have been used in the home, as well as for pouring out libations in a religious context. They often appear depicted on Roman altars and on coin types illustrating priestly equipment. Often there was a decorative mask where the handle joined the body of the vessel. This has a respectable history in the classical world. Greek jugs (which were copied by the Iron Age Celts), tended to have a head of Silenus the wine god at the join. Other Greek jugs had palmettes on the handles; this appears on one example (probably imported from Italy) found at

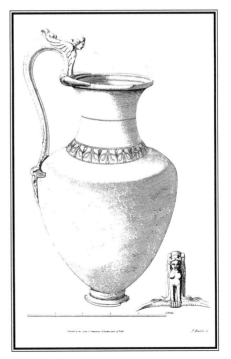

Bronze jug from Bartlow Hills, Essex. Height: 24.5 cm. (From a drawing by J. Basire, 1836)

65

Cornhill, London.[28] Two jugs from Threadneedle Street, London, display a female bust, perhaps of Ceres, and a male one, probably Oceanus.

Some jugs were decorated not only at the base of the handles but also where they joined the rims. One from Canterbury has a female mask on the base of the handle and a horse, its forelegs gripping the rim of the jug, at the top.[29]

Even more ornate were jugs with classical myths illustrated on their handles. One from Bayford, Herts., depicts the madness of Ajax; from Faversham, Kent, we have the story of Diana and Actaeon; and from Welshpool, Powys, the boy Hercules. A jug from Carlisle, Cumbria, has a sacrificial scene, presumably relating to the jug's function.[30]

POTTERY

Pottery in Roman Britain comprises a mixture of fine and coarse wares, while the artistic repertoire indicates a range of tastes from the frankly earthy to the culturally refined. Although most was mass-produced and therefore might represent not so much the taste as the income of the buyer, it nevertheless gives spirited impressions of several aspects of the period. If the images were not deliberately sought, but unintentionally acquired, they must, after exposure to usage, have had a psychological effect on the users. As subliminal advertisements for *Romanitas*, they would have been insidious and successful.

Samian Pottery

The bulk of the fine ware comprises red-gloss (or sometimes black) vessels imported from Gaul (and, around the time of the Conquest, from Italy). This is known as samian since it was believed to have originated on the Greek island of Samos. Its presence is usually taken to indicate a relatively high degree of Romanization, though it has been found not only on the majority of Roman sites south of the Antonine Wall, but also in northern Scotland and Ireland.

At the beginning of the first century AD the samian industry was focused on Arezzo in northern Italy. Arretine vessels were intended as cheap versions of richly decorated metal counterparts, and had moulded relief designs. A few Arretine pots reached Britain before the Conquest, but the ware is extremely rare in Britain.

By the time of Claudius, samian ware was being mass-produced in southern Gaul, notably at La Graufesenque, and South Gaulish samian dominated the market until *c.* 110. By the second century, however, factories in Central Gaul, especially around Lezoux near Clermont Ferrand, were dominating the industry, and these remained the main exporters into the third century, though towards the end of the period they were supplemented by East Gaulish samian from the Rhineland, mainly from Rheinzabern. The trade died out early in the third century, but samian survives as site finds long

Castor ware beaker with gladiators, Colchester, Essex. Height: 21.59 cm. (Colchester Museum)

after, and is found sometimes on post–Roman Dark Age sites.[31] For a brief period in the second century, samian was also produced in Britain, at Colchester.[32]

Samian can be found in both decorated and plain forms, the former mostly comprising bowls with relief modelling. The vessels were moulded, and then finished off by hand. The overall design was achieved by using individual stamps to build up the

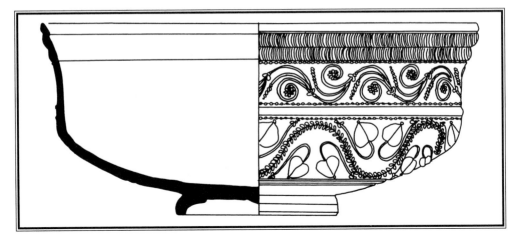

South Gaulish samian bowl from Richborough, Kent. (Drawing: Cilla Wild)

pattern, and while 'freestyle' designs are found, more often the decoration comprises individual elements framed in panels or roundels, sometimes in zones. Individual stamps seem to have been used by more than one potter, and detailed study of samian pottery over the best part of a century has meant that the output of individual factories and even potters (who signed their products) is known. As a result samian can often be dated quite closely.

The motifs on samianware are generally in the mainstream of classical tradition and seem to owe nothing even to Gaulish taste. The subject matter[33] ranges from plant motifs, shells, trees and bushes through hunt scenes to depictions of Venus, Cupid, Minerva, Apollo, Diana, Vulcan, Pan, Bacchus and other gods and myths, including episodes from the story of Hercules and depictions of Victory. Particularly popular were depictions of gladiators or animal fights and hunting scenes. On the freestyle pots the figures process in a circle, in much the same way as the figures on Mesopotamian cylinder seals. The iconography can sometimes be matched on coins or on gems, as well as metal vessels (in some cases the stamps seem to have actually been produced by taking impressions from metal prototypes), and no doubt also followed sculptural and other renderings.

The quality varies. The moulding on Arretine was often very precise, but South Gaulish samian is coarser and Central Gaulish samian is often roughly modelled with an imperfect impression from the mould. Among the pieces of Arretine from Britain is an exceptionally pleasing sherd with a maenad and vine leaf from the Jewry Wall site in Leicester.[34]

Some vessels were produced by moulding the complete vessel. On others, a pad of stamp-impressed clay was affixed to the surface by luting. The quality of appliqués is often much higher than that of stamps applied directly to the mould. Mixing bowls with lion-head spouts were invariably made in this manner, but a number of other figural appliqués have been found in Britain with different designs. The collar of one lion-head mortarium from York bears a representation of a river god reclining against an overturned urn. In the centre is a fluted chalice piled with fruit on which a bird perches, while to the left is a running Cupid.[35]

A third technique of decoration on samian involved tracing out patterns *en barbotine*, that is, by squeezing soft clay on to the surface of the vessel. It was most commonly used to apply ivy leaves to the rims of platters, but more elaborate designs are known on globular pots, including one from Felixstowe with a hunt scene of a hound chasing a stag and a hind.[36]

A fourth technique was similar to that used in the production of cut glass – a fast-moving wheel was used to incise the designs, usually of stylized leaves and flowers. A figural composition involving a gladiator can be seen on a bowl from York.[37]

Romano-British Coarse Ware

Relief decoration was not confined to samian, and some of the most interesting examples are to be found in native coarse ware,[38] where local artists made a distinctive response to classical models. On the native products, the *en barbotine* techniques were perfected by the potters working in the Nene Valley, producing what has sometimes been termed Castor Ware, after the place where it was first recognized. Nene Valley Ware is a dark-slipped pottery inspired by beakers produced in the Rhineland in imitation of metal vessels. The pots have a white fabric, and sometimes almost metallic finish, and were at the peak of production in the late second to third century, though production continued until the end of the Roman period.[39] It seems quite possible that the industry was begun by immigrant potters from the Rhineland. The finest are the hunt cups which, as the name suggests, have depictions of hounds chasing hares, though a very rare type depicts charioteers. An example in the British Museum has the charioteer in the armour of a gladiator, perhaps suggesting a lack of familiarity on the part of the artist with both pastimes, or possibly producing a deliberate amalgam. The finest of the hunt cups, however, is possibly one from Verulamium, showing hounds chasing a hare amid floral scrolls.[40] Claims are sometimes made about surviving Celtic spirit in these vessels. The models that lie behind them come from the Roman Continent, but the designs indubitably create a 'Celtic' sense of movement.

There is considerable variety in the subject matter employed on the relief decorated pots – they include myths such as the labour of Hercules, erotic scenes (such as a woman driving a phallic chariot, on a vessel from Great Casterton, Rutland) and festivals. It has been suggested that they were produced as gifts at seasonal festivals, or sold at fairs at religious foci.[41]

Vessels in the same tradition as Nene Valley ware were sometimes produced elsewhere in Britain. The Colchester Vase, a beaker on which appliqués are combined with *en barbotine* details, was probably a product of the Colchester kilns. Two gladiators named Memno and Valentinus are associated in the inscription with the German-based Legion XXX. Valentinus indicates that he has been beaten, and the name of Memno is followed by the number viii, perhaps the total of his victories. There are in addition two further figures (named Secundus and Mario) fighting wild animals, including a bear. The Colchester Vase dates from the end of the second century and it has been suggested that it depicts stars of the arena who were associated with the Thirtieth Legion, famed throughout the western provinces.[42] Another vessel in the same tradition (from Verulamium), has a depiction of Mithras, Hercules and Mercury.[43]

Of Rhenish inspiration is a series of vessels made in the Nene valley; they have white-painted decoration, sometimes with inscriptions and sometimes combined with *en barbotine* work. The Rhenish prototypes tended to have exhortations along the line of 'Cheers!' or 'Drink Up!', though some were coarser. The figural work on the Rhenish models was much less varied than the British, which were often highly accomplished. One example is represented by a sherd depicting the Syrian god Jupiter Dolichenus.[44] Another sherd from Wroxeter, Shropshire, is decorated by a spirited horse which, probably fortuitously, comes close stylistically to horses that adorn Iron Age Celtic coins, particularly from the area of the Trinovantes.[45]

Coarser pottery was also on occasion decorated with relief ornament. It seems likely

'Harry Lauder', cast from a mould from Corbridge, Northumberland. Height: 14.60 cm. (Photo: Jennifer Laing)

that local factories started producing relief-decorated wares towards the end of the second century when the flow of imported products was diminishing. A mould designed for making appliqués to attach to pots, and a group of grey ware sherds with relief decoration, all from Corbridge, are interesting in this context. The mould is for a bearded figure in a conical hat bearing a crooked club, an oblong shield and with a wheel – the so-called 'Harry Lauder'.[46] It has been suggested that he is the Celtic wheel god Taranis. He has a counterpart on a sherd – a smith, again bearded, with anvil and hammer – who may be Sucellos. Neither, however, need represent gods, but could be caricatures of local personalities – the smith and the wheelwright. Another sherd from the site has been seen as depicting Jupiter Dolichenus. One of the sherds names the potter as Alletio, and all date probably from the third century.[47]

A series of face-urns depict either human faces on their sides, or are in the form of human heads. Some are fully modelled, such as one from Fishergate, York, in the form of a woman's head with a hairstyle like that of Julia Domna, which dates the vessel to the beginning of the third century.[48] One from Lincoln, again of a woman, has painted features – her daubed mouth makes her look as though she has been eating a jam sandwich. Two pots from Colchester have amusing faces modelled on them, but they may well have been funerary.[49]

Antefixes

Related to pots are the ceramic antefixes made to adorn roofs in Roman buildings. The best known of these are the examples produced in the kilns at Holt for the fortress of the twentieth legion at Chester; these depict the legionary badge, a running boar. Antefixes also, however, occur on civilian sites.[50] They were designed to ward off the evil eye, and frequently depicted masks. They are probably the equivalent of the 'severed' heads of the Iron Age and the more recent past – in parts of Yorkshire, stone heads are still reputedly affixed to barns for this purpose. Among the most interesting are those from the fortress at Caerleon, Gwent, where the subject matter seems predominantly Celtic – one crude depiction is of a Celtic goddess perched above two inverted dolphins.[51] Another from Dorchester, Dorset, has a male Medusa which is a less refined version of the famous Bath pediment example (page 26).[52]

GLASS

Glass was fairly common in Roman Britain, and was used for a variety of purposes from window panes to artificial gems. It usually survives only in very small fragments. Although it was probably quite expensive, it was used for a range of utilitarian vessels such as bottles and jars. Small bottles (often erroneously called 'tear bottles' after the Victorian custom of burying bottles of tears in graves), are found in burials and were used for precious unguents. In the early Empire cremations were also sometimes deposited in glass jars. Glass was produced in many centres in the Empire: in Syria, Egypt, and in the Rhineland, Gaul and Italy. In Britain glass-working was carried out at Mancetter, Wroxeter and Caistor-by-Norwich.

Glass could be decorated in a number of ways. Blown glass became common from the first century BC onwards, and a variety of effects could be achieved. Heads of black men found at Caerleon (with a head of Sol on the base) and reputedly at South Shields, could have been produced by mould-blowing.[53] Cut glass was also produced, such as the example from Wint Hill, Banwell, Somerset, and glass could also be decorated *en barbotine*.

One first-century AD engraved glass vessel from a cemetery at Girton College, Cambridge, displays Nilotic scenes. A Bacchic scene of maenads is engraved on a glass

Cut glass bowl from Wint Hill, Somerset. Diameter: 19 cm. (Ashmolean Museum)

piece from Colliton Park, Dorchester, Dorset (fourth century AD) and from Wint Hill, Banwell, Somerset, comes an engraved hunting scene with an inscription in Greek (fourth century AD).[54]

A series of glass cups have mould-blown scenes of chariot racing and gladiatorial combats. The finest, from Colchester, names the victor (Crescens) and the losers (Hierax, Olympa and Antilocus). Other vessels depict and name other gladiatorial stars. Produced in Gaul in the first century, they were clearly 'souvenirs' akin to present-day pop or film memorabilia.[55]

Glass beaker, with moulded scenes of chariot racing, from Colchester, Essex; first century AD. Height: 8.3 cm. (British Museum)

COINAGE

Such sumptuous belongings as those outlined in the previous pages were produced and paid for by a very sophisticated society, with a highly developed monetary system. Coins not only introduced the Romano-British to fiscal matters but also, through art, to many new ideas and concepts. Coinage was therefore of paramount importance to the Roman world. With rare exceptions Roman coinage was imported, so it is likely that the majority of Britons were introduced to Roman art through this medium. Constant bombardment with their imagery and propagandist messages would have had a profound psychological effect. The coin types were subject to frequent change and in the absence of other mass communication methods, were excellent and rapid transmitters of news, propaganda and ideas to a very large sector of the community.[56] Periods of abundant coin loss (i.e. when coinage was so plentiful that losses were sustainable), for example in the later third and fourth centuries, would have led to increased exposure to the imagery, even if the total value of the coins was not necessarily great. In contrast, in the first and second centuries, the life of coins seems to have been prolonged, and the impact of coin designs may have been significant owing to the longevity of circulation.[57]

Pre-Roman British Coins

Coins were introduced to Britain around the late second century BC, and throughout the Iron Age were mainly circulating south-east of a line between the Severn and the Humber.[58] The precise functions of coins in the Iron Age are not yet fully understood – the earliest pieces were mostly gold and probably not used as regular currency but rather in high-level exchanges and possibly religious ritual. Until the time of Julius Caesar Celtic coins were uninscribed, but increasingly they bore the names of individuals, most of whom are otherwise unknown to history. While most of the uninscribed coins (and many of the inscribed) had designs that were Celtic versions of Greek prototypes, during the last years of the first century BC and the early years of the first century AD, prolonged contact with Gaul led to the issue of coins with very Romanized designs. Some seem to be copying Roman Republican denarii, others bear portraits based on those of Augustus and Tiberius, and a few seem to be inspired by classical gems and metalwork. Yet others are without known classical models, but are Roman in style if not subject-matter. These coins were particularly struck in the region of Hertfordshire and Essex, by Tasciovanus and Cunobelin and some of their close contemporaries, and in Hampshire and adjacent areas by Verica, Tincommius (Tincomarus) and Eppillus. By this period coins were being issued in gold, silver and bronze, and served probably in regular trade, as were those of the succeeding Roman period.

The Language of Coinage

After the Conquest, coins had very definite functions and purposes. The language of coin types in the Roman world is distinctive. The challenge for the artist lay in communicating often complex messages clearly, using a single, small-scale visual image and aided by the minimum of written words. Although literacy seems to have been quite widespread in Roman Britain, not all the people who used coins would have been able to read the inscriptions, and therefore the image had to be as self-explanatory as possible. To achieve this, die-sinkers (coin engravers) developed a complex symbolism in which the most common element was personification. Although personifications had appeared at an early stage in the development of Roman Republican coinage, the idea was not fully developed until the time of Augustus.[59] The matter is complicated by the fact that some of the personifications seem to have roles as minor deities – Victoria (Victory), Fortuna (Fortune) and Bonus Eventus

(Happy Outcome) are examples of this, and reflect a tendency in Roman religion to believe that some supernatural force presided over each aspect of life and experience. For purposes of differentiation, the personifications were given attributes – thus Pax (Peace) holds a palm branch and sometimes a sceptre, a horn of plenty or the caduceus, the serpent-twined sceptre of Mercury. Fecunditas (Fertility) is, predictably, shown with children. Pudicitia (Modesty, Chastity) is shown veiled. Securitas (Security) sits back relaxing in a chair, while Fortuna holds a rudder, among other attributes.[60]

Three phases of design in Roman Imperial coin types are discernible. During the first and second centuries types were comparatively varied, communicating a diversity of messages. In the third century personifications predominated, usually in the form of a single figure with attributes which provided immediate explanation and a legend (inscription) which reinforced it. In the fourth century coin types were much more monotonous, and were concerned primarily with reinforcing Imperial power using the language of State ceremonial.

It has been estimated that between a quarter and a half million coins were excavated in Britain in a twenty-year period up to 1987.[61] These must represent only a small proportion of those in circulation in the province. (The collective value of the 1,387 coins from Corbridge, for example, is a mere twenty-four gold aureii, whereas the real coin 'population' of the site in the period concerned, based on calculations of army pay, is likely to have been the equivalent of 240,000 aureii.)[62] In the Empire as a whole, coins were struck in hundreds of millions.[63]

Coins did not flow steadily into Britain, nor did they circulate evenly within the province at all periods in Roman times. Some emperors and periods of issue are barely represented, while others turn up in copious numbers. Rural sites produce almost no coins from the early days after the Conquest, whereas urban and military sites seem to have had coinage from the outset. Coins were introduced initially in army paychests and spread out from the forts and fortresses, though some currency must have entered the province through traders.

In the first and second centuries, most of the coin coming in to Britain was from the mint of Rome. Subsequently the currency was mostly derived from the western Gallic mints, notably those at Trier, Arles, Lyons and sometimes Trieste.[64]

Coins and the British Artist

Disc brooches which imitated Hadrianic sestertii were made in the second century[65] – clear demonstration that coin design had a direct impact on art in the province. Imperial portrait heads clearly borrowed from coins also appear on pendants and other items of jewellery. Additionally, a number of gems have designs which they share in common with coins, though whether both were dependent on a common source for their iconography cannot be determined.

A coin appears to be the inspiration behind the design on a cake mould from

Silchester, which shows a scene of Imperial sacrifice involving the emperor Septimius Severus and Julia Domna, though the precise model is not known.[66] A bronze mirror-cover from Coddenham in Suffolk has a medallion copied from a coin of Nero, with a portrait bust on the obverse and a scene of *adlocutio* (the emperor addressing the troops) on the mirror itself.[67]

At certain periods coins were issued in Britain, sometimes officially, sometimes not. Coins were also struck to inform the Empire (and perhaps sometimes particularly Britain) of events in Britannia. Most of the coins relating to Britain use a personification of Britannia, represented as a lady sitting on a pile of rocks, or a depiction of Victory with a record of events in Britain on a shield.

Earlier than these are coins of Claudius, which commemorate the conquest of the province and depict a triumphal arch surmounted by a statue of the emperor flanked by trophies and with the inscription DE BRITANN. This coin type probably refers to the arch set up in Rome: a portion of its inscription survives.[68] Although coins of this type were issued intermittently during Claudius' reign, they were not specifically intended for circulation in Britain. This is less certainly the case with the Britannia issues of Hadrian and Antoninus Pius. The coins of Pius in particular are roughly struck and are exceptionally common in Britain but rare elsewhere. It has been suggested that some or all of them were struck in Britain, perhaps in a travelling mint, or that they were imported in bulk.[69]

The last commemorative coins were issued to celebrate Septimius Severus's successful campaigns in northern Britain in AD 208–9. One stylized depiction probably represents the bridge used to cross the Tay – the legend TRAIECTUS explains that it indicates a crossing.

Coins Struck in Britain

The relatively few coins that were struck in Britain are of considerable interest for the study of Romano-British art since it is likely that they were the work of locals. They begin with unofficial copies of Claudian bronze coins, struck to meet a shortage of low denomination currency in the years immediately following the Conquest. It is clear from the best coins that local moneyers could copy Roman art well enough to fool most of the people most of the time; the poorer copies show, very significantly, that they did not always feel it necessary.[70]

Leaving aside the plated and cast denarii of the time of the Severi, which were made by hubbing (taking impressions) from original coins, the next main series of British-made issues were the so-called 'barbarous radiates' of the third century. Produced at a time of shortage of small change, the best copies are faithful to the prototypes (Gallic issues which themselves were often rough-and-ready), the worst are abysmal by artistic standards. The coins they were imitating were base metal pieces distinguished by a head with a radiate crown on the obverse, and usually (though not always) a

British imitation of an as of Claudius, with Minerva advancing on the reverse. Enlarged. (L. Laing)

'Barbarous radiate' – British imitation of an antoninianus of the third century AD. Enlarged. (L. Laing)

personification on the reverse.[71] No in-depth study has been made of the art displayed in these coins: the subject is complex since (except for a few in hoards), no two 'barbarous radiates' are alike. Some of the radiates are so aberrant that in the past they were believed to have been the products of the Dark Ages (see attitudes to barbarians, page 2). Some look suspiciously like Anglo-Saxon sceattas, others have an almost surreal quality. A radiate copy from Dinorben in North Wales, for instance, represents a copy, of a copy, of a coin of Aurelian. The portrait just about passes muster, but on the reverse an 'alien' holds aloft a giant fish. It represents, as Boon has said, a rationalization of something not understood.[72] None of the radiates was produced outside the third century, and it used to be thought that they were entirely a token currency for local use. However, research on die-linked pieces from hoards in the Midlands has shown that issues travelled as far afield as southern and western England. This is particularly well demonstrated by issues from a mint which supplied Calverton, Notts. Furthermore, a few British coins have been die-linked with finds on the Continent.[73]

Barbarous imitations were also produced in the fourth century. Mostly, they copied coins, the reverse type of which showed a soldier spearing a fallen horseman and the legend FEL TEMP REPARATIO ('the renewal of happy times'). The copies were of widely differing standard and their main effect in the present state of art historical research is to confuse the beholder.

The Coins of the British Usurpers

A different situation prevails when consideration is given to the official coins of the British usurper Carausius and his successor Allectus at the end of the third century.[74] Carausius's portrait is usually like a caricature, even on coins with meticulously designed reverses. His bust also appears juxtaposed with those of Constantius Chlorus and Maximianus (rendered in a form that was faithful to their own coin portraits) on a remarkable jugate portrait obverse on an antoninianus. This has a legend describing them as CARAVSIVS ET FRATRES SUI (Carausius and his brothers).[75]

The reverses that Carausius employed, however, show how far classical learning had infiltrated the province. For example, the reverse depicting the emperor being greeted by a personification of Britannia bears the legend EXPECTATE VENI (Come thou

Quinarius of Allectus from the Colchester mint, with a galley on the reverse, AD 293–6. Enlarged. (L. Laing)

Antoninianus of Carausius from the London mint, with Pax on the reverse. From the Little Orme's Head hoard. Enlarged. (L. Laing)

long awaited). This phrase comes from Book II of Virgil's *Aeneid*, and was spoken by Dido to Aeneas on his arrival in Carthage.

A series of coins also imitate the tradition established by Mark Antony of paying tribute to legions in the emperor's service. The tradition had been revived nearer Carausius's time by the Gallic Emperor Tetricus and, as with the triple-headed coin, it was an attempt to claim legitimacy.

The London mint continued to strike under Carausius's successor Allectus, who also coined from Colchester. The overall artistic quality of Allectus's coins was much higher, and compared favourably with those struck by the legitimate emperors.

Coins were struck in London at various times during the fourth century. In the early fourth century (under Constantius Chlorus, Diocletian, Licinius I, Maximinianus, Maximinus Daza and Constantine I) the style of the London mint is very distinctive, and can be identified even when the coins do not carry a mint signature. Portraits tend to be flat and angular.

CHAPTER FOUR

JEWELLERY

The jewellery used in Roman Britain is a subtle indicator of the extent to which Romanization penetrated the province. It is also one of the few records that is almost exclusively feminine. The jewellery ranges from the magnificent goldwork discovered, for example, in the Hoxne Treasure (page 57), to mundane examples of pins that reflect contemporary fashion. Safety-pin brooches are notable for being a Celtic form that survived throughout the Roman period, and many pieces of jewellery reflect native Celtic decorative taste. The majority of individual items of jewellery would have been inexpensive and, unlike other art forms, were unlikely to have been used as political statements. Undoubtedly this was a market in which Celtic decorative artists could make a good, if unspectacular living, without facing the difficult artistic decisions of their more ambitious colleagues, such as sculptors.

WOMEN IN ROMAN BRITAIN[1]

Although it is possible to build up a general picture of the role of women in Roman society from documentary sources, it is less easy to determine the status of women in Roman Britain, since Celtic women had been considerably more powerful and 'liberated' than their Roman counterparts, and logic suggests that this situation probably continued.

Romano-British women certainly retained a tribal identity – a woman buried at Ilkley, Yorkshire, was commemorated as belonging to the Cornovii (in the Welsh Marches), while Verecunda Rufilia, buried at Templebrough, was described as a tribeswoman of the Dobunni in the Cotswolds.[2] A curse tablet from Bath designated Veloriga as the head of a family, and other curse tablets from the same site show that through to the fourth century women owned property in their own right and took part in transactions.[3] Tombstones show that women could live to be ninety, but the evidence from the cemetery at Poundbury, Dorset, suggests a high mortality among adolescent girls.[4]

Red hair was much admired in Roman circles, and there is evidence that it was more common in Britain than in provinces nearer the heart of the Empire. Boudicca had red hair, according to Cassius Dio, and red hair as well as blonde and brown was found at Poundbury.[5] Since red hair is traditionally the result of a union between dark and blonde parents, the possibilities of Celts intermarrying with Germanics and Scandinavians, even at this early stage, cannot be precluded, though no work has been done on this fascinating area. There is also evidence for the occasional use of a wig or hairpiece, woven from hair-moss, for example at Vindolanda or Newstead, Roxburgh.[6] The generally dark or reddish hair colouring of Romano-British women doubtless had an effect on the popularity of certain colours of beads or metals in jewellery.

The many glass bottles which have been found in Romano-British contexts would usually have contained perfumes, and a fragment of a flask from Silchester, containing face powder, was in the shape of a bird and had been imported from North Italy.[7] A series of boat-shaped pestle-and-mortar sets from Britain were probably used for grinding down minerals for the ancient equivalents of mascara and eye-liner. Toilet articles, such as cosmetic scoops and nail-cleaners, are common in Britain.

Most women seem to have worn a calf- or ankle-length tunic with sleeves known as the 'Gallic coat'; men wore a knee-length version. Other types of dress are also known.[8]

BRACELETS

Perhaps the finest examples of Romano-British jewellery are gold bracelets. Particularly noteworthy are the nineteen examples from the Hoxne Treasure which constitute the largest group known. All are rigid bangles, including two sets of four, and a pair. A technique employed on several of them has been termed *opus interasile*, and is essentially openwork with a thin web of lace-like gold. The largest of the bracelets made in this manner was intended to be worn on the upper arm, and weighs nearly 140 grams.[9] Another of the openwork bracelets has an inscription, which reads UTERE FELIX DOMINA IULIANE ('Use this happily, lady Juliana') – clearly it was a special commission. The pair of bracelets has a relief pattern of animals and hunters. Of the two sets of four, one set has a ribbed and corrugated pattern rather like basketry. A similar pair was found in the Thetford hoard.[10] *Opus interasile* became very popular in the late Roman Empire, and continued to be fashionable into the Byzantine period. The holes were cut using a chisel.

Two massive gold armlets, fashioned into coiled serpents, were found at Dolaucothi in south Wales. It seems likely that these were produced locally since this was the location of the only known gold mine in Roman Britain. The armlets may have been worn by men, though there is little evidence for males wearing bracelets in Britain after the early Iron Age. Snake bracelets, usually of silver or bronze, are very common in Roman Britain (and were known in the Iron Age, too). They were seen to be protective and were associated with rebirth and healing, and with the god Aesculapius. Snakes were also deployed on finger rings, and both rings and bracelets figured in the Snettisham hoard (page 85). A gold snake finger ring came from the cache at Backworth.[11]

A different type of gold bracelet is represented in another south Wales find, from

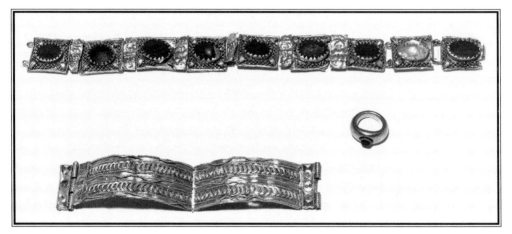

Gold bracelets and ring from Rhayader, Powys. Length of two sections of bracelet: 9.8 and 9 cm. (British Museum)

Rhayader. This takes the form of a hinged strip, and is decorated with filigree patterns of interlace. Filigree (fine twisted gold wire soldered on to the base plate) was particularly fashionable in the Dark Ages. It was not generally common in the Roman period, though it had been fashionable in the fifth and fourth centuries BC in Greece.[12] The Rhayader bracelet is additionally noteworthy for having a Celtic-style pattern with trumpet scrolls at the ends, and touches of enamel inlay. Dated to the second or third century, it is probably a local product. Silver was sometimes used. From Greatchesters on Hadrian's Wall there is a silver bracelet with a hinged central section set with a single cabochon garnet.

Most bracelets were made of copper alloy. Romano-British women could choose from a considerable variety of styles, but the most common are decorated with stamped ring patterns and chiselled terminals. Some have stylized animal heads, and an almost baroque design. A large number of bracelets (datable to the fourth century) were found at Lydney Park, Glos., where they were probably given as offerings to the local god, Nodens.[13]

Some northern British women appear to have liked glass bracelets – typically these have cabled patterns, and seem to have been made from cullett (recycled glass). There are different types, one being yellow with blue and white cables or inlaid scrolls.[14] Many types of plain bracelet are also found in iron (rarely), bone, ivory and shale.

NECKLACES AND BODY CHAIN

The Hoxne Treasure is a valuable source of information about neckwear in Roman Britain. This was so extravagantly flamboyant as to be comparable only with modern designer items that never reach the high street shops. There were six gold necklaces and an ornate gold body chain in the hoard. The body chain is unique in Britain, and consists of a harness with four straps of loop-link chain which went over the shoulders and under the arms, with a central element on the chest and in the corresponding position on the back. One of its roundels was made from a gold solidus of Gratian (AD 367–83). The other roundel was set with gems: a central cabochon of amethyst, four garnets and four further settings, probably once containing pearls. A heavy and thus costly item (it weighs nearly 250 grams), it was probably intended for a relatively young woman. This type of body chain is known from depictions on late Roman terracottas from Egypt, and is worn by Venus in the mosaic from Low Ham, Somerset.

The necklaces from Hoxne are also chains, made in loop-in-loop goldwork – effectively, these were knitted straps of gold. They were intended for pendants (which were not buried with them). Animal heads (lions and dolphins) adorn the fastenings on two, while another has a filigree Chi-Rho.[15]

Other gold chain necklaces of earlier date were found in the Backworth Treasure. The jewellery in this find comprised a bracelet (set with gold beads) and two necklaces, all of ordinary chain-link construction. All three have central openwork medallions in the form of a wheel executed in filigree with granular work – tiny gold beads soldered to the base in another precursor of Dark Age techniques. The necklaces had hook fastenings. Although it has been suggested that the Backworth wheels are Celtic sky god symbols, it is equally likely that they are simply ornaments in the mainstream of Roman decorative art. A similar necklace and clasp with wheels were found at Dolaucothi.[16]

Along with the bracelet mentioned above, a gold ring and a necklet with filigree details and set with cabochons of carnelians and blue paste, was found at Rhayader. Other gold chains, set with emeralds or green glass, have been found at Wincle, Canterbury, London and Thetford.[17] Another, from Richborough, had sapphires.

A gold necklace from Newtown, Cumbria, has a cross-shaped centrepiece, while a necklace from the Wall fort of Greatchesters has three silver chains of double loops with a rectangular box at each end and an oval carnelian in a cable-edged setting in the centre.[18]

Most necklaces were made of beads, usually worn round the neck rather than dangling on to the chest.[19] They had hook fastenings, or were continuous strands. The beads sometimes matched, but more often comprised an assortment of different colours. Blue melon beads were common types in Britain – sometimes they were made of glass, sometimes of a type of faience. Glass beads with gold foil appear to have been imports from Egypt. A necklace from London was made of seventy beads of Baltic amber.

PENDANTS

Medusa jet pendant from Strood, Kent; fourth century AD. Width: 1.75 cm. (Drawing: L. Laing)

A number of pendants show pictorial subject matter. The most interesting series is of jet and comes from York, where a jet workshop, found at Station Yard, manufactured pins and bracelets. Jet beads and finger rings also appear to have been made in the city. Whitby jet enjoyed a particular vogue in the nineteenth century, when it was made into, for example, mourning jewellery. In Roman times it was often fashioned into pendants with pictorial scenes, sometimes of animals, sometimes of human figures. Similar jet items, believed to be British exports, have been found in the Rhineland.[20]

Betrothal pendants depict the happy couple face to face. A fine example from Vindolanda depicts a woman with a late third-century hairstyle, similar to that worn by Salonina, wife of the Emperor Gallienus (d. AD 268).[21] A pendant from a grave in Colchester has two Cupids facing one another, one of them pushing something into a bag held by the other. Three pendants depict the facing head of the gorgon Medusa, and a fourth, from Strood, near Rochester, Kent, has a Celtic-looking head reminiscent of the Bath Medusa.[22]

Of the portrait medallions, three come from York. One of these has a confronted pair, like the Vindolanda pendant, one a family group of parents and child, one a facing bust of a woman.[23] Some medallions were made of more precious materials. The finest of these were cut from chalcedony, and a superb example was found on the Roman road (Akeman Street) near Blenheim, Oxfordshire. Probably carved in a Mediterranean workshop, it may depict a maenad.[24]

A pendant may have been the mounting for a cameo of Indian sardonyx from South Shields, Tyne and Wear. It depicts a bear, carved in white against a dark brown ground. The bear seems to be attacking a goat, and the pendant is likely to be an import.[25]

PRECIOUS MATERIALS

Among the precious materials used in Romano–British jewellery, coral is of interest since it was believed to ward off the evil eye. Necklaces of coral were found at Cirencester and York.[26] Pearls were much admired for their shape, and were worn in groups on ear-rings which clinked when the owner moved. Pearl does not survive well, but an ear-ring from Gloucester still contains its four pearls.[27] Other precious materials used were emeralds, jasper, sapphires, amethyst and garnet. Rarer stones include variscite and chrysoprase.[28] Diamonds were exceptionally rare, and rubies even rarer, but the various members of the quartz family were popular because they were easy to work and varied. Types selected included rock crystal, amethyst, citrine, chalcedony, carnelian, sard, prase, chrysoprase, plasma and jasper. Agates were also used, as well as onyx and nicolo.[29]

RINGS[30]

A burnishing implement of chalcedony, found at Snettisham, Norfolk, was among the treasures that formed the tool-kit of a jeweller. The hoard was coin-dated to the Antonine period, and the cache was hidden in a pottery jar. Among the objects were snake rings and bracelets, gem-set rings, and wheel and crescent necklaces. The silver was obtained by melting down denarii, of which there were over a hundred in the hoard. Silver ingots that had been produced from coins were also present. The treasure contained 110 carnelian gemstones for setting in rings, as well as a large number of finished, set, rings. The cutting of the gems was comparatively crude, but included figures of such classical subjects as Mars, Ceres, Fortuna and Bonus Eventus.

Snettisham jeweller's hoard, Norfolk. (British Museum)

The finger rings from the Snettisham find are representative of some of the multifarious types found in Roman Britain. Rings were worn by both sexes, and ranged from gold to iron, the latter probably worn by men. Some very tiny rings have been found which may have been worn by toddlers, or, somewhat precariously, on the top joint of the little finger.

Betrothal rings are known from fourth-century contexts at Richborough and from the Thetford Treasure. One from Groveley Wood, Wilts., was associated with another ring, pottery and coins which suggested a deposition date around 395.[31]

Those from Richborough and Thetford are of gold, that from Groveley Wood of silver with a gold setting in the bezel. All have bezels depicting clasped hands. There is evidence that such rings were placed on the third finger of the left hand of the woman by the man during the betrothal ceremony, since it was believed this finger was directly connected to the heart – when this still prevailing custom reached Britain is not known.[32]

The simplest rings were plain bands or hoops, sometimes in a spiral which could expand to fit the finger. In the second and third centuries a flat band with a cup-shaped setting for a green glass 'stone' was popular. In the fourth century gold *opus interasile* rings occur, sometimes with mottos.

Among the later gold rings is an *opus interasile* example from Corbridge, Northumberland, which bears a Greek inscription PHILTRON POLEMIOS, indicating that it was a love-token from Polemion.[33] Other inscriptions on rings are likewise in Greek, which was apparently regarded as the language of love. One from Stonham Aspal, Suffolk, is of gold with a central sapphire, and the inscription on the shoulders reads, OLYMPEI ZESAIS ('Life to Olympis'). Other inscriptions include EUSEBIA VITA ('Life to Eusebia') on a gold ring from Bedford, and DA MI VITA ('Give me life') on an iron ring inlaid with strips of copper alloy inscribed with niello letters.[34]

The Thetford Treasure also contained some twenty-two noteworthy gold rings. One example has a pair of woodpeckers on the shoulders, and a central bezel in the shape of a vase with a blue-green glass stone in the centre, representing water. This relates to the cult of Picus, the father of Faunus. (Faunus himself appears on another gold ring in the treasure.) The rings include a multi-jewelled example with the bezel gripped by a pair of dolphins, reminiscent of those found on some late Roman buckles (see below). The rings from the Thetford Treasure show a considerable diversity of techniques, but filigree and granular work are both very much apparent, as is chasing and openwork. An unusual device employs gold wire inset in glass. Associated with the hoard was a group of eight intaglios destined for rings, depicting Fortuna, Spes, Diana, a bird, a dolphin and a corn measure (modius) with corn ears.

Rings and stones seem to have been associated with the same workshop, though some of the stones were old and reset in new rings. None of the jewellery appears to have been used, and the cache may have been a votive deposit.

Some rings were used as signets, for example one from New Fresh Wharf in

London, on which the initials of the owner (A.P.D.) were engraved backwards.[35] Filigree was used extensively on the rings from a small hoard found at Silchester,[36] and on two fine rings found at Newgrange in Ireland.[37] An interesting group of very late silver rings was found in 1843 at Amesbury, Wilts., with coins, of which the latest was of Theodosius (AD 379–95). The bezels have engraved designs, one of a griffin-like creature, one with four helmets facing one another in pairs, and one with a fallen stag and bird. The animals are a foretaste of creatures to be seen in the Dark Ages.[38]

INTAGLIOS

A considerable number of intaglios have come from Roman Britain, betraying the social aspirations of their owners. They were personal signets, used for stamping property and letters. Clearly there was a correlation between the quality of the items and the prestige of the owner.[39] Poorer people made do with glass substitutes for real stones, but the rich used various stones (particularly carnelian), which were set as ring bezels.

The intaglios were cut with a bow drill, and their subjects were drawn from the standard range of classical motifs: gods and goddesses, their attributes and animals. Similar designs were found all over the Roman world. Apart from individual stray finds, collections of stones have been recovered from hoards (such as those from Snettisham and Thetford); from collections of votive offerings (such as those at Bath); and from stray finds (such as those from the legionary bath-house at Caerleon) seemingly lost by bathers. The subject matter of the gems reflected personal tastes – soldiers, for example, tended to favour Mars, Minerva, Fortuna and Victory, as well as a legionary standard or eagles. They also favoured heroes such as Hercules and Alexander the Great. Some display the classical learning of their owners, such as the gem from Colchester which depicts Jupiter feeding Amaltheia, the Cretan goat who looked after him as a baby.[40]

The finest gems were probably imported, but the majority were undoubtedly the work of British artists. One group from Bath seems to have been the work of a local first-century workshop. A second-century workshop operating in the north of England seems to have used red jasper as its material.[41]

The Bath find comprised a cache of thirty-three gems, perhaps thrown into the water in a now-perished bag. Subject matter is varied, and includes horses, Ceres, a portrait bust and a Cupid.[42]

EAR-RINGS

Ear-rings were exclusively female adornments, and ears were probably pierced in very early youth. Mostly they take the form of simple rings of gold or silver, or on occasion copper alloy, sometimes with a bead suspended from them. A few late ear-rings have their terminals twisted together and may thus have been permanent 'sleepers', to which various types of pendant might have been attached. More elaborate ear-rings with semi-precious stones in box settings are also known. A gold ear-ring with a carbuncle inset as a centre-piece was among the votive offerings at Bath.[43]

Most ear-rings in Roman Britain were simple penannular rings and hoops, usually of bronze.[44] Some 82 gold ear-rings, 25 in silver and over 450 in bronze are known.[45] Gold ball ear-rings of the type found in Pompeii and depicted on Egyptian mummy portraits are sometimes found, as are 'Hercules club' ear-pendants. These took the form of an elongated cone, sometimes with filigree, and with settings of gems or enamel. It has been suggested that they were love-tokens, based on the story of Hercules and Omphale (the queen of India with whom he fell in love and to whom he gave his club while he dressed up in women's clothes to please her).[46] Some may have been worn as necklace pendants. Gem-set gold rosette ear-rings were similarly common in the Roman world but in Britain are comparatively simple.[47]

BROOCHES

Most Romano-British brooches were fairly utilitarian, mass-produced items, with little artistic merit, but there are some noteworthy exceptions. A few brooches carry inscriptions, in particular a type of safety-pin fibula known as the 'Hod Hill' type after a site in Dorset. A 'Hod Hill' brooch from Richborough, Kent, has an inscription SI AMAS EGO PLUS ('If you love me I love you more').[48] Brooches fall mostly into three categories – the safety-pin, the plate and the penannular, with crossbow brooches being developed out of the safety-pin models, towards the end of the period under review.

Trumpet brooch, late first/early second century. (Drawing: L. Laing)

Safety-pin Brooches

The most common type of brooch used in Roman Britain was the safety-pin or fibula, which had been current in the Iron Age.[49] The earliest found in the province are the direct descendants of these, usually constructed from a single piece of wire which incorporated the spring, pin and bow. A number of types were imported from the Continent in the first century, but few of the imports are of artistic interest. Two types of safety-pin – the trumpet and the fantail brooch – were sometimes fairly elaborately ornamented. The first of these has the head expanded into a trumpet shape which concealed the spring. They are distinctively Romano-British, and appear to have often been worn in pairs, joined together with a chain. They begin soon after the Conquest, and continued to be made through the second century.

The finest trumpet brooches were of silver, sometimes gilt. One, mercury gilt, from Carmarthen has classical-looking acanthus mouldings on the trumpet, and a catch-plate with Celtic-derived pellet-and-leaf ornament executed in openwork.[50] Trumpet scrolls ornament the body of the brooch. It was one of a pair, and has a rosette on the headloop to carry the now lost chain. Other paired brooches are known, for example from Great Chesterford, Essex, from where came two simple silver examples, linked by a chain. At Red House, Corbridge, a pair of brooches were originally joined by a chain. Two brooches from the Tyne, although not matching, are still linked by a chain.[51] A pair of extremely elegant silver trumpet brooches from Chorley, Lancs., were originally linked by a silver foxtail chain. They are dated by coins to around AD 140.[52]

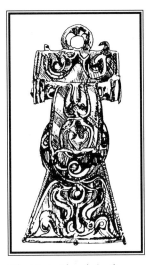

The 'Aesica' brooch (a gilt bronze fantail brooch), from Greatchesters, Northumberland. Length: 103 mm. (Drawing: Marie Crook)

Fantail brooches represent another type, with a fan-tail foot, that seems to have been developed by Romano-British artists in the mid-first century out of imported 'thistle' brooches. The finest example, the 'Aesica' brooch, from a cache found in the strongroom of the fort of Greatchesters on Hadrian's Wall, was found in 1894, and seems to have been linked to a second.[53] Of gilt bronze, it has lyre and trumpet patterns with borders, and was probably made in the north of England under native influence in the later first century AD.

Plate Brooches

The second major type was the plate or disc brooch, which had a flat plate, variously decorated, and a pin at the back. These were popular in the second century, and are frequently inlaid with enamel or glass. They continued, however, to the end of the Roman period, when circular brooches with a cabochon glass setting were quite popular.

Dragonesque brooches are distinctive enamelled plate types that began in the late first century and were particularly fashionable in the second.[54] With double heads, ultimately derived from the 'crested bird' of Celtic Iron Age art, they have a sinuous outline and look not unlike double-headed sea-horses. The earliest, from Lakenheath, Suffolk, seems to have a connection with the Iceni, though most are probably Brigantian products from Yorkshire. They have been found exported as far afield as Hungary, France and Germany, and seem to have continued into the third century.

'Trompetenmuster' brooch with confronted trumpets, from near Sleaford, Lincolnshire; second century. (Drawing: L. Laing)

Trumpet patterns – which are distinctively Celtic – are an element in their decoration.[55]

Some other types of disc brooch seem to reflect native taste. A series of brooches is decorated with relief patterns of triskeles made up out of trumpet scrolls. The finest is from Silchester, but several others show that they were fashionable from the second through the third century and into the fourth. They are interesting pieces of evidence for the survival of native Celtic artistic taste within the province and, equally significantly, are related to the plate brooches that appear to be modelled on coins of Hadrian.[56]

Triskeles (which are characteristic of Celtic art), executed simply in relief against an enamel ground, are also found quite frequently on second-century Roman disc brooches. Typically Celtic too, are trumpet patterns – a devolved type occurs on the footplates of some Romano-British fantail brooches.

A form of openwork ornament using slender-stemmed trumpets is usually associated with harness fittings in the north of the province. This type of work, known as *trompetenmuster*, is found all over the Empire, but may have originated in northern British workshops. A brooch with an openwork S-scroll of trumpets was recently found in Lincolnshire.

A large series of enamelled plate brooches was made in the shape of various animals and objects.[57] Particularly common are those shaped like hares, though dolphins, dogs, flies, birds, fish and horses also occur. In the second century one series of such brooches was in the form of a horse and rider. A related series of disc brooches bear depictions of objects such as the soles of shoes, daggers, axes, cornucopiae, phalluses and swastikas. They have been seen as lucky charms, and the animal brooches in particular occur as finds on religious sites. They are often very colourful, and with their stylized lines

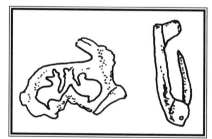

Hare brooch, second century. (Drawing: L. Laing)

represent another strand of native art persisting under Roman rule.

Eastern England in particular has produced bird brooches in the round: particularly common are those in the shape of a duck or hen. Some enamelled brooches are pelta (i.e. shield) shaped, with a horse and rider motif in reserve against an enamelled field.[58] A particularly interesting variant is a brooch of a cat chasing a hare. Hounds chasing hares are common on Roman knife-handles, but this is the sole such feline depiction from Roman Britain. Found at Baldock, Herts., the cat probably originally had stripes inlaid with niello.[59]

Penannular Brooches

Each penannular comprises a broken hoop with a pin which swivelled loosely on it.[60] These had been current in the Iron Age, and remained typically native in the Roman period. The only scope for decoration was provided by the terminals, which were sometimes fashioned into animal heads. They continued with ever increasing elaboration into the post-Roman period.

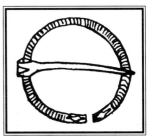

Penannular brooch, fourth century, from Birdoswald. (Drawing: L. Laing)

Crossbow Brooches

In the fourth century the range of brooches was reduced, and it seems likely that particular types were indicators of social status. The most important of these are the so-called crossbows, which are essentially elaborate safety-pin brooches with solid arms terminating in knobs, sometimes made separately and screwed on. Crossbow brooches were made in a range of materials from gold to copper alloy. The finest (but incomplete) example in gold was found on the line of a Roman road at Erickstanebrae in Dumfriesshire. It carries an inscription indicating that it was a gift from the Emperor Diocletian – it may have reached Scotland as part of some buy-off to a barbarian chief. The inscriptions IOVI AUG and VOT XX (a reference to vows taken) allude to the emperor's vicennalia of his accession, and a graffito suggests that at one time it was owned by someone called Fortunatus.[61]

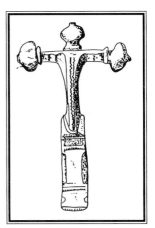

Crossbow brooch, fourth century (Drawing: L. Laing)

Others penetrated Pictland – a fine intact gold example was found at the Moray Firth, with engraved triangular leaf patterns and openwork scrolls,[62] and a native imitation was found on a broch site at Carn Liath in Sutherland.[63] It is known that such cross-bow brooches were worn on the right shoulder by high-ranking men, and there are depictions of them being worn in late Roman art. A very unusual silver crossbow brooch from Sussex has a boar (or more probably a horse), on the bow, and a flattened plate with a punched Chi-Rho. It may date from the beginning of the fifth century.[64]

PINS

Stick pins probably served a variety of purposes including the fastening of clothes but were employed most commonly for pinning up hair. Most were of bronze or bone and are comparatively simple,[65] but a few are more ornate, of gold, silver or jet, and with heads moulded into various shapes. Some seem to be portrait heads, others miniature sculptures.

One bone portrait pin (of uncertain provenance) shows a lady with an ornate Flavian hairstyle. A jet pin from York bears a comical mask.[66] A silver pin from London is surmounted by a tiny statuette of Venus, leaning on a column and raising her foot to fasten her sandal.[67] A bone pin of outstanding workmanship from London has a tiny statue of Fortuna.[68] Among the more unusual subjects represented on pins is an oil lamp with green glass insets that surmounts a silver pin.[69]

CHAPTER FIVE

THE COUNTRYSIDE

The economy of Roman Britain was firmly rooted in the countryside, where the majority of the population lived. The rural areas supplied the towns and the army with basic foodstuffs and raw materials such as iron, timber and slate and supported numerous essential industries from tile making to gold mining and pottery production. Even water was often ducted from the countryside into towns (for example at Wroxeter, Dorchester and Lincoln).[1] Unlike today, the towns offered relatively little employment, though they were the focus of local administration and imperially administered power.

In the past, emphasis has been laid in archaeology on the villa estates of the rich, at the expense of humbler rural settlements. Villas probably accounted for a mere 15 per cent of the total number of rural habitations,[2] and represent the country residences of the Romanized élite. However, it was in such homes that the most numerous, impressive and informative artworks were to be found, so this chapter will display a traditional emphasis.

Aspects of the personalities of individual owners have endured — mostly in the cases of the rich rather than the humble. Through art, architecture and the decor of the houses, levels of education, hopes, aspirations, religious beliefs, fears, occupational and leisure preoccupations and even political affiliations can be glimpsed.

Rural settlements are recognizable in a very wide variety of forms from the most sumptuous stone-built palatial mansions of the southern rich to the round timber-built huts of the peripheral areas. In the less Romanized areas, it is notable that there is relatively little variation between rich and poor homes in either style or size. Frequently, as families became more prosperous, their homes were adapted and extended, although the alternative of building afresh for the new lifestyle was also an option.

The extent to which a new house layout was required must have been connected to the rapidity with which the household adopted Roman ways — a simple agricultural lifestyle did not require, for example, a dining room, bedrooms, a suite of baths, mosaic floors or wall paintings. The general dearth of artwork that survives from Celtic-style dwellings is probably indicative of the lower standard of living enjoyed by the less Romanized population, though as always such deductions must be tempered with the fact that lavish furnishings do not often survive the ravages of time and that quality of life is not necessarily to be equated with the possession of durable *objets d'art*.

The Roman occupation saw the widespread adoption of stone, tile and slate as building materials. Houses with Roman influence were commonly half-timbered on stone plinths, which partly accounts for the survival of only the lower parts. The distribution of Roman-style architecture was partly economic and partly a reflection of the political developments.

THE PATTERN OF RURAL LIFE

Recent estimates suggest that the population of Roman Britain was about four to six million,[3] with around 420,000 living in towns or forts (including the small towns which grew up outside them).[4] In some areas fieldwork suggests that density was high – perhaps one settlement to every 0.4–0.5 sq. km, for example in Northamptonshire and Bedfordshire.[5] Even in the sparsely populated areas, such as the Wear Lowlands of northern England, communities were probably no more than 3.3 km apart.[6] This density is closely comparable with that of medieval England on the eve of the Black Death.[7] Within the Roman period there were undoubtedly fluctuations in the population – there is evidence for a peak in the second century, with a gradual decline in numbers thereafter.

The Romans introduced new elements into the basic rural economy. The endemic warfare of the Iron Age gave way to a time of relative peace and stability, particularly in the south, while Romanization opened up wider markets and boosted trade partly through the increase in a coin-based economy.

There is, however, a growing conviction among scholars that the settlement pattern of the pre-Roman Iron Age endured to a much greater extent than has previously been thought. This is partly the result of highly developed archaeological techniques which have enabled investigators to distinguish as Roman, more humble dwellings. Certainly, at the level of subsistence farming, the differences between Iron Age and Roman-period rural dwellings can be slight.

As far as can be established, Celtic society was based on the extended family.[8] It has been suggested that this system persisted through the Roman period[9] and certainly the layout of some Romano-British villas appears to reflect the fact that two or more families were living under the same roof.[10] There is also no doubt that many villas acquired their Roman features at a secondary or tertiary stage, presumably as new generations became more Romanized.

BASIC CELTIC RURAL ARCHITECTURE

At the Conquest, British architecture (except in parts of the west and north) was almost exclusively of perishable materials – wood, and wattle and daub with thatched or turfed roofs were the norm. The Celts do not appear to have been innovative architects. Generally speaking, the layout of their dwellings differed little according to function – the chief's house, stores, farms, animal shelters usually sharing a common, very practical, circular design. Undoubtedly, we would be correct to guess that the more important buildings must have been distinguished by the additions of furnishings or carvings, but the evidence for this is sparse, whereas, perhaps misleadingly, such details of Roman lifestyles are extremely well documented from a number of sources.

Some areas (notably in the North, Wales and some parts of the Imperial Estates, page 121), paid little heed to Roman-style architecture throughout the period. Even in the most Romanized south, domestic subsistence-level architecture often adhered to traditional British wooden forms. In the north of England (especially Northumberland and Cumbria), Roman period civilian settlements continued the traditions of the pre-Roman Iron Age, with round houses, often in small groups of two or three, often within enclosures. These may reflect the social organization of the extended family.

Here and there settlements stand out as being slightly larger than the rest. Thus in Cumbria the settlement at Ewe Close is larger than most,[11] while in North Wales the enclosed hut group at Din Lligwy on Anglesey seems to be comparable with villas in the more Romanized zones, and is unusual in having produced a silver ingot and numerous coins.[12]

Within the network of native farmsteads, there are hints that a few families enjoyed more power than others. An inscription found near Vindolanda, Northumberland, to the south of Hadrian's Wall, was dedicated to the goddess Sattada by the assembly of the Textoverdi. Presumably these were a regional group (pagus) within the tribal territory of the Carvetii.[13]

In the more Romanized areas the character of rural settlements was correspondingly less Celtic. In Nottinghamshire a settlement at Dunston's Clump, which was occupied from the first to the third century, comprised a group of buildings in an enclosure amid a network of rectangular fields, roughly laid out east–west.[14] The main farmhouse was replaced first by a series of stock pens, then by at least three buildings. Sites such as this, or those at Dragonby, Lincs.,[15] or Braughing, Herts.,[16] seem to indicate that compound settlements comprising a family farm and subsidiary storage and domestic buildings were fairly commonplace in the Romano-British landscape. As well as cattle-rearing and corn-growing, some farmsteads diversified. At Wollaston in Northamptonshire, for example, there is evidence for an extensive vineyard.[17]

Apart from such compound settlements, hamlets, small villages and sometimes larger villages are all to be found in the province. Catsgore in Somerset[18] had twelve farm compounds in a village complex; Chisenbury Warren in Wiltshire was even larger[19], and both seem to have been arranged with deliberate planning along a village street.[20] At Neatham, Hants, when about 2.6 ha. of the settlement was excavated, it was calculated that there was a population of between 2,270 and 3,972 people in the later Roman period. This settlement covered an area of between 8 and 14 ha., and was thus approaching the size of a small town.[21]

Celtic Interior Decoration

No structural wood-carvings have survived from native contexts in Iron Age or Roman Britain. That intricate wood-carving was employed in the pre-Roman Iron Age is apparent from a carved tub from Glastonbury, Som., and wooden figurines are known from religious contexts. Similarly, a range of tools from both Iron Age and Roman Britain seem to have been designed for wood-working, though it is fairly certain that this extended to the decoration of buildings.

VILLAS

Into this relatively simple repertoire the Romans introduced architecture that had been developed in the Mediterranean, in the form of the villa. Villas, as identified by archaeology to date, represent the highly Romanized country estates of the élite – about a thousand are known. The term 'villa' can itself be misleading since it includes a considerable diversity of sites. Villas and their associated estates probably operated in conjunction with local market centres in the distribution of local produce. The variations in their distribution and the speed of their construction have consequently been seen as a mirror of regional prosperity.[22]

Typically, villa owners invested wealth in domestic architecture and both interior and exterior decoration.[23] The plans and features indicate the extent of the Roman lifestyle adopted or followed – thus hypocausts, bath buildings, dining rooms, atria, formal gardens and verandas could all be found, along with a complex of outlying buildings such as barns, granaries, animal houses and workshops which were the working parts of the economic unit.

The distribution of villas is broadly speaking in a zone south and east of the Tees at Middlesbrough, south-westwards across to the Bristol Channel and south to the Exe at Exeter. The villas outside this region are comparatively few and mostly modest.

Although villas were built in the first century (and indeed, the most sumptuous villa found to date, at Fishbourne in Sussex, was begun during that century), the first main phase of building took place in the second. This was followed by a lull in the third century with a noteworthy expansion in the fourth.

It is becoming increasingly clear that villas were not necessarily occupied or even owned by one family, and that they were usually the centre of considerable estates with subsidiary buildings. Early excavators often failed to find the complete complexes, which led to the view that villas were simply luxury houses in isolation from the countryside around.

There are many variations to villa plans, though most conform to a few basic layouts. Many started out (and some finished) as a simple line of rooms under the same roof alignment. Another simple plan was a barn-like structure, sometimes with aisles. By the second century the winged corridor villa had evolved, with lateral wings added

to the central strip element, while in the fourth, the complex courtyard villa developed.

Although for convenience Roman villas have been grouped into different styles, there is considerable variation, and such features as courtyards, usually associated with sumptuous fourth-century villas, are also found early in the period. Essentially courtyard villas were simply elaborations of basic corridor houses.

Early Villas

The earliest villas were often comparatively grand, and represent the sudden investment in the province and the extent to which the local population accepted Roman domination. Nowhere is this more clearly seen than in the 'palace' at Fishbourne, built on the site of an early military base, perhaps connected with the Claudian invasion. At the time of its discovery, the palace was thought to have been the residence of King Cogidubnus of the Regnenses, and as such a tribute to the early Romanization of some pro-Roman chiefs. More recently, however, it has been suggested that it was more likely to have been the palace of the Roman governor of Britain.[24] It rapidly evolved to reach its greatest extent at the end of the first century. It was designed to impress, with a formal garden (discovered in excavation) occupying a central court. A grand colonnaded entrance ensured that the visitor would be suitably impressed when walking through it and the gardens to the audience chamber at the opposite end.

Comparable with Fishbourne, though not as sumptuous, the villa at Eccles, Kent, is another example of the large complex built with outside money and expertise in the early days after the Conquest. It was a corridor house with twelve rooms, put up by AD 65, with mosaics, baths and a garden court with an ornamental water basin.[25]

At Rivenhall, Essex, an early second-century villa replaced a rich Iron Age chieftain's residence, and was laid out around a courtyard – it has been argued that it was the work of Romanized locals rather than immigrants.[26] At Angmering in Sussex there was another of comparable standard.

The winged corridor villa is fairly widespread in the Roman Empire (and in modified form, saw renewed popularity in Tudor England). In essence the layout created an imposing porticoed entrance with public rooms, and with one wing containing such essentials of civilized living as the triclinium (dining room) and suite of baths, while the other wing contained the domestic accommodation. The provision of a veranda (the corridor) to give individual access to a basic strip of rooms caused complications over light which then had to be provided by windows at the back. To allow for clerestories and dormers the elevations had to be taller. Where a second range was built behind the first, the problems of lighting must have posed challenges to architects or builders.

The classic sites for demonstrating the developments of winged corridor houses are Lockleys, near Welwyn, and Park Street, outside Verulamium, both in Herts. At

Lockleys, a pre-Roman circular house was replaced by a timber Roman rectangular structure between AD 50 and AD 120.[27] This was updated in stone in the fourth century. The wings were added after AD 340. At Park Street the winged corridor plan evolved much earlier in the site's history – the wings were added to a strip house sometime around the middle of the second century.[28] The villa at Boxmoor, Herts, had symmetrical wings and a veranda from the outset, perhaps influenced by architectural trends infiltrating from Gaul. These three villas (and a number of others, such as Gorhambury) were close to St Albans. This has led to the suggestion that after Boudicca's rebellion, the local Catuvellaunian gentry built them as their country residences, perhaps with financial rewards from Rome for their loyalty during the troubled period.[29]

Villa building continued during the second century, despite upheavals in Britain when the usurper Clodius Albinus made a bid for the purple. He was defeated by Septimius Severus, and it is likely that the estates of Albinus's supporters were sequestered in the aftermath. Some villa buildings, such as Ditchley, Oxon., and Lullingstone, Kent, show signs of abandonment around this time, though the reasons for this are not known.[30]

Third- and Fourth-Century Villas

The third century was a period of political and economic uncertainty, but towards the very end of the century the situation stabilized and villa building began again. The fourth century was the golden age for sumptuous domestic architecture in Britain – with rebuilding, extensions and new constructions for builders to covet.

The courtyard villa is a particular feature of this period. That at Frocester Court, Glos., started as a strip building which faced on to a walled courtyard (page 101). Some of the elaborate courtyard villas, such as Brading on the Isle of Wight or Stroud in Hampshire, had various buildings grouped around a central court. Some villas, however, such as Chedworth, Glos. and Bignor, Sussex, have double courtyards. At Bignor the second court seems to have been for farm buildings but the function of the second court at Chedworth is less certain. The Bignor complex has an enclosing wall surrounding an area of 1.8 ha. Other complex fourth-century villas include Rockbourne in Hampshire (which in its final stage comprised forty rooms) and Woodchester in Gloucestershire. The Woodchester complex is palatial, and laid out in a manner more akin to Mediterranean planning, with a columned reception room.[31]

On occasion, villas which had grown up piecemeal were given a unifying facade. One example is the assymetrical Gadebridge Park in Hertfordshire, at which a porticoed entrance was built to obscure the sprawl of its outdoor swimming pool and two turriform granaries, built to utilize the heat from the hypocaust beneath.[32]

Some fourth-century villas had elaborate features. For example, the villa at Littlecote, originally excavated in the eighteenth century, seems to have had a summer triclinium (dining room) within a triconch hall. To construct it, one corner of the

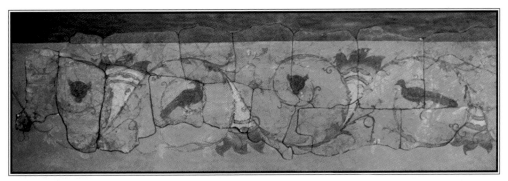

Section from a painted plaster wall with a leafy scroll with panther heads and birds. Verulamium, second century AD. (British Museum)

The Water Newton, Cambridgeshire, treasure of Christian plate. Fourth century AD. The chalice (back, right) may be the earliest surviving liturgical vessel in the Roman Empire. Height of chalice: 12.5 cm. (British Museum)

Silver mirror back, Wroxeter, Shropshire, with 'Gordian knot' handle. Fourth century AD. (Rowley's House Museum, Shrewsbury)

Two platters with Bacchic designs from the Mildenhall treasure, Suffolk. Fourth century AD. Diameters: 18.8 and 18.5 cm. (British Museum)

Group of six gold bracelets from the Hoxne treasure, Suffolk. Late fourth century AD. (British Museum)

Group of carnelian intaglio gems from the Snettisham Hoard, Norfolk. The subjects represented include Fortuna (top right), Diana (right centre), Spes (Hope, upper centre), a modius (corn measure) with corn (lower right), a bird (bottom) and a dolphin (bottom left). Mid-second century AD. (British Museum)

A group of twenty-two gold rings from the Thetford treasure, Norfolk. Fourth century AD. (British Museum)

Mosaic roundel with a head of Christ in front of a Chi-Rho and flanked with pomegranates. Hinton St Mary, Dorset. Fourth century AD. (British Museum)

The mosaic in the triconch hall, Littlecote Roman villa, Wilts. Fourth century AD. (Bryn Walters/Association for Roman Archaeology)

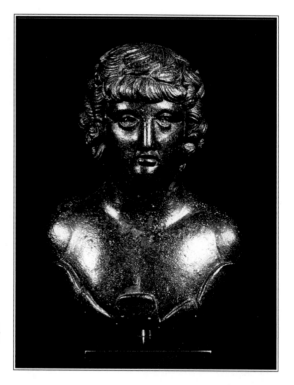

Bronze appliqué of Antinous, favourite of Hadrian, disguised as Bacchus, from Littlecote, Wilts. Second century AD. Height: 11.6 cm. (Luigi J. Thompson/Association for Roman Archaeology)

Reconstruction of the south gate of the fort at South Shields, Tyne and Wear. (Lloyd Laing)

Wall plaster from Colchester, Essex, depicting a gladiator. First century AD. (Colchester Archaeological Trust Ltd)

baths was removed, and access seems to have been through the remaining part. It was built with a central tower supported by four piers with arches. Claims have been made that it had a religious function.[33]

A few villas seem to have had architecturally accomplished bath suites attached to them in the fourth century. At Lufton, Somerset, the baths had an octagonal frigidarium (cold room), with an ambulatory. Over this it would appear that there was a tall clerestory – subsequently the whole structure had to be reinforced with buttresses.[34] At Holcombe, Devon, a similar arrangement was also employed in the bath suite, though in this case the rooms were arranged in an octagon.[35] At Littlecote there was an ornate gatehouse. A recent study has suggested that these features, all of which are found in south-west Britain in the mid-fourth century, were inspired by Mediterranean or North African models.[36]

Some villas were provided with detached religious buildings. At Chedworth, Glos., there was a shrine and a nearby temple – it has been suggested that the site may have been a fourth-century cult centre of Mars Lenus, with a guest house connected with healing.[37] At Lullingstone a circular shrine was built, and later demolished when a mausoleum was constructed. At Bancroft, Bucks., a detached octagonal building may have been a shrine or possibly a summerhouse.[38]

A building at Chalk, Kent, possibly a villa outbuilding, had traces of a wooden staircase to a cellar, which had niches for lamps and a ramp probably for rolling barrels down.[39] Two other cellars are known in Kent: the 'Deep Room' at Lullingstone, and one at Plaxtol, where a drain had been constructed to counter flooding.[40] There is growing suspicion that some villas had an upper storey, though no evidence of ladders or staircases has been found. Fallen gables, found at Meonstoke, Hants, Redlands Farm, Stanwick, Northants and Carsington, Derby, suggest that some villas had elevations of 15 m or more (page 103).[41]

Gardens

Roman gardens were not identified until relatively recently in archaeological terms, but it is evident that many country homes enjoyed cultivated settings which would have required considerable horticultural knowledge and gardening labour. Although gardens have other functions – especially the growing of herbs or produce for the kitchens, and keeping children safe from marauders and farm animals – their distinguishing feature is that, unlike yards or fields, they are intended to be aesthetically pleasing. Gardening is the prime method of creating a visually pleasing outdoor environment which can additionally appeal to the other senses.

Much of the evidence in early excavations was missed or misinterpreted, and not until the investigation of the gardens at Fishbourne was attention focused on this aspect of archaeology. At Apethorpe, Northants, a feature in the central courtyard was probably for a water feature but was misinterpreted in 1859 as a 'dipping well'.[42] At Pitney, Somerset, structures interpreted as pigsties were probably pavilions.[43]

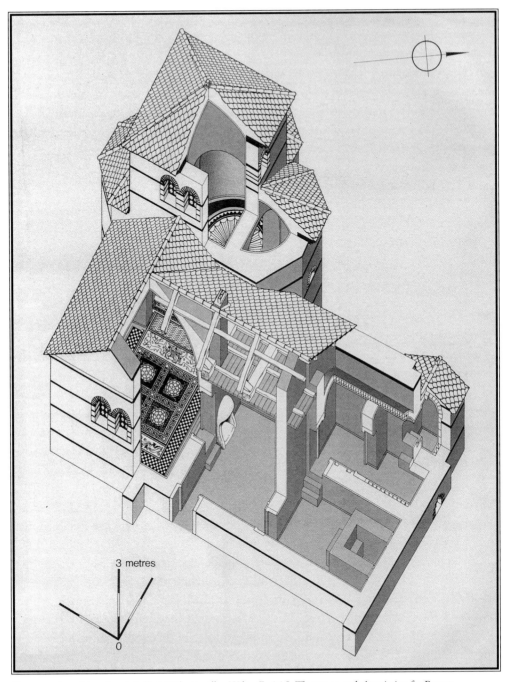

Reconstruction of the triconch hall at Littlecote villa, Wilts. (Luigi J. Thompson and Association for Roman Archaeology)

Replanted Roman garden, Fishbourne, Sussex. (Jennifer Laing)

Of the more recently excavated villas, that at Sudeley, Glos., seems to have had garden terraces within the main courtyard, with a paved pathway down the middle. At Frocester Court, Glos., the drive to the main entrance of the villa was flanked in timeless manner by turfed verges with flower beds which bordered a gravel path. There is evidence for two gardens, one for vegetables and one for flowers, laid out in formal beds.[44] The villa also had what seems to have been an orchard, and box hedges had been planted. Box was also found at the villa of Farmoor, Oxford.[45] At Rockbourne, Hants, there was a square walled garden with gravelled paths as well as an ornamental pond. At Gorhambury a walkway was probably covered with climbing plants, while at Brading there was a water feature, or possibly an alcove with seating.[46] The villa at Ditchley was reached by a drive through paddocks and orchards.[47]

By far the most extensively excavated garden, however, was the formal one in the central court at Fishbourne. Here colonnaded walks led around the outside while the path which divided the courtyard was flanked by bedding trenches. These were alternately semi-circular and rectangular and were planted with shrubs, probably box. A statue base was found at the end of the path in front of the 'audience chamber', and there were probably other statues and trees. The main area was probably grassed.[48]

These fragmentary and elusive remains prove that gardens known from wall-paintings elsewhere in the Empire were also enjoyed in Britain.

Exterior Decoration

At Piddington, Northants, a variety of techniques were used to create an interesting exterior elevation. The original villa was the work of the early second century: the main range had a veranda with a low wall supporting columns made up of stacks of stone discs. The wall had been plastered and painted plum red; the columns, which

Part of fallen facade, Meonstoke, Hants; early fourth century AD. (British Museum)

were painted the same colour, had been plastered with crude mouldings to represent bases and capitals worked into the plaster. The bases and capitals were painted white, and the purple-brown bands of paint just below the capitals were relieved by dabs of white. The tiles on the veranda roof were over-fired to sky blue juxtaposed with others which were pale yellow. The main roof had red tiles, some of which had been painted to achieve the desired uniform shade. In a subsidiary range to the south, a corridor with an exterior wall furnished with windows was painted with vertical stripes. These were about 10 cm wide in a sequence of plum, white, khaki, white and pale green, with traces of trailing branches and flowers painted between.[49]

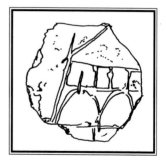

Graffito of a building elevation on wall plaster, Hucclecote, Glos. Height: 9 cm. (Drawing: L. Laing)

The end wall of a late Roman aisled building at Meonstoke collapsed forwards, thus enabling modern excavators to reconstruct the original. A clerestory rose above the height of the side aisles and it appears to have been a subsidiary building in a comparatively ordinary villa complex. Its function is not known, though it may have been at least partly domestic since it had a small mosaic over a hypocaust and some painted wall plaster.[50] The Meonstoke elevation was colourful, and the materials employed (flint, brick, stone, and pink and white mortar) were combined to give an effect rather reminiscent of the late Victorian era.

A building not totally dissimilar to that at Meonstoke, though lacking the side aisles, was sketched on a piece of wall-plaster from the villa at Hucclecote, Glos. At Redlands, Northants, collapsed masonry aids a detailed reconstruction of the exterior appearance of the villa. Here a wing of an entirely stone-built structure seems to have had an upper storey added to the lower; the lower floor had herringbone-coursed masonry, the upper was laid in straight lines. String courses were used as well as quoins, and there was evidence for windows.[51]

INTERIOR DECORATION

The interior decoration of villas reflects the aspirations of their owners, their personal tastes and personal wealth, as well as the availability of materials and skills. It is to be noted, however, that expensive though wall paintings and mosaics were, they were highly durable if reasonable care were taken. Artwork and furniture was diverse and more important in Roman decor, both outside and in, than archaeological finds might suggest.

Marble veneers were sometimes used in interior decoration, and at Fishbourne they included white marble from Turkey, green and white veined marble from the Pyrenees, a yellow and white marble from the Haute-Garonne, and at least a couple of types from Greece, one from the island of Skyros.[52]

Wall paintings went through a number of discernible fashions during the Roman period, the earliest styles being named from those at Pompeii in Italy. Rooms were small and windows tiny or non-existent, so a major function was to give the impression of space and light. Murals can vary from garden scenes with flora and fauna to overpoweringly regal architectural vistas.

Although paintings of all periods are known in the Roman Empire, they are best documented in Pompeii and Herculaneum where the eruption of Vesuvius (AD 79) led to their preservation.[53] Wall painting in Roman Britain tends to follow the trends apparent at Pompeii and later elsewhere in the Empire, though there are signs of a time-lag with older styles still fashionable in Britain after they had fallen from popularity elsewhere.[54]

Due to climatic conditions as well as the robbing-out of stone for later building, Britain has yielded relatively few wall painting remains, the vast majority having been preserved during excavations of the past two or three decades. Nowhere is the ostentatious display of wealth more clearly apparent than at Fishbourne, which was decorated in line with contemporary Italian taste. Little remains of the wall paintings that once adorned the palace, but it is likely from the fragment of a harbour scene, not unlike similar harbour scenes discovered at Stabiae in Italy, that imported pattern books were available in Britain.[55] This painting dates from the last quarter of the first century. Another fragment of wall plaster from the early palace of c. AD 60–70 shows a detail probably from an ornate candelabrum with a red plate with white tassels and fillets on which are yellow fruits. Another fragment appears to show a carefully painted shrimp, while fragments (probably from a ceiling) have eight-petalled pink rosettes not dissimilar to a scheme employed in the Forum Baths in Pompeii or the Herculaneum Palaestra.[56] At Fishbourne yellow was used for the main field, a feature of the late Third and Fourth Styles at Pompeii.[57]

Of slightly later date is a section from Boxmoor, Herts., which dates from the end of the first century. Here the plaster decorated a timber building. It has a pink, spotted dado divided into panels with black stripes, above which was an orange zone with a horizontal red stripe. Above this were red panels with green borders ornamented with candelabra. Part of a frieze was also recovered. The overall decorative scheme is one found commonly in the western provinces of the Roman Empire, for example at Trier in Germany.[58]

Not until the late second century are large-scale figures apparent in Romano-British villa paintings. The earliest are a group of three water nymphs from a niche in the so-called 'Deep Room' at Lullingstone. The background is a neutral white, but the nymphs are delicately modelled, with linear draperies.[59]

Comparatively little wall painting survives from villas datable to the third century, though there are fragments from Collingham, Yorkshire, and Sparsholt, Hants. The Collingham fragments come from a ceiling with octagonal panels containing roundels, in which patterns were printed with stamps, a very unusual technique. This type of ceiling pattern is probably derived from stucco work.[60]

To the earlier part of the fourth century can be ascribed paintings from Iwerne Minster in Dorset (where the walls had panels demarcated by lines and stripes); Bignor in Sussex (where the fragments included those of a column with scale decoration and a volute capital); Gadebridge (where there were trellis patterns); Tarrant Hinton in Dorset (where there were high-quality figural compositions and marble effects); and Brantingham, Humberside (where there were busts with halos in roundels. The halos were perhaps to indicate that the portraits were those of members of the Imperial family, or possibly mythological figures).[61]

The number of rooms that were painted varied according to the income-bracket of the owner. Iwerne, a relatively modest establishment, had only one while at Winterton in Lincolnshire eleven of its sixteen rooms were so decorated.

A device seemingly confined to Britain is wall painting designed to simulate mosaic. At Sparsholt a guilloche pattern in mosaic on the floor was continued on the wall in paint, possibly to make the room look bigger.[62] Other instances of painted mosaic were discovered at Bignor and Lufton.

Aquatic themes are reflected in wall-paintings. The Tarrant Hinton paintings may have included Narcissus looking at himself in a pool (a subject well known to readers of Ovid), while the paintings from a presumed villa at Otford, Kent, datable to the late first or earlier second century, have small-scale figures illustrating episodes from Virgil's *Aeneid*, with inscriptions which seem to have been quotations from the poem, pointing to the literary pretensions of the owner. One inscription appears to read *bina manu* [*lato crispans hastilia ferro*].[63] A bust from Sparsholt might be a portrait of the lady of the house.[64] Other subjects include a very classical Cupid from Southwell, Notts., and a fish from Sparsholt.

Techniques of the Wall Painters

Roman wall plaster, which was made with slaked lime, was built up in layers. A gritty material, usually sand, was added to the base, in the ratio of 2:1 or 3:1, and several layers were built up before the addition of a final, fine coat which contained calcite or, ideally, powdered marble.[65] The Roman architectural writer Vitruvius advocated six layers of sand-based plaster followed by three finishing coats, though in Britain the usual was two base coats followed by one final coat. Additions to the plaster included powdered brick, which helped to make the plaster waterproof.

Each layer of plaster was applied before the last had dried, and the final painting was done in fresco, that is, when the plaster was still damp. This helped to fix the paint as it became coated with a fine layer of calcium carbonate during the drying process. The final surface was polished with stones and last-minute detail was added. Wall painting had to be executed in sections so that the plaster did not totally dry out.

Wall painting of female bust from Sparsholt, Hants; fourth century. (Winchester Museum)

Most of the pigments used were earth colours, but some costly dyes were imported on occasion – cinnabar is known from York, Leicester and London and from a villa at Piddington, Oxon., and gold leaf is known from Colchester, Lincoln and London.[66] Apart from being painted, wall surfaces were sometimes decorated with stucco work. This has survived at Gorhambury, where there are female figures,[67] and at Fishbourne, where there are birds with fruit in their beaks on each side of vases of fruit.[68] The latter is datable to the Flavian period.

Floors

Floors were treated in various ways. Although no carpets have survived from Roman Britain, the designs of some mosaics seem to be imitating them. Some houses probably had wooden floors. At the villa at Piddington red and yellow tiles were laid in a

Stucco moulding from Fishbourne, Sussex; first century AD. (Sussex Archaeological Society)

herringbone pattern. *Opus signinum*, produced by mixing crushed tiles with mortar to create a tough surface reminiscent of modern reconstituted stone, was employed in some buildings.

It is for their mosaic pavements, however, that Roman villas are renowned, partly because it is mostly the floors that have survived and partly because it is through the instantly recognizable mosaics that villas are often noticed during building or farming activities. It is also through mosaics that firm dating evidence can often be obtained since such floors can give archaeologists the assurance that datable objects are securely stratified.

Of the 400-plus mosaics known in Britain,[69] most are abstract rather than pictorial.

About half the British villa mosaics are found in the south-west of England. The mosaics are a mine of information about the tastes and aspirations of the owners. They reveal a highly Romanized society with a thorough grounding in classical literature and values, who revealed their education in their choice of subjects.

The 14 m² mosaic at Woodchester, Glos., known since the seventeenth century and periodically exposed, is the largest north of the Alps.

Only about a quarter of villas had mosaics and comparatively few had more than one.[70] Normally, this was to be found in the dining room. Where there was more than one, private family rooms were probably next endowed, then ante-rooms and corridors, and finally servants' quarters. At Great Weldon, Northants, there was a mosaic, albeit much simpler, in the servants' hall.[71]

The earliest villa mosaics from the province, however, are modest by later standards. At Fishbourne, where there are more mosaics than on any other known site in Britain, two types of mosaic are encountered in the earliest phase – *opus sectile,* in which abstract patterns were built up with geometrically shaped tesserae, and abstract mosaics executed in simple black and white. The mosaics in rooms W8 and N12 at Fishbourne have counterparts at Valcamonica in Italy and Besançon in France.[72]

Of the other first-century mosaics, perhaps the most interesting, although

Black and white mosaic from Fishbourne, Sussex; first century AD. (Jennifer Laing)

Mosaic roundel of Cupid riding a dolphin, Fishbourne, Sussex; second century AD. (Sussex Archaeological Society)

unfortunately very fragmentary, are those from the governor's palace in London. Simple mosaics can also be seen in early villas at Eccles, Kent, datable to *c.* AD 65, which has some colour work and a figured panel in the centre showing gladiators.[73] Tesserae showed that the villa at Angmering, Sussex, had black and white mosaics (destroyed) which may have been by the same workshop that produced those at Fishbourne.[74]

By around AD 100 a new style of mosaic was being employed at Fishbourne, for a coloured floor was laid down at this time with a head of Medusa as a subject. Pieces of distinctive south Gaulish samian pottery cut down to make tesserae helped to date the mosaic, which was laid on top of one of the black and white ones. Samian tesserae also provided a date of *c.* 150–200 for a fine mosaic at Fishbourne with a central medallion depicting Cupid riding a dolphin, with lunettes containing winged sea-horses and sea-panthers. Another mosaic, of comparable date, is very much clumsier.

Cupids as gladiators; fourth-century mosaic from Bignor, Sussex. (Jennifer Laing)

Most of the known second-century mosaics have been found in towns (page 130), but they also exist at, for example, the villas of Winterton, Lincs., and High Wycombe, Bucks. Large numbers of samian tesserae were used at the latter.[75] The High Wycombe mosaic work seems to have been excuted by mosaicists from nearby Verulamium, who were also responsible for mosaics at Boxmoor, Herts, and (well outside their immediate area) at North Leigh in Oxfordshire.[76] At Great Witcombe, Glos., the second-century mosaic work seems to have been commissioned from the mosaic school which served Cirencester (page 131).

Few villa mosaics can be ascribed with any certainty to the third century, though those from Rudston, Humberside, may belong to this century rather than the next, and some poor quality work at King's Weston, Bristol, may belong to the end of the third rather than the fourth century.[77] In contrast, the fourth century was a period of opportunity for competent mosaicists in Britain. More than fifty mosaics have been firmly dated on archaeological evidence to this time.

Even in the fourth century, elaborate pictorial mosaics were far less common than mosaics with abstract patterns, presumably because the skill and the variety of raw materials necessary put the cost up. The range of subjects for pictorial mosaics was, however, wide and reflects distinctly British preferences. In North Africa, for example, favoured subjects were scenes of blood sports – hunts or arena spectacles – but in Britain these are extremely rare. There are scenes of gladiators at Brading, and at Bignor (where they take the form of cupids, thus softening the subject). Hunting is depicted at East Coker in Somerset and at the villas at Frampton and Hinton St Mary (best known for the Christian content of their mosaics). Scenes of chariot racing were found at Horkstow, Humberside, and Colerne, Wilts. British patrons preferred subject matter which reflected the rural life, such as personifications of the Four Seasons, the Winds, a river (perhaps the Stour) at Hemsworth, Dorset, a spring of water (Brantingham and Woodchester), and the days of the week as at Bramdean, Hants. The list of mythological personages represented includes cupids making garlands (Horkstow), maenads (Bignor), satyrs and maenads (Brading, Chedworth, Fullerton and Horkstow) and a shepherd and nymph (Brading and Rudge).[78]

Mosaic Schools

It is likely that mosaics were laid by groups of mosaicists. Since several 'schools' have been identified as producing floors in or around towns, it has been assumed that the mosaicists were urban-based. However, it is notable that no *officina* (workshop) has been found. This leads to the logical suspicion that perhaps mosaicists were based at quarries near their markets, thus ensuring that any remains of their activities have long since been swept away.

The main schools so far identified are the Corinian, traditionally based on Cirencester in the Cotswolds; the Durnovarian, based on Dorchester, Dorset; the Durobrivan, possibly based on Water Newton, Cambridgeshire (a more recent suggestion is that it was based on Leicester); and the Petuarian, based either on Brough in Humberside or on Aldborough. Additionally, a 'Central Southern Group' of mosaicists was responsible for the work at Bignor,[79] and may have been based at Winchester, Chichester or Silchester. The style of their mosaics is very closely comparable to work in Gaul, and the workshop may have been set up by immigrants.

Different 'trademarks' distinguish the various schools. At Cirencester there were probably two schools at work, the 'Orpheus' and the 'saltire' (their distinguishing marks), operating in succession. In all about forty mosaics have been attributed to this, the largest school, which specialized in a distinctive type of Orpheus design, perhaps modelled on a wall painting.[80]

The Petuarian school specialized in concentric circle designs, while the Durobrivan school worked entirely in abstract patterns. The Durnovarian school was responsible for the Christian mosaics at Frampton and Hinton St Mary, and probably also for the mosaics at Fifehead Neville, Dorset, with more veiled Christian content.

Signature, probably of mosaicist, at Bignor, Sussex; fourth century AD. (Jennifer Laing)

Various suggestions have been made about the organization of the mosaic industry. Early mosaicists were almost certainly Italians who travelled to Britain specially for commissions, but by the second century the industry was developing along insular lines. Whether the 'schools' represent individual workshops, or local traditions shared by several different workshops, cannot now be discerned, though claims have been made for 'offshoot' schools, for example at Ilchester, Somerset, seen as derived from the Durnovarian school.

The Mosaicist at Work

The mosaics were made with small cubes, 10–12 mm², fashioned out of local materials: limestone, chalk, sandstone, shale, fired clay and sometimes glass. As previously noted, too, tesserae were sometimes made from pottery – samian, or less commonly, pieces of amphorae. Borders were composed of much larger tesserae, usually set directly on prepared mortar.

The main account of mosaic production can be found in the writings of Vitruvius, who set out an ideal and complex method of construction that was seldom followed in Britain.[81] There were three main methods of construction employed in the province. The direct method entailed laying individual cubes or tesserae *in situ* on a bed of cement (a method employed for the simplest designs). In indirect prefabrication the tesserae were laid face-up in sand on which the design had been sketched. A sheet of linen was glued over them to hold them in place and the panel was then inverted. The undersides of the tesserae were coated in fine mortar and then the panel, thus prefabricated, was turned the right way up, set into the mortar bed and the linen peeled off. In reverse prefabrication the tesserae were laid face-down on a glued linen surface on which the design had been sketched and cement was then poured over the undersides; once this had set, the panel was inverted and the linen removed.[82] The latter method was the most favoured for fine work. The prefabricated panel is known as an *emblema*. On the Continent *emblemata* were made from very tiny tesserae, about 2–3 mm², the resultant work being known as *opus vermiculatum*. The only instance of it known in Britain is at Fishbourne. True *emblemata* are not found in

Mosaic of Aeneas and Dido at Low Ham villa, Somerset; fourth century AD. (Taunton Museum)

Britain, though prefabricated panels, sometimes wrongly set, are frequently encountered, for example at Bignor and Brading. Marks left by abutting prefabricated sections were found at Cirencester; guidelines scratched on the base cement were encountered at Rudston and Hinton St Mary; and red pigment outlining marine creatures, possibly part of the original cartoon or guidelines for direct work, were found at Littlecote.[83]

A feature of many mosaics both in Britain and elsewhere is a line of one or two tesserae which follow the outline of the main picture – this is presumably the result of laying the background separately, but it also gives the appearance of slight movement and vitality.

Floors may have been oiled or waxed for added lustre. The basic colours in Britain are red, white and blue, though pink, black, grey, purple, green and brown are also found. On occasion imported marble offcuts were turned into tesserae (for example in the Seasons mosaic at Cirencester), and glass (usually from bottles) gave variety. Although the main cutting of slabs must have been done in the base workshop, temporary workshops were clearly set up on the site of the commission – tesserae cut from rods and piles of tesserae sorted according to colour are known from Littlecote. Some 750,000 tesserae were used in the main Woodchester mosaic, and there are indications that designs were scaled up or down from the pattern book – at Middlesbrough the mosaic was built up in units of 2.5 Roman feet,[84] and it would appear that mosaics were paid for by the foot.

Indirect laying seems to have been quicker and thus less costly than the direct method. A reconstruction of the head of Venus at Bignor (a design 59.96 cm in diameter) took 7,500 tesserae and twenty-seven hours of work including cutting the tesserae and matching the colours. A reconstruction of the Orpheus mosaic at Woodchester progressed at the rate of 0.18 m² per day using tesserae about 0.8 cm².[85] Diocletian's Edict of AD 301 indicated that the most highly paid mosaicist earned 50 denarii a day plus maintenance.[86] Restoration of the Littlecote mosaic cost over £100,000.

THE VILLA OWNER'S PRIVATE ART GALLERY

Since expensive artworks are usually the last items to be abandoned by their owners, British villas have yielded a surprising number of artworks, particularly in stone. Some statuary may have adorned gardens and simply been forgotten and overgrown during hard times. Other, especially heavier pieces may be evidence for the hurried abandonment of villas in the late Roman period owing to unrest.

Perhaps the finest examples of villa statuary are the pair of second-century portrait busts from Lullingstone, which were buried by a respectful later owner of the villa in the 'Deep Room' with votive offerings before the cellar was sealed and the upper rooms converted to Christian usage.[87] The two busts show bearded men, carved out of Pentellic marble, probably in the Mediterranean. It has been suggested that they were part of the portrait gallery of a successful official transferred to Britain. One dates from around the second quarter of the second century, the other is slightly later, perhaps around 155–65.[88] Fishbourne has yielded the head of a youth, larger than life-size, which perhaps represented a member of the owner's family. Another outstanding piece of sculpture in marble is from the villa at Woodchester, and depicts the goddess Luna, her draperies billowing. She stands 43.5 cm high.[89] Other Woodchester sculptures include a Cupid and Psyche, which may have graced a garden (a similar group adorned a courtyard of a house in Ostia, the port of Rome).[90] Two pedestals from the bases of statues, one with the feet of the statue and an animal's feet were also found at Woodchester. These were found with Luna in room 25; in room 26 there was part of the drapery of a bust, with some small columns of local stone.[91]

Other examples of larger sculptures from villas include a marble of Bacchus from Spoonley Wood, Glos., a relief of Fortuna from Stonesfield, Oxon., and reliefs of Fortuna and a genius from Llantwit Major, Glam. A now-lost head of Ceres was found at Bignor and fragments of statues came from Hucclecote and Wadfield in Gloucestershire and Tracy Park and Lansdown near Bath. Other statues include one of Venus from Froxfield, Wilts., and a panel, perhaps representing Mercury and two mother goddesses, from Wellow, Somerset.[92] Some of these, particularly the reliefs of Fortuna, may have come from household shrines.

Marble statue of Luna from Woodchester villa, Glos. Height: 43.5 cm. (Drawing: L. Laing)

A number of fragments seem to have been elements of decorative architecture, such as a frieze from Longstock, Hants, and a first-century slab with scrolls and cornucopias from Ashtead, Surrey.[93]

Among the small bronzes from Roman Britain are figures of household gods – Lares. A good example was found at Lakenheath, Suffolk, but none as yet has been found in a villa.[94]

FURNITURE

Most information about furniture in Roman Britain has come from tombstones, which depict couches, chairs, tables and stools. Cupboards and sideboards, known from representations elsewhere in the Roman world or from literature, are absent. There are some archaeological traces of furniture, such as Kimmeridge shale legs from couches or

Marble bust from Lullingstone, Kent; second century. Height: 71.12 cm. (British Museum)

tables and the remains of folding stools, a good example of which was found in a Roman burial mound at Bartlow, Essex. Made of iron, it had bronze feet and bronze caps on the ends of the seat bars, and when discovered still had traces of its leather seat. The front of the seat did not have a continuous bar, but had a break, possibly to provide greater flexibility when the stool was piled with cushions.[95] Another folding stool was found in a barrow at Holborough, Kent, in 1953, but lacked the bronze fittings.[96] Related are tripods. Part of one was found in a house at Caerwent, Gwent, and took the form of a bronze claw foot.[97]

Strong boxes appear on some tomb reliefs, and remains of them have been found at Silchester and in a villa at Brislington in Somerset.[98] The fittings for boxes and caskets have been found on many sites, and include those for the box associated with the Hoxne Treasure (page 57).

Couches are well represented in sculptures. One of the most informative is that of Victor from South Shields which depicts the deceased lying on a mattress with a bolster-like cushion. The legs of the couch are lathe-turned, and the seat rails are incised with a pattern of rectangles. A simpler couch appears on a tombstone commemorating a lady called Julia Velva from York. Couches appear on a variety of other tombstones, from Kirby Thore in Cumbria, Lanchester in Co. Durham, and

Table leg constructed from Kimmeridge shale, Colliton Park, Dorchester, Dorset. Height: 48.26 cm. (Drawing: L. Laing)

Chester, where several different types of couch are represented.[99] From this it has been deduced that two types of couch were current, those with backs and those without. The chairs depicted in sculpture seem to suggest that the type most commonly used in Roman Britain had a solid, rounded back, made in one piece with the sides, and placed on a rectangular or semi-circular base. The most common were wickerwork.[100]

Furniture was sometimes decorated. There is, for example, from Littlecote, Wilts., a fine appliqué of Bacchus or possibly Antinous (Hadrian's favourite) which was probably attached to a piece of furniture.[101] Particularly notable are the table legs in animal shapes, which in Britain were carved out of Kimmeridge shale, a soft material worked in Dorset from the Iron Age. One example, discovered at Rothley, a Leicestershire villa, was surmounted by a lion with a prominent mane. Another fragment comes from the Frampton villa. A table leg from a villa at Preston, Dorset, has the head of a fantasy animal at the top and another apparently climbing up the leg underneath.[102]

THE VILLA OWNERS

Many early villas were probably built new or adapted from earlier Celtic-style houses by local leaders whose objectives were to demonstrate ostentatiously their new allegiance. Some may have been the homes of people with important urban connections. Others seem to have been the bases of immigrant traders. There was a vast diversity of occupations, from Imperial officials to local entrepreneurs. What villa owners had in common was sufficient money to spend on non-essentials and a taste for skills, objects and fashion imported from abroad.

It is notable that many villas are clustered round major towns, suggesting that it was useful for their owners to be near the centres of local administration. Many probably served in official capacities on the town councils. The pattern is far from uniform, however, since some large towns such as London have few villas in their proximity, while some small towns such as Ilchester in Somerset have many. In the case of London, this dearth may be due to destruction by later building developments. By and large, civitas capitals (local market towns) have more villas round them than administratively less significant urban foci.[103] Almost certainly high status necessitated having more than one home – perhaps a town house and a country seat.

Many early villas may have been constructed as homes for local chiefs – those around St Albans, for example, probably belonged to the Trinovantian potentates. The villa at Gorhambury started out before the Conquest as a complex of timber buildings including a rectangular house, granary and aisled 'barn' of a type found later in Roman Britain. A victim of the Boudiccan uprising, it rose out of its ashes as a stone-built dwelling in the mid-second century. The 'barn' was rebuilt several times in the Roman period on the same site, and was probably (as was the case with other 'aisled barns') the residence of the farm workers. It continued in use until the fourth century.[104]

The villas at Eastbourne, Folkestone and Mersea are all near suitable anchorages,[105] suggesting that their owners were either foreign traders or had close connections with the import/export business. That at Fingringhoe, Essex, which was close to the Claudian supply base near Colchester, may have been owned by an immigrant.[106]

The *Antonine Itinerary* (a list of routes with mileages, initially compiled around AD 220[107]) mentions a villa (located somewhere between Caistor-by-Norwich and Peterborough in East Anglia) called the Villa Faustini – presumably the owner was called Faustinus. The Barnsley Park villa had an inscription FIRMINI which might have meant 'the villa of Firminus', though whether this is the name of the owner or the builder is not known.[108] A text on a tablet from Chew Park villa seems to relate to the sale of land.[109]

A recent suggestion is that many of the early villas were built by army officers.[110] It has been argued that the Park Street type of villa may have been modelled on the first-class accommodation found in *mansiones* (inns) built by the Roman army, and a military model may also lie behind the bath suites in villas. This fact has been seen to account for military equipment found in some villas, such as at Gorhambury, Herts.

A number of villa mosaics appear to reflect the education of their owners. Eight bear inscriptions, two of them metrical (one from Lullingstone being an allusion to an episode in the *Aeneid*, and another from Frampton with a couplet about Neptune). It was suggested by Sir Ian Richmond that the couplets were the outcome of an impromptu versification during a meal.[111] One at Thruxton, Hants, was apparently the name of the villa owner (alas incomplete) – it read QUINTUS NATALIUS ET BODENI. His name is Romano-Celtic, and the rest of the inscription may have related to a private religious group.[112] Another, at Colerne, Wilts., apparently named the successful charioteer depicted in the mosaic. (Compare this with the hunt cups in castor ware, page 69.) Had the villa owner paid for the mosaic with a win at the races? An inscription at Woodchester seems to have been a request to the viewer to worship Bonus Eventus, while one at Bignor appears to have been the signature of the mosaicist, TER[tius].[113]

Some mosaics show scenes from Roman literature. Thus a mosaic at Low Ham, Somerset, depicts the story of Dido and Aeneas from the *Aeneid* which was probably copied from a manuscript original. (A similar model exists in the Vatican Virgil.) From East Coker, also in Somerset, there is a scene of the birth of Bacchus which seems to have been copied from a manuscript illustration of Ovid's *Metamorphosis*.[114] Ovid's book may also be one of the sources of inspiration for the mosaic at Brading which depicts scenes with Ceres and Triptolemus and the story of Perseus. This mosaic has other allusions: Orpheus appears with the Gnostic deity Abraxas, and the elements have been noted in a mosaic of around AD 200 in the House of Dionysus and Ariadne at Antioch.[115]

The other figure-subjects of the mosaics extend the evidence for classical literacy among villa-owners, as well as displaying the Roman liking for dramatic subjects.[116] Apollo and Marsyas appear at Lenthay Green in Dorset; the rape of Ganymede was found at Bignor; Hercules and Antaeus were depicted at Bramdean (Hants) and Hercules with the Hydra was chosen by the villa owner at Pitney (Somerset). Lycurgus and Ambrosia appear at Brading, and Theseus and the Minotaur are to be found in a group of sites of which the most northern is at Oldcoates in Nottinghamshire.

A personification of Astronomy appears at Brading, and one possibly of Providence at Winterton. Among classical deities depicted are Mars, Mercury, Neptune, Venus and Bacchus.

Aquatic themes occur most commonly in bath suites, for example at Witcombe in

Gloucestershire. In these cases the choice of dolphins, fish and sea-horses was probably purely ornamental rather than symbolic.

Some mosaics seem to reflect the religious convictions of their owners. This is particularly the case with mosaics concerned with Christian or Orphic subject matter. The specifically Christian mosaics at Frampton and Hinton St Mary (which has the earliest depiction of Christ known anywhere, in a mosaic), have been noted previously (page 37), but a number of subjects may be less obviously Christian in significance. Doves pecking at fruit or holding a twig appear at Chedworth (Glos.), Keynsham (Somerset), Rudston and Stonesfield (Oxon.), while grapes between confronted peacocks appear at Horkstow, Lincs. A cantharus (a wine-mixing bowl which looked like a liturgical chalice) appears associated with dolphins, fish, peacocks or panthers at several villas. Peacocks were symbols of everlasting life, and dolphins (which were regarded as fish) and fish were also popular early Christian symbols.

The story of Orpheus was commonly used to teach the Christian message, as he descended into the Underworld to rescue Eurydice (a symbol of Christ opening the gates of Hell). Orpheus as charmer of the animals with his pipe-playing was similarly symbolic of the Good Shepherd. Orpheus appears on the mosaic at Woodchester. In the centre was an octagonal pool design, with the legendary hero in the first circle then a frieze of birds encircled by a ring of animals. It seems to have been the work of a Cirencester workshop, though elements are shared with mosaics in Trier in Germany.[117]

Similarly veiled is the possible reference to the triumph of Good over Evil in the depiction of Bellerophon slaying the Chimaera at Hinton St Mary and Lullingstone.[118]

How far the subject matter of mosaics was simply dictated by a choice made after looking through a pattern book has been much debated. No doubt the ability and repertoire of the artist as well as the availability and cost of particular raw materials played an important part. The final choice may have been no more than a general reflection of taste. In all probability the abstract patterns were chosen simply as 'wallpaper' but figured mosaics were probably selected because the patrons had more personal motivation. The idea of 'pattern books' for mosaic design in the Roman world has often been suggested. It is recently seen as less convincing than the view that basic patterns would have been learned by apprentices who kept alive a traditional repertoire.

It seems likely, however, from the wide variety of scenes, that a patron would have demanded more than a cheerful verbal assurance of the likely outcome before investing heavily. It is notable that the mosaics in general are thoroughly classical. So far, no depictions of Celtic deities, or native treatments of classical themes have been recognized. Even the purely ornamental have patterns that belong in the mainstream of classical decorative art – guilloches, Greek key patterns, chequers, stellate patterns, scrolls and the like. A few mosaics which are rather cruder in execution may reflect the natural tendency to stylization found among British artists – for example in the treatment of the eyes in the figures of Apollo and Marsyas at Lenthay Green.

At Rudston, Humberside, a mosaic depicting Venus is exceptionally stylistically drawn, and is surrounded by animals of which two, a lion and a bull, are labelled. The inscriptions are not grammatical, and usually the mosaic is taken as an example of how crude Romano-British art could be. But another explanation for the mosaic is the possibility that the design was really the work of a child, whose fond parents had the design preserved for eternity in the stone floor. The main argument against this is that the subject matter is to be found in North Africa. No such argument can be advanced against the equally childish Romulus and Remus with the she-wolf that appears at Aldborough, Yorks.

ECONOMIC FUNCTIONS OF VILLAS

Most villa owners would have run their estates as farms though the units may have served other economic as well as social functions. At the extensively excavated villa at Barton Court Farm, Oxon., it proved possible to calculate that around 160 ha. were farmed; 40 per cent of the land was arable, the rest being used for cattle and sheep. Ten permanent staff would probably have been needed.[119]

Some villas are in areas where minerals were mined or the pottery industry was strong, such as in the Nene Valley or in the Mendips. Britannia was not able to develop its rural potential uniformly – some areas were notably richer than others, supporting the greatest numbers of fine houses for example. Other regions were surprisingly impoverished. This phenomenon has been explained by the demands of the army which, rather than creating wealth, drained areas which were deliberately used to supply it. The units producing timber, stone or corn for example were likely to have been run not by private individuals but by tenant farmers or bailiffs who rarely achieved riches.

Perhaps the most important motive behind the Roman Conquest was the acquisition of wealth. The extent to which the Imperial machine plundered new territory can be seen from the three areas of Britain which appear to have been huge Imperial estates: the Fens, Salisbury Plain and the Cotswolds. The first two never became prosperous and the Cotswolds did not support rich villas until the later Roman period, presumably because all produce was channelled out to the army as it moved north and then attempted to stabilize the frontier.

CHAPTER SIX

TOWNS

Roman towns were novelties in Britain. Although many grew up piecemeal outside forts for example, some were deliberately planned, using traditional planning systems. They introduced the British Celts to entirely new ways of life and social organization in which forum, basilica, public baths, aqueduct, amphitheatre, theatre and paved streets had roles to play. Houses, sometimes with cellars[1] and perhaps two storeys, rows of shops, and fountains were key elements. Since many Roman towns have been built over, such features have come to light at random and are often 'rescue'-excavated under difficult conditions. Those which were not developed in later periods are by definition atypical and have rarely been excavated – the town of Silchester in Hampshire is a notable exception.

Major towns were sited at strategically important locations for communications and local resources as well as administration. Towns were automatically the focus of much artistic and architectural endeavour, both public and private. Almost certainly the towns of Roman Britain were adorned with statues and monumental arches, but for the most part these have not survived. The rationale behind the deliberate development of towns in Roman Britain was to spread classical ideals. Tacitus opined that the growth of towns was the outcome of Agricola's educational policy of spreading the use of language, dress, porticoes, bathing establishments and dinner parties.[2] In contrast to other parts of the Empire, planned towns were comparatively rare in Britain. In Roman Italy there were about 480 towns, in Gaul about 60.[3]

CELTIC 'URBAN' SETTLEMENTS

The closest Celtic equivalent to towns were called 'oppida'[4] by Julius Caesar. They existed mostly in the south-east and share a number of features such as planned street layout and zones for different uses, which probably accounts for the enthusiasm with which the Romano-Britons appear to have taken to urban life proper. However, after the Claudian conquest in AD 43, any budding Celtic architectural or town planning development was subordinated to the classical ideal.

Many oppida show signs of pre-conquest Romanization in the adoption of rectangular building plans, though rectangular building had been a minor feature of earlier periods in the Iron Age, for example at Crickley Hill, Glos.[5] Since they were built from perishable materials, it is hard to know whether they displayed the kind of civic art and ostentation common in Roman towns. The evidence may simply not have survived.

Both hillforts and oppida – the chief foci of Celtic tribal society – were deliberately replaced by Roman towns. For example, the oppida of Wheathampstead and Prae Wood were probably the antecedents of Roman Verulamium (St Albans), while that at Silchester underlay the Roman town of Calleva Atrebatum.

THE STATUS OF TOWNS

Romano-British towns fall into different categories according to status. Coloniae (for example, Colchester and Gloucester) were chartered towns intended for legionary veterans. They originated as legionary fortresses and were show-pieces wholly dedicated to Roman ideals. The municipiae of Roman Britain, which were also chartered, are poorly documented, the only certain example being Verulamium, although London (Londinium) may have achieved this status before perhaps being promoted to a colonia in the early fourth century.[6]

The unchartered 'cantonal capitals' were essentially straight replacements of the tribal centres, and by the mid-second century fifteen had been created.[7] Some help was given for this purpose – a few governors made grants, and some emperors, such as Hadrian, may have remitted taxes.[8] Such towns were built by and for the locals.

In addition to these categories there was an amorphous group known to archaeology somewhat uninventively as 'small towns', which amount to about eighty sites. They are by far the most numerous urban settlements.[9] There is very little evidence of deliberate planning among these, as they tended to grow up as ribbon developments along roads, with the growth of side streets from the main artery. Their origins were diverse. A few started as vici attached to forts, perhaps focused on an inn or posting house as was the case with Catterick or Wanborough. A few such as Bath or Buxton may have developed round a healing spring. Some may have evolved around a local market. A few were probably granted the official rank of vicus later in their development. They generally lacked amenities such as fora and basilicas, and few had key public amenities, though such luxuries were occasionally found. In the third or fourth century some, such as Ilchester, Water Newton, Bath, Towcester or Carlisle may have been upgraded. The small towns could be any size from a village to a settlement 40–50 ha. in extent.

Town planning was generally less ambitious in Britain than in Gaul. Where a town had been deliberately planned, a grid-iron street layout was employed, dividing the area into blocks termed *insulae*. The towns of Roman Britain were small, comparable to their medieval successors. The largest was London, with a population of about 30,000, and an area of about 160 ha. Colchester and Verulamium had populations of around 15,000 in the time of Boudicca, but later Colchester only housed about 4,400. Even at their greatest extent, the largest towns such as Verulamium and Corinium sheltered no more than 20,000 people, while the small towns had populations ranging from 300–1,500, and the civitas capitals around 2,000–3,000 inhabitants.[10]

Elsewhere in the Empire, rich individuals endowed towns with public buildings and statuary. In Britain there is little direct evidence for this, though there is some evidence for officially approved remission of taxes on occasion to allow towns to complete a municipal building. Certainly public building was in hand soon after the Conquest, and by the mid-second century most towns had at least some of the amenities of civilized urban life.

TOWN DEFENCES[11]

In the early years after the Conquest, few towns were defended. The purpose of town defences in any age is always debatable – were they erected in order to repel physical attack or for symbolic reasons such as state or civic pride expressed through artistic or architectural endeavour? The erection of Roman town walls reflects official policy since permission had to be sought from the emperor. Since burials were not permitted within the walls, there was also strong moral and religious reason for defining boundaries.

Roman townspeople certainly felt the need for walls or banks, sometimes with elaborate gateways, from the earliest period in Britain and scholars have long pondered on their motives, attempting with varying degrees of success to equate political upheavals with phases of building or strengthening defences.

Those towns with defences before the end of the second century in Britain usually had military origins. Towards the end of the second century defensive schemes were more methodical and it has long been postulated that the increase in urban defences around the late second century was connected with political upheavals which culminated in the uprising of Clodius Albinus (page 98).[12]

Widespread replacement of the earth-and-timber defences with stone walls began in the third century, before the development of the new types of fortification in the forts of the Saxon Shore (page 142). At London forgers' moulds found in a tower dated the construction to before 225–30,[13] and similar gates at Silchester, Caerwent, Canterbury and Brough were probably roughly contemporaneous. At Verulamium the Silchester gate had a coin hoard of 227–9 in a wall tower, proving that it was built some time after this date.[14] During this building programme the coloniae were generally neglected, though the early narrow walls were replaced by more substantial ones at Lincoln and Gloucester.[15]

The fourth century saw a renewed programme of fortification. In the middle years of the century, bastions were added to existing walls to take catapults – seemingly incontrovertible evidence that these defences were motivated by fear of outside attack rather than aesthetic considerations. In the earlier defensive schemes town gates were made of wood, but at Verulamium and Corinium monumental stone gates were constructed with double carriageways and drum towers.[16] These suggest that, as in medieval times, there was a strong element of ostentatious display in the motivation of their builders.

ARCHITECTURAL FEATURES OF ROMANO–BRITISH TOWNS

Fora

A Gallic forum (market square) had a double precinct with an oblong court furnished with two entrances on the long sides and with a temple and altar located on one of the short sides and a basilica (town hall) on the other. In Britain only Verulamium followed this plan; elsewhere fora were simple squares with porticoes around three sides and a basilica on the fourth.[17] Although fora were likely to have been the focus of much architectural and artistic achievement, very little evidence in Britain has withstood the test of time.

Public Baths

Bath buildings in Roman towns in Britain often had a military appearance. These public baths differed from the Mediterranean model, where the various rooms were clustered round a *palaestra* or central exercise yard. In Britain the rooms were set in line one behind the other, and by the second century the open exercise yard was replaced with something more suitable for the British weather – a covered hall. Examples have been discovered at Wroxeter, Caerwent and possibly Leicester.

Governor's Palace

A building that has been identified as the governor's palace has been partially excavated in London. It seems to have been built on three terraces above the Thames in the late first or early second century, and had a large ornamental garden (with a pool) dominated by a hall.[18] Round the garden were arranged rooms that probably served some official purpose. The complex extended to some 130 m, the main hall being over 24 m long and over 13 m wide. It would probably have had a Thames-side wharf. A rival claimant is represented by the Huggin Hill baths. Both sites have produced tiles stamped P P BR LON ('Procurator of the province of Britain at London'), showing that both were official.[19]

Inns

There are a few inns known from Roman Britain; most of them connected with forts, such as the *mansio* at Vindolanda (Chesterholm) and that at Chester. Within towns, examples are known at Chelmsford (Essex) and Wall (Staffs.), but the finest is perhaps that at Silchester; this was a large courtyard building on a road to the forum, with a fine bath suite and a granary.[20]

Arches

Three arches stood in Verulamium. An arch was later converted into the Balkerne Gate at Colchester, and another example from London is known from sculptural evidence. A major arch stood at the gateway to the province at Richborough but is known only from its foundations (page 143). The London arch appears to have had a single span, like the Arch of Titus in Rome, with an upper panel depicting the gods of the week. The pillars bore full-length figures including Minerva and Hercules. A wind god was shown at one end, above a scroll. The stones from the arch were found near Blackfriars and had been rebuilt into the city wall in the fourth century. The arch has been dated on art historical grounds to the second or third century.[21] The Verulamium arches were single-span and comparatively simple. Two arches spanned Watling Street and were intended to mark the first-century limits of the town when the third-century walls were erected.[22]

Public Statuary

The appearance of magnificent Roman town statuary in Britain has to be pieced together from fragments and conjecture. The most impressive example is the head of a bronze statue of Hadrian, found in the Thames in 1834, which probably adorned the London forum. It is evident that the statue was originally more than life-size. The head itself is 41 cm high, and the statue may have been erected on the occasion of Hadrian's visit to Britain in 121 or 122.[23]

London has also produced a number of other bronze fragments, presumably from Imperial statues. A colossal forearm and right hand, originally gilded, was found in Seething Lane. Other pieces include two hands, one of which, from Lower Thames Street, may have come from the same statue of Hadrian as the head found in 1834 (above).[24] The bronze head of Claudius from the Alde in Suffolk which was found in 1907 (page 27) had a tilt of the head which has suggested it may have come from an equestrian figure.[25] From London has come a battered bronze head, probably of Nero, found in 1906 at Great Eastern Street, outside the city walls of Londinium.[26]

Stone Imperial statuary is also known – a marble bust of Trajan was found in a modern garden at Bosham in Sussex. It is probably far too large to have been a 'Grand Tour' trophy, and it may well have been from a work which graced the palace at Fishbourne or a public place in nearby Chichester.[27]

A colossal head of Constantine the Great (roughly twice life-size) was rediscovered in the basement of the Yorkshire Museum in 1944 (*illus.* page 18). Although the stone is extremely weathered, it is clearly a sensitive portrait, and may have been erected in a public building in York when he was declared emperor there in 306.[28]

Although the statue is lost, an inscription which probably comes from a statue plinth in London[29] reads: NVM C[AES AVG] PROV[INCIA] BRIT[ANNIA] ('To the divine power of Caesar Augustus, the province of Britain [set this up]').

The historian Suetonius commented that 'numerous statues and busts' of Titus were put

Bronze hollow cast bust of Hadrian from London. Height: 42 cm. (British Museum)

up in Britain in the late first century, though none has survived.[30] Other public statues from Roman Britain are not necessarily Imperial. There is a fragment of the mane of an equestrian statue from the forum in Gloucester,[31] and the life-size leg of a horse from Lincoln, which was also probably displayed in the forum there.[32] At Cirencester excavators found a larger-than-life eye from a statue that seems to have stood in the apse of the Flavian basilica.[33] The famous bronze eagle from Silchester was made the subject of a children's novel by Rosemary Sutcliffe, *The Eagle of the Ninth*. It probably adorned a statue group, perhaps depicting Jupiter, in the town basilica (where it was found).[34]

A pedestal from Caerwent has an inscription commemorating the fact that the (now lost) statue which surmounted it was erected in honour of Tiberius Claudius Paulinus, legate of Legio II Augusta at Caerleon by the town community, in around 213.[35] The legate subsequently became governor of Britannia Inferior.

Theatres

Theatres are not well represented in Roman Britain though there are excavated examples at Verulamium, Colchester and Canterbury, and an inscription mentions one at Brough-on-Humber.[36] Theatres served a variety of functions, some of which were religious, and the one at Verulamium may have also served some of the functions of an

Verulamium theatre, St Albans, Hertfordshire. (L. Laing)

amphitheatre since there are suggestions that animals were baited there. Tacitus refers to a theatre at Colchester at the time of the Boudiccan uprising, but the theatre that has been partially excavated there was a second-century building outside the town.

Roman theatres had a semi-circular auditorium facing a stage. The Canterbury theatre was built in the later first century, with third-century rebuilding, and was adjacent to a temple complex.[37] The Verulamium theatre was put up on a site apparently left clear for it in the earlier days of the city. The first structure, which was near a Romano-Celtic temple, had an almost circular orchestra with earth banks for wooden seats. In the late second century additional seating encroached on the orchestra and in the third century staircases were added. In the fourth century the extra auditorium seating was removed and a perimeter wall built – subsequently it was used as a rubbish dump.[38]

Ivory mount in the form of a theatrical mask from Caerleon, Monmouth. Height: 10.8 cm. (Drawing: L. Laing)

Of theatrical remains, there is a fragment of a life-sized theatrical mask from Baldock, Herts., made of fired clay. Only the grotesque grin survives.[39] A nearly complete miniature theatrical mask made of ivory also survives from Caerleon, where it was found in the amphitheatre. It was probably used with other panels to ornament a box.[40] Three theatre masks are also known from London.[41]

Amphitheatres

Amphitheatres are known from both military and urban contexts. The best-known in Britain are at Caerleon and Chester, but others can be seen at Dorchester-on-Thames (where a neolithic henge was remodelled for the purpose), Silchester[42] and Cirencester, and others are known at London and Charterhouse-sub-Mendip. The most northerly is military, at Newstead in Roxburgh. They are circular or oval, with (in Britain) banks of earth which supported wooden seating. The Silchester amphitheatre had niches, perhaps shrines to Nemesis (Fate), and the Cirencester amphitheatre was used into the fifth century.

There is little direct evidence for gladiatorial contests in Britain from the amphitheatres themselves, but such finds as the castor ware pots with gladiatorial combat scenes (page 69), and a tinned bronze gladiator's helmet from Hawkedon, Suffolk,[43] probably of the first century, attest their popularity. In addition, there are a number of figurines of gladiators, of which the finest is an ivory from South Shields.[44] It originally formed a knife handle. Two bronzes from London depict Samnite gladiators, done in a provincial style.[45] Apparent evidence, often quoted, for an ancient love-affair is the graffito on a potsherd from Leicester which records Verecunda the actress and Lucius the gladiator.[46]

Town Houses

Early town houses were usually rectangular timber buildings end-on to the street, with shops, workshops and accommodation under the same alignment. Sometimes the dwellings could be spacious – at Watling Court in London one house had eleven rooms, one with a mosaic, and with a floor area of nearly 300 sq. m.[47] In the first and early second centuries there is little evidence for a rich urban élite, but substantial residences were increasingly erected. By the fourth century towns were dominated by the mansions of the rich, and the homes of the ordinary citizens are much more elusive to the archaeologist's techniques.

By the second century a few town houses were being built along Mediterranean lines, notably in places with military connections. Two examples have been excavated – at Gloucester and Caerwent. Both had a central court – that at Caerwent had a veranda which looked out on to a small garden that occupied the court.[48]

One outstanding house in Roman Britain is the 'Painted House' at Dover, which seems to have been associated in some way with the British Fleet, the *Classis Britannica*. Possibly it was the home of a military official, or perhaps was used as a residence for important visitors from the Continent. As the name suggests, it has a suite of richly decorated rooms.[49]

The later town houses were stone built and laid out round courtyards – the urban counterpart of rural villas.

Interior Decoration

The town houses of Roman Britain were decorated in the same ways that the villas were (pages 103–4). Walls were adorned with painted plaster and some floors were embellished with mosaics. Mosaics were being laid down in London before the end of the first century – the Watling Court complex included polychrome mosaics, one with a marine scene,[50] but generally speaking such luxuries were absent from Romano-British urban homes until the boom of the second century following the Emperor Hadrian's visit in 121 or 122. One (or more probably two) mosaic school(s) apparently operated in or near Verulamium and Colchester, being particularly active in the Antonine period. Before this, in the period *c.* 130–150, at Verulamium a superb fluted scallop-shell design with wave border was laid down in the apse of a dining room, with a border of plain red-brick tesserae.

Figural work was employed by the Verulamium mosaicists in the period 150–190. Of exceptional merit was the Stag floor, which had a central square depicting a stag's head being carried off by a lion. This may have been made elsewhere as an *emblema* which was laid in place before the chalices (canthari) and guilloche were built up round it. The whole was set within a background of coarse tesserae. At Colchester similar schemes were in operation.

The recently discovered and badly damaged Middlesbrough mosaic had a central panel depicting two wrestling cupids watched by a bird. This panel may have been prefabricated, but the surrounding area was probably worked *in situ* since the outermost border, an inhabited vegetal scroll with birds and lotus flowers, contains a number of mistakes in its arrangement.

The mosaicists also favoured geometric designs. An attractive mosaic in a courtyard house in Insula XIV at Verulamium, dated to the mid-second century, had hexagons with skewed swastikas between, and motifs which included canthari and ivy leaves. In the second century the high-quality mosaics at Leicester were predominantly abstract. One from Blackfriars is datable to the middle of the century by the samian tesserae used. Compasses were employed in its layout.

At Cirencester figural work is found in the second century. The finest of the Corinium mosaics at this period were discovered in a house at Dyer Street. Here the subject matter of one mosaic was the Seasons, depicted in male guise. Autumn takes the form of a portrait of Dionysos, with windswept hair intertwined with fruit. Glass tesserae were used in this mosaic. In another room was the Hunting Dogs mosaic, with a central roundel, repaired in antiquity, showing Actaeon being dragged down by canines. A third mosaic in the Dyer Street house was decorated in a carpet style, with marine subjects randomly scattered in the field – a sea-leopard, sea-horses, a nereid and a cupid holding the wheel of what was probably Neptune's chariot all figured in the composition. All these Cirencester mosaics probably date from the last years of the second century. Dionysos reclining on the back of a tiger embellished the centrepiece of a fine second-century mosaic from Leadenhall Street, London, with a border of peltas. The small northern town of Aldborough (Yorkshire) was somewhat surprisingly adorned with predominantly geometric mosaics in the second century.

Business for mosaicists was not good in the third century, although it has been suggested that some mosaics have been erroneously assigned to the second century instead of the third. None the less, few can be assigned with any certainty to the third century. The naively charming, grinning wolf and twins from Aldborough may belong to this period (page 121, *illus.* page 133). The fourth century saw a boom in mosaic-laying that accompanied the expansion in villas. It has been assumed that this was based on an extension of the activities of the urban *officinae*, but this seems to be negated by the dearth of urban mosaics. Six fourth-century houses at Cirencester were fairly well endowed with mosaics, however, including a charming example with a central roundel

Mosaic showing Actaeon being pulled down by hounds, from Cirencester, Glos. (Corinium Museum)

depicting a hare (from House XII). This may corroborate the theory that the Corinian School of fourth-century mosaics was based on (or near) this town.[51] One of the later pavements from the Dyer Street house depicted Orpheus surrounded by birds, animals and trees, a hallmark of the school.

Wall Painting

Wall paintings are well represented from Roman town houses, and span the period of the occupation. The finest are those from Verulamium and Leicester. At Verulamium there were wall paintings in existence before the Boudiccan sack. At Six Bells a dado was found showing a still life with a lyre, quiver and bow.[52] Much more extensive is the scheme represented in a courtyard house in Insula XXI which dated from the second century.[53] Located in a corridor, it had a yellow ground frieze with a green and black vegetal scroll with panther heads and birds, above red panelling with

Romulus and Remus with the she-wolf; mosaic from Aldborough, Yorks. (Leeds City Museum)

candelabrum and birds. The ceiling had an all-over coffered pattern with yellow on a purple-red ground, the panels containing floral patterns, birds and panther heads.

Also of the second century is a section of wall painting from a timber house destroyed in a fire in around 155–160. Here the decorative scheme imitates veneers of breccia and alabaster, with *trompe l'oeil* columns.[54] In Insula XXII another corridor painting was found. It too was designed in panels, with stylized 'balconies' above. It dates from the third or fourth century.[55]

The Leicester wall paintings are very varied. Some of the finest come from the

Detail from a mosaic showing a lion with the head of a stag. Verulamium, second century AD. (Verulamium Museum)

peristyle of a courtyard house dating from the mid-second century in Insula XVI. The ornament is close to the Fourth Style at Pompeii, with illusionistic architectural settings. There is an illusionistic projecting podium, painted yellow, with a curving recess. Above this is a columnar building on a black ground, and above that, a black frieze with various motifs, including a theatrical mask. The little building (*aedicula*) has plant fronds and birds, including what seems to be a dove and a peacock, labelled in a graffito. Another section has an architectural theme but with figural work in the panels. The colours are varied, and the artist possessed considerable skill.[56] From the Market Hall at Leicester has come a section of ceiling decoration with a pattern of roundels.[57] Fragments of wall paintings have survived in Winchester, Wroxeter, Cirencester and Catterick.

Household Adornments

Some Romano-British urban householders were rich in worldly possessions. The bronze lampstand Cupid from Cirencester, for example (page 32, *illus.* opposite), dates

Bronze Cupid, possibly a lampstand, from Cirencester, Glos. Height: 41 cm. (Ashmolean Museum)

Bronze Venus from Verulamium, Hertfordshire. Height: 20 cm. (Verulamium Museum)

probably from the second century AD. The eyes were inlaid with silver and (now lost) enamel or glass and there are slots on the shoulders for wings to be attached. It is skilfully modelled, and is probably a Mediterranean import.[58] Nearly as competent, and of similar date, is the bronze figure of Venus from Verulamium, found abandoned in the cellar of a house (page 29, *illus.* opposite). The eyes were originally silvered, and it was probably made in Gaul. She is nude apart from a cloak round her thighs, and the artist has captured the sense of the drapery fluttering in the wind.[59]

URBAN ARTISTS AND CRAFTSMEN

Towns have produced the largest amount of evidence about the working life of artists and craftspeople. Although it has been postulated that mosaicists were based on towns, this is based more on logic than on firm proof (page 111). Sculptors too may have been based on towns. Evidence for this is particularly strong at Cirencester, where a (probably) Gaulish sculptor may have set up his business and produced such works as a head of Mercury, the head of a river god, and a relief of the Tres Matres.[60] It has been suggested that one sculptor worked in both Cirencester and Bath – Sulinus, son of Brucetus, set up altars in both places, and his occupation is mentioned in the inscription from Bath.[61]

Although no workshop can be identified, a series of sculptures found on sites around Cirencester are in the same simplistic but vigorous style, and generally depict the Tres Matres, sometimes the *Genii Cucullati* (page 44), and would be explicable in terms of products carved in a Cirencester workshop.

At Wroxeter after a disastrous fire in the second century, a bronze-smith seems to have bought out his neighbours and amalgamated their workshops into his own. From most of the original shops came evidence of bronzeworking – ovens and furnaces for example. It would seem that small bronze busts and brooches were both manufactured using *ciré perdue* casting, and a fragment of a failed cast showed that two rather than one hole had been left for the melting wax to run out. Silver was also extracted from lead in cupellation furnaces, and silverwork produced.[62] To the west of the baths at Wroxeter was another workshop used by a smith. Nearly half the floor in the back room of the workshop was covered with fine sand for mould making. A small furnace was located on top of a beehive-shaped block of clay, and a column base may have been used for an anvil. Quantities of slag were recovered, as well as powdered granite and glass, perhaps used in enamelling.[63] Also from Wroxeter has come a large iron die, decorated on both faces, for producing stamped sheet metal.[64] Another such die is known from North Wraxall, Wilts.[65] Such dies were used for the production of 'casket ornament' work.

Coppersmiths are known to have worked at Verulamium and Catterick. A goldsmith had his workshop at Verulamium, and others are known at Norton (Yorks.)[66] and

Cirencester. A silversmith operated at Silchester (page 55). Prior to a fire in 155, bronze-smiths worked at Verulamium.[67]

Glass-working was carried out at Mancetter, Wilderspool and Caistor-by-Norwich, where the main product seems to have been window glass.[68] At Leicester a glass-worker set up shop in the market hall in the fourth century, where he melted down silver coins.[69]

In London a jeweller lived behind the quays and worked gold. Here were found two crucibles for refining gold, three lids, and the luting from crucibles stamped with his 'hallmark', a confronted lion and a boar.[70]

One of the characteristics of metalwork in Britain is the colourful use of enamel inlays. Although lumps of crude frit have been found on a number of sites such as Caerleon and Wroxeter[71], there is a dearth of positive evidence relating to enamellers' workshops. Enamel was in use in pre-Roman Britain as well as in the Roman period, but Romano-British enamel employed a wider range of colours.[72] Enamelling appears to have been carried out at Colchester and London – from the former came pieces of blue and red frit.[73] Finds from London include an unfinished enamelled plaque from the Thames, crude lumps of green enamel and balls of blue frit.[74] The best evidence comes from the site of Wilderspool at Warrington, Cheshire, where tuyères (clay covers for the nozzles of bellows), crucibles, raw materials, slag and waste products were found, together with lumps of coloured enamel or frit. No moulds were discovered, however, though a lead model of a trumpet brooch probably for making moulds was among the finds. Enamelled brooches were discovered, and it seems likely that these were being produced there.[75] The best evidence for broochmaking comes from a rural site near Prestatyn in North Wales, where unused clay moulds were found for a type of trumpet brooch, penannular brooches and horsegear.[76]

CHAPTER SEVEN

THE ARMY

Military architectural remains are uncompromisingly Roman in nature and intent: military installations were designed to dominate the British Celts. Since auxiliary units were always stationed in the border areas where Celtic resistance was likely to be greatest, and where the army pay-rolls had fewest outlets, it was also where the interaction between Celtic and Roman cultures can most readily be discerned. The army recruited from all parts of the Roman world so border areas in particular were subject to cosmopolitan influences (Chapter 2).

Conversely, because legionary fortresses were built well behind 'enemy lines' and legionaries were all of citizen status, they were the focus of the most orthodox Roman influences. Army installations of all types were also the centre for much propagandist art, and the legionary fortresses in particular contained a considerable number of highly literate and skilled artisans. These factors are well attested in the artistic remains.

CELTIC FORTIFICATIONS

The Celts did not produce dedicated military architecture – warfare was carried out on an *ad hoc* basis and permanent field armies were unknown. Some large settlements (hillforts) were defended, but they were little more than ordinary rural settlements enclosed by banks and ditches and possibly palisades. Such settlements were forcibly abandoned in favour of new towns in any area held securely by the Romans, and therefore they play little part in the development of Romano-British architecture. Winchester (Venta Belgarum) for example, replaced the Iron Age hillfort of St Catherine's Hill; Dorchester in Dorset (Durnovaria) replaced Maiden Castle; and Wroxeter (Viroconium) replaced the Wrekin. Some were reoccupied apparently through necessity at the end of the period (page 157). There is some evidence that the gateways to such settlements were elaborate and intended to impress, but generally architectural considerations seems to have been of minimal importance.

THE ROMAN ARMY IN BRITAIN

The size of the army in Britain fluctuated. The legions amounted to a fighting force of about 5,300 men each, with additionally a large number of administrators.[1] As there were normally four legions in Britain, the number of legionaries varied between 18,000 and 24,000 men. The evidence of military diplomas and inscriptions suggests that there were 65 auxiliary regiments amounting to a further 36,000 men in the early second century.[2] As citizens, the legionaries were rarely in the front line; thus Tacitus, writing about Agricola's campaigns, could state that the battle of Mons Graupius was fought without loss of Roman life, though 360 auxiliaries perished.[3]

The legionaries built impressive permanent fortresses which often contained architectural features of considerable merit and splendour. On occasion, surviving wall paintings and artworks are comparable to those found in towns or villas. After the abandonment of such bases as Lincoln, Colchester and Wroxeter, the three legionary fortresses were York, Chester and Caerleon. A fortress at Inchtuthill in Perthshire was systematically demolished, presumably when it was evident that the area so far north could not be held. York was visited by the emperors Septimius Severus and Constantius Chlorus, both of whom died there.[4] Constantine the Great was declared emperor there.

The Roman army was primarily recruited to conquer and then maintain the Pax Romana, so most of its achievements were functional. It dug and metalled roads, worked quarries and mines, and constructed the two northern frontier works – Hadrian's Wall and the Antonine Wall.[5] It threw up marching camps each night when moving into new territories, and practice camps when on manoeuvres. The army built signal stations[6] and auxiliary forts in strategic places in the frontier areas and as it moved northwards during the first century, it left behind its military installations to be used in some cases as the sites of towns. The type of units stationed in particular forts can be ascertained from the size and interior arrangements.

Army personnel included not only soldiers and administrators, but also carpenters, masons, tilers, blacksmiths, hydraulic engineers, glaziers, medical orderlies, surveyors, armourers and shipwrights.[7] In addition there were the wives and families of centurions and other high ranks, though it is unknown to what extent these enjoyed married quarters or had to live outside. Hairpins are frequent finds in the sewers of fortifications, however.

Individual personnel had likes and dislikes; emotional, physical and intellectual needs; and personal lives. Above all, soldiery enjoyed high rates of pay in areas where, initially, there were few opportunities for spending. Ordinary soldiers were not permitted to marry, and were on call at all times for the policing of the frontier areas. The intensity with which military life was lived is apparent from the many surviving works of art, especially religious.

Many civilians were attracted by the opportunities afforded by the army so townships called vici grew up beside fortresses to absorb any surplus money and supply goods and services of all kinds. These traders, artisans and suppliers, as well as the unofficial family groups, provided a further market for commodities including luxuries and artworks. The more regular towns outside legionary fortresses are termed canabae.[8]

The highest ranks (who were not soldiers but administrators) were permitted to take their families with them, and Vindolanda (Chesterholm, Northumberland), a fort near Hadrian's Wall, has provided a series of documents including letters between the womenfolk which make particularly diverting reading.[9] The wooden tablets were preserved in waterlogged conditions, and a couple of thousand came to light between 1973 and 1989. They relate to the period between AD 90 and AD 130. The documents cover information about the strength and activities of the units at Vindolanda, military accounts and the domestic accounts of the commandant's house. Personal letters are also included, notably from one Flavius Cerialis, prefect of the Ninth Cohort of Batavians, and his wife Sulpicia Lepidina.[10] Sulpicia received an invitation to her friend Claudia Severa's birthday party. The letter was written by a scribe, but as was the custom, the lady added three terminal lines in her own hand – 'I shall expect you, sister. Farewell sister, my dearest soul, as I hope to prosper, and hail.' A letter from Cerialis himself seems to be by his own hand and of some literary merit.[11] Several hundred different hands have been distinguished in the Vindolanda tablets, proving that literacy was widespread, at least among army society. Some letters seem to have been the work of soldiers from the lower ranks.[12] The divide between Roman and Celt at this point is demonstrated by the Roman use of the term, 'Brittunculi', 'little Brits'.[13]

MILITARY ARCHITECTURE[14]

More evidence for military than for civilian architecture survives in Britain. Though few examples are preserved above foundation height, those which do exist are formidable and have often been preserved because they were incorporated into later defences. Evidence for features above the lower courses (windows, architectural sculpture and so on) is inconclusive since little is preserved *in situ*. Parapet walks, the presence or absence of crenellations and the construction of roofs are equally elusive (see below).

Most of the buildings within forts and fortresses were strictly utilitarian – barracks, workshops, granaries, hospitals and the like, but more scope for impressive building was provided by gates, principia (headquarters), praetoria (commanders' houses), bath-houses (normally located outside forts because of the fire risk) and amphitheatres. In front and behind the central buildings lay barracks and stables blocks. In each legion, 120 men were mounted,[15] but some auxiliary units were composed mostly of cavalry. Stables are remarkably difficult to identify archaeologically, though the presence of drains helps. They have been identified at Ilkley and Halton Chesters.[16] The first military installations were built of wood, which was gradually replaced by stone, starting in the late first and early second century. Stone was used for bath houses in the late first century, and masonry was employed in the building of the legionary fortresses in the early years of the second.[17]

Roman military architecture was designed to be impressive as well as to repel physical attack. This is well exemplified by the fortress at York. It had eight substantial towers and bastions along the front facing the River Ouse, built around the beginning of the fourth century, of which the 'Multangular Tower' still survives beneath a medieval topping.[18] Highly skilled stonemasons used a variety of tools to achieve fine ashlar blocks. Until the later Roman Empire, fortresses were built to a standard architectural plan[19] in the shape of a playing-card. Interior layout was equally stereotyped, though numerous slight variations have been observed, particularly through aerial photography.

Fort and fortress walls were often incorporated into the medieval defences – at Chester for example both the town walls and the main streets are based on the Roman layout. Recent work on the fortress wall has shown that it was topped with a decorative cornice which also served to deflect rainwater. It has also produced evidence for the crenellated parapet crowned with capstones – one such (probably from the wall top) is decorated with a Romano-Celtic bearded face.[20]

There were two main frontier works in Roman Britain: Hadrian's Wall and the Antonine Wall.[21] The appearance of the walls has been discussed many times and their functions were several – as a physical barrier to tribal movements; to repel attack from outside; to create a physical statement of intent and delimit the extent of the Roman world; and to overawe. They are important in a discussion of Roman art in that they were located at the raw edge where cultures met.

In late Roman forts, notably those which defended the 'Saxon Shore' coastline, strength and aesthetic considerations were met by the addition of tile bonding courses, for example at Burgh Castle in Norfolk, Richborough in Kent and Pevensey in Sussex.[22] In the later third and fourth centuries forts were afforded a thick high wall, with few and narrow entrances. Some had the rounded corners of earlier forts, on occasion with bastions – massive platforms of masonry designed to carry catapults. Other types had sharp-angled corners or were of very irregular shape: the most notable of these belonged to the Saxon Shore defences where walls and bastions have often survived nearly to their original height, most notably at Portchester, Hants, Burgh Castle, Norfolk, Pevensey and Richborough, Kent. Other forts designed for coastal defence at this period were built at, for example, Cardiff, at Caer Gybi on Holyhead, at Caernarvon and at Lancaster.[23]

Arches and Gates

Typically, arches were so well made by legionaries in Britain that they were sometimes reused. The chancel arch in the church of St Andrew at Corbridge, Northumberland, was clearly taken from the Roman station adjacent to it,[24] while it is likely that the arch at Escomb, Co. Durham, was similarly reused. Roman arches may also have been reused in early Anglo-Saxon churches in Kent.[25] Vaulting was not unknown – the strongroom vault at Chesters fort on Hadrian's wall survives.

Monumental arches are uncommon in Britain; evidence of the most splendid comes from Richborough. Probably erected around AD 85 to mark the place where the Claudian army landed, it stood at the start of Watling Street. It was a four-way arch, covered in marble and crowned with bronze statues, fragments of which were found. By the mid-third century it had been converted into a signal tower, and subsequently it was levelled to make way for a Saxon Shore fort. It probably stood about 28 m high.[26]

Gates were afforded special treatment since they were symbolic of the might of Rome. One was generally provided in each fort wall – centrally in the short sides, but in the long sides placed towards the front to allow room for the central administrative buildings. Their position could vary according to expediency. The west gate of the fort at South Shields has been reconstructed on the site. Probably built in the second century, it has a double entrance passageway with flanking towers and a crenellated walkway over the passages. Crenellations are attested in sculptures on Trajan's Column in Rome,[27] and on the camp gate depicted on Constantinian coins. Gates usually had inscriptions commemorating the building of the fort, for example that at Risingham, in Northumberland.[28] Some also displayed sculpture, such as the Victory relief recovered from the east gate at Housesteads.

Exterior Features

Baths and temples normally stood outside fortifications. The baths for the forts of Bearsden and Duntocher on the Antonine Wall lay within annexes for added protection. Religious observance normally took place outside the military walls, with the exception of that associated with Jupiter and Mars which was probably carried out in the sacellum of the headquarters building.[29]

Outside cult practice was more diverse, and nowhere is this more apparent than on Hadrian's Wall where the intensity of life attracted rigorous beliefs. The temple of the Celtic deity Antenociticus at Benwell has a simple rectangular cella and a small apse, in which stood the cult statue with two flanking altars to the god.[30] Mithraic temples are particularly associated with the military (page 33).

Some Roman parade grounds are known in Britain, for example at the precipitously placed Hardknott in Cumbria. At the Lunt, near Bagington in Warwickshire, a feature that has been interpreted as a *gyrus* for exercising cavalry horses has been found, while the amphitheatres outside some fortresses, such as Chester and Caerleon, were probably used for exercises as well as for animal baiting and gladiatorial contests. The only auxiliary fort with a small amphitheatre (almost certainly a ludus for games), is at Tomen-y-Mur in Gwynedd.[31]

ART AND THE ROMAN ARMY

The Roman army was an important patron of the arts. Many of the decorated tombstones of Roman Britain come from military contexts. They recorded military service, or were the memorials of the wives and men who had served in the Roman army. Some art comes from shrines and temples erected by soldiers. Some comprise personal items owned by soldiers or their wives, or emanate from the civilian settlements that grew up outside Roman forts.

Interior Decoration

It is extremely likely that official statues stood in the praetoria of major forts, though apart from the occasional base, little evidence survives. Fragments of at least one bronze statue have been found at Caerleon, Gwent, and part of another at Caernarvon, Gwynedd.[32] Some of the walls of an unusual building at Vindolanda were decorated with relief sculpture showing Sol in his chariot. Small statues which were attached to a background were lost during the Second World War before they could be fully examined.[33]

It is clear that the praetorium of an auxiliary fort reached the standard of a civilian home in terms of mural decoration, though floor mosaics are not known. Other military buildings with painted wall plaster include the principia at Brecon Gaer and Caerhun in Gwynedd, the gatehouse at Brecon Gaer and the baths at Chesters, Lancaster, Gelligaer and Loughor.[34] Even the northern fort at Newstead in Roxburghshire had painted wall plaster. What was probably a *mansio* at Catterick in Yorkshire had panels and motifs including a tree.[35] Not surprisingly, the fortresses are more richly decorated than the auxiliary forts; for example, at York the centurion's quarters were also painted.[36]

MILITARY EQUIPMENT

Most military equipment takes the form of pieces of armour, buckles and miscellaneous horsegear, much of which was strictly utilitarian. Recent work has refined dating and suggests that at first it was imported (or made by forming moulds from imported pieces). This was followed by a period when it was produced locally. Finally, in the late Empire, it was imported again from government sources.[37]

Military equipment was subject to fairly frequent changes of fashion, and sculpture can help in its dating. A relief from Croy Hill on the Antonine Wall, for example, shows three legionary soldiers and can be dated to the second century.[38] The equipment can shed much light on how soldiers saw themselves and were seen generally, and can distinguish the different provincial units. What is known of the production and distribution of equipment can also be very informative.

In the first century the army manufactured most of its equipment in *fabricae* (workshops) within forts. Some ornate pieces seem to have been commissioned from private craftsmen – possibly retired soldiers. In the first century brass was the main material used, and was recycled. At the end of a term of service, legionaries sold back their equipment to the army, who reissued it, with the result that some items bear the names of more than one owner.[39]

In the second century the army increasingly produced its own equipment (by then of bronze rather than brass), and an Egyptian papyrus records that legionaries, auxiliaries and civilians all worked on the production of armour and arms in a legionary *fabrica*.[40] In the third century a fabrica at Caerleon was producing various items, and at Corbridge spearheads, javelins and arrows were made and repaired at this time. In the fourth century, although some fort *fabricae* still operated, for example at Housesteads on Hadrian's Wall, around AD 300 Diocletian set up an organized system for supplying the army.[41] Of particular interest are the fine buckle plates decorated with millefiori and enamel that were fashionable in the third century. Millefiori (literally 'thousand flowers') was a type of glass produced by fusing rods, stretching them, then slicing them after the manner of lettered seaside rock. The slices could then be set in enamel. Although workshops employing bought-in millefiori are known from Namur and from Nornour in the Scilly Isles, it is still not known where the millefiori was produced.

To judge by the number of Celtic horse trappings found in Roman military contexts in North Britain, these were manufactured by natives and traded to the army by local entrepreneurs.

Standards

Standards were used as rallying points, in organizing the striking of camp, and as religious talismans.[42] What is assumed to have been a plain, leaf-shaped silver military standard was found at Caerleon in 1928. The tip of a standard was also found at Vindolanda,[43] where a bronze horse attached to a finial was originally interpreted as a standard but later re-appraised as a vehicle attachment.[44] With one foreleg raised, it is a spirited, native rendering of its subject. A bronze hand holding an eagle, from Dover, may have been from a standard belonging to the *Classis Britannica*, the British fleet.[45]

Arms and Armour

The equipment of legionaries was standardized, but that of auxiliary troops varied according to the unit in which they served. Legionaries carried a short sword known as a *gladius*. One was found in its richly decorated scabbard in the Thames at Fulham.[46] The scabbard has a floriate acanthus scroll of the type made popular in the Augustan period. It is inhabited by hares, birds and butterflies, and includes a depiction of Romulus and Remus with the wolf in a cave, above which a stag is shown being pulled down by two dogs.

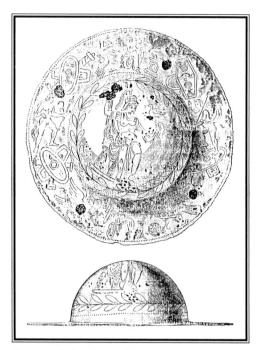

Bronze shield boss from Kirkham, Lancs. Diameter: 10 cm. After Watkins, Roman Lancashire, *1883.*

An even more remarkable iron sword was found at South Shields, and has inlaid gilt-bronze figures of Mars on one side and legionary standards on the other.[47] A couple of decorated shield-bosses probably came from parade shields and were thus never intended for active use. One from the River Tyne is rectangular with a circular central dome, with punched figures on a niello background. The central roundel is decorated with an eagle and surrounded by eight panels, four containing personifications of the Seasons (a popular subject with mosaicists in Britain), a warrior (presumably Mars), two standards and a bull (the badge of the Eighth Legion). Inscriptions note that the owner was Junius Dubitatus who was from the century of Julius Magnus, in the Eighth Legion – a detachment of which is known to have been posted to Britain in the time of Hadrian.[48] Another circular shield-boss from Kirkham, Lancs., is engraved with a seated Mars surrounded by eagles, spearmen and trophies. It seems too delicate to have seen active service.[49]

An auxiliary shield-boss from London carries the inscription COCILLUS F[ecit] ('Cocillus made it'). It has been suggested that it might have been produced by a civilian working for army contracts.[50]

Parade Helmets

A bronze parade helmet found near the Roman fort of Ribchester, Lancs.,[51] is one of the most evocative pieces of art from Roman Britain. This was designed for ceremonial use in the Roman equivalents of military tattoos, the *hippika gymnasia*. The second-century writer Arrian[52] described some of the spectacular shows that involved parade armour. He said that 'manes' were attached to the helmets to billow in the wind, and that oblong, brightly painted shields were carried. (Some painted wooden shields have been found at Dura-Europos on the Euphrates.) Arrian reported that the men wore coloured tunics rather than body armour, and tight trousers, while their horses had chamfreins (head armour).[53] Pennons were carried, decorated with snake-like creatures, and all in all, the effect must have been similar to that of a medieval joust.

The Ribchester vizor depicts a young idealized face, and as such has something of the quality of a theatrical mask. It is almost intact, bar a few holes in the bonnet and a piece missing from the top of the mask. It has imitation ears and is surmounted by a mural crown with a frieze of seated human figures, sea-monsters and facing heads above. Appropriately, the crown of the bonnet is decorated with relief figures of foot-soldiers and cavalrymen armed with short swords. The mask has a fringe of curls and rounded features. The style of the mask is very similar to that employed in a group of three parade helmets from a pit which was filled in at Newstead, Roxburgh, sometime before AD 100.[54] All four may have come from the same

Parade helmet from Ribchester, Lancs., after Watkins, Roman Lancashire, 1883. Height: 28 cm.

workshop, and are closely related to an example from Nicopolis in Bulgaria, though arguments have been advanced that the British finds were manufactured in the province.

One of the Newstead helmets is of silver-plated iron, one of brass and one of bronze. The silver-plated iron example retains the helmet and the vizor, though a substantial part of the latter is now missing. It has a ring, perhaps for a streamer. The bronze find consists of only the vizor (more or less intact). The brass lacks its vizor but is otherwise complete. It is decorated with relief cupids, one in a two-wheeled chariot pulled by leopards. Both this and the Ribchester helmet carry ownership inscriptions. A helmet from Guisborough, Cleveland, was found in the bed of a dried-up watercourse by the Cleveland moors, and is made of thin brass. It has a false upturned peak with two confronted snakes at the crest. A series of figures, appropriate to a military piece (a Victory with wreath and palm; Minerva with a spear and shield; Mars, and a further Minerva and Victory) were lightly incised on it. The deities stand in stylized buildings. A similar helmet was found during dredging work in the River Wensum, at Worthing in Norfolk. This had a false peak, with a bird-headed snake on each side. On either side of the helmet-cap is a sea-dragon, and its crest is adorned with an eagle head. An inscription XII on it refers to a cavalry squadron which, it has been suggested, may have been based at the Saxon Shore fort at Brancaster, 29 km away.[55] It dates from around the third or possibly fourth century AD, when the earlier type of vizor helmet

Parade helmets from Newstead, Roxburghshire. Height of tallest: 24.13 cm. (National Museum of Antiquities of Scotland, Edinburgh)

with human features was out of fashion. Of similar date is a vizor from another helmet found nearby in the same river. This is decorated with representations of Mars and Victory, as well as a Medusa mask.[56] The Guisborough and Worthing helmets were pierced for the attachment of cheek-pieces which did not survive, although ornamental cheek-pieces from similar helmets are known in Britain. The finest is one from the fort at South Shields, which has a delicately drawn representation of one of the Dioscuri (Heavenly Twins). A similar Dioscurus appears in relief on a cheek-piece from Brough, near Newark.[57]

Who owned the parade armour of the types described above is debatable. Did it belong to the army unit, or did it belong to the individuals who wore it? The XII on the Worthing helmet points to that one at least being regimental, but there are engraved personal names on others. CARAU(sius?) engraved his abbreviated name twice on the Ribchester helmet. While some of the subject-matter of the helmets is suitably military in its connotations, other elements, as Jocelyn Toynbee pointed out,[58] are more suited to Roman funerary monuments. Were these parade pieces also involved in Roman ritual and belief?

SCULPTURE AND INSCRIPTIONARY ART

Much of the sculpture from Roman Britain has been found in the vicinity of Roman forts and fortresses. The majority comprises military tombstones and altars, but there are a number of other works, of which the most notable are reliefs associated with inscriptions commemorating building works. Much is known about the movements of the army in Britain through the habit of marking everything with inscriptions – thus it is known for example that the headquarters building at Birdoswald was rebuilt in the time of Diocletian (*c.* 296–300).[59]

Among the most informative military inscriptions are the distance slabs from the Antonine Wall, which commemorate sections of the work as they were completed. The most substantial is the Bridgeness Distance Slab, which records a portion of the wall, about 6.9 km long, erected by soldiers from the Second Legion. The slab is 2.8 m long and 1.2 m high. The inscription is flanked by highly modelled relief work – at the end of the tablet are peltas with griffin heads (peltas were stylized depictions of shields, seen in profile) and compositions set within columned frames. On the left a Roman cavalryman rides down a group of four barbarians, presumably Caledonians, while on the right is a scene of sacrifice with pig, sheep and ox and with five male figures in the background, one of whom is sacrificing at an altar. Another figure is playing a double pipe. This is not the work of a professional military sculptor, but something carved on the frontier probably by a native Briton. Yet it is a forceful work, large in scale, dynamic in its depiction of the triumph of Rome over the barbarians, one of whom has been beheaded.

The image of the horseman riding down the vanquished is one which was taken up on fourth-century coinage, but at this period it was a subject apparently peculiar to provincial British sculpture. Of the other distance slabs, one in the Hunterian Museum in Glasgow is far more classical in style, with a figure of Victory reclining under a architectural frame. She holds a wreath and a palm, and the inscription makes it clear that this commemorates work done by the Twentieth Legion. A further distance slab from Hutcheson Hill, Dunbartonshire, has a female figure, believed to be Britannia, with a signifer (standard-bearer). Beneath is a running boar, the badge of the Twentieth Legion, which also appears on the Victory slab described above. A slab from Duntocher has two facing Victories holding the inscription panel, flanked by figures of Mars and Virtus. [60]

There are a number of other building reliefs from Romano-British forts. These include a slab from the fort at Benwell on Hadrian's Wall, depicting the standard of the Second Legion and its emblems, a capricorn and Pegasus, the flying horse.[61] A slab from Halton Chesters has a wreath encircling the information that LEG[IO] II AUG[USTA] F[ECIT], with pairs of juxtaposed eagle heads.[62] At High Rochester a slab records work done by a vexillation of the Twentieth Legion, probably in the third century. On either side of the inscribed panel are depictions of Hercules and Mars, with the legion's symbol, the boar, underneath.[63]

Tombstones

Tombstones amount to a major category of military relief sculpture. In the early Empire, normal burial practice involved cremation, but by the late first century inhumation was becoming increasingly popular. In the frontier area of Britain,

Detail of distance slab at Bridgeness, West Lothian. Second century AD. (National Museum of Antiquities of Scotland, Edinburgh)

however, cremation probably had a longer vogue, well into the second century, and tombstones continued to be erected over cremation burials. The idea of erecting tombstones was widespread in the classical world, having been common in Greece. Four main types of subject matter are usually encountered in Britain – standing frontal figures of the deceased, seated facing figures, reclining figures and soldiers riding down fallen horsemen.

The earliest military tombstones from Roman Britain include some from the colonia at Colchester. Of these the tombstone of Marcus Favonius Facilis is a classic example.[64] Standing 1.8 m high it is carved from Bath stone, which demonstrates that it was the work of an immigrant sculptor. It was possibly thrown down in 61 at the time of the sack of Boudicca, and the fact that Facilis is not recorded as being a veteran suggests it dates to the period when Colchester was still an active base, not yet a colonia. Facilis is shown facing forward in a niche in the full gear of a centurion, and his round, strong features are clearly intended as a portrait, not merely a stylized rendering of a soldier. Traces of plaster on the stone suggest that it was originally painted. A depiction of a centurion came to light in London in 1669. Another, from Chester, depicts Marcus Cornelius Nepos, who stands stiffly next to his wife – the rendering is both crude and native, and a date in

Tombstone of Facilis at Colchester, Essex; first century AD. Height: 1.83 m. (Colchester Museum)

Tombstone of Flavinus, probably from Stanwix, Cumbria, now in Hexham Abbey, Northumberland. (Andrew Poulter)

the earlier third century has been suggested for it.[65]

The auxiliary cavalryman riding down a fallen foe is also represented among the early monuments from Colchester. Here a certain Longinus is described as *duplicarius* of the First Thracian Squadron, and it is believed that his monument was toppled over at the time of the Boudiccan revolt. The figure was originally believed to have been deliberately damaged, until his face turned up in 1996 on the site where the tombstone had been found.[66] Longinus's horse stands with one hoof upraised, while the rider originally faced the viewer. A naked barbarian crouches under the animal. Above the niche in which it is set is a sphinx flanked by lions.[67] The same general composition is displayed in the tombstone of Rufus Sita, a Thracian cavalryman from Gloucester. Here the niche is square and the barbarian prone but clutching a sword. The horse is starting to rear, and Sita is about to plunge his spear into his victim. Above, a sphinx and two lions rise above the top of the tombstone. It dates from around the late first century.[68]

There are a few other early tombstones of cavalrymen, but none as fine as that now in Hexham Abbey which dates from the second century and depicts a standard-bearer on a spirited horse with the barbarian beneath putting up a good fight. The standard-bearer, whose name was Flavinus, carries his standard and seems to be wearing a ceremonial helmet of the type described above. A remarkable monument of the later first century at Colchester takes the form of a sphinx in Oxfordshire stone, with a portrait head between her paws, and the bones of the deceased protruding from beneath. But this sphinx is serene, the guardian of death, and the head is far from troubled. It is almost certainly the work of an immigrant Mediterranean craftsman.[69]

Military tombstones shed interesting light on the places of origin of the men serving in the army in Britannia. At Wroxeter a soldier of the Fourteenth Legion emanated from Vicenza. At Lincoln one serving in the Ninth Legion came from Heraclea in Greece. An auxiliary from Cirencester was far from his home at Augst in Germany, while a soldier of the Second Legion at Lincoln hailed from Hungary. At Caerleon in south Wales a soldier called Gaius Valerius Victor originated in Lugdunum (Lyons, France). Although later purely a spa town, Bath in the first century may have had a fort – this would account for the tombstones of a Spanish cavalryman and two other soldiers of the Twentieth Legion there. Some military tomb-stones post-date the presumed fort, and may have been of soldiers sent, in vain, to take the curative waters. They include monuments to Julius Vitalis, from Belgic Gaul, and Murrius Modestus, from Forum Julii in southern France.

Tombstone in the form of a sphinx, at Colchester, Essex; first century AD. Height: 83.82 cm. (Drawing: L. Laing)

CELTIC ARTISTIC ENTREPRENEURS IN THE NORTH

Several different Celtic art styles were current on the fringes of Roman Britain. Significantly, the Roman army took up some of the language of Celtic artists – slender-stemmed confronted trumpet patterns, triskeles, peltas and the like – and started manufacturing its openwork horsegear. This has been found throughout the Empire, from Hadrian's Wall (and further north, where one item made its way to a native fort in Fife) to Dura-Europos on the Euphrates. A workshop was set up by a craftsman signing himself Gemellianus in Switzerland. One northern style seems to have been the preserve of warlike northern tribes at the time of the resistance against Rome in the first century AD. The richness of the objects shows that despite the presence of Rome, some native patrons in the fringe areas had sufficient funds to pay for non-essentials.

The style probably developed out of the relief modelled work of the Iron Age style represented by the Snettisham torcs. This style, typified by slender-stemmed trumpets

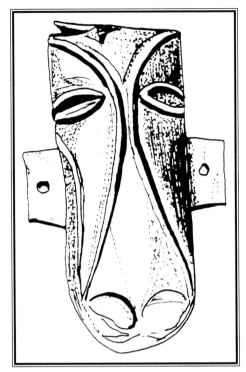

Bronze mount in the form of a horse's head, from the Stanwick hoard, Melsonby, Yorks. Height: 10.9 cm. (Drawing: L. Laing)

Uninscribed tombstone from Ribchester, Lancs., found in 1874. Height: 152.4 cm. After Watkins, Roman Lancashire, *1883.*

and high relief modelling, is found first in the territory of the Brigantes of north-east England. It is best known from a hoard of metalwork found at Melsonby in Yorkshire (also known as the Stanwick Hoard on account of its proximity to the Iron Age fortress and settlement there).[70] The hoard comprises a diversity of objects in differing styles, deposited some time after AD 70 during the Roman advance into the area. Much of the hoard comprises items of horsegear, together with a number of other pieces of which the most significant are two sheet-metal mounts, one in the form of a lugubrious horse head, the other a moustached human face. Other items in the hoard include openwork harness mounts with lips borrowed from terrets (guide-rings for harness) and with peltas taken from Roman art. These additionally display slender-stemmed trumpets.

Also Brigantian is a very unusual terret from Aldborough, Yorkshire, the ring (now broken so it resembles horns) extending from the head of a fearsome humanoid.[71] The terret had an apron (a Roman feature), decorated with a lyre pattern with trumpet scrolls round enamel bosses (now missing). The pattern is perhaps derived from Iron Age mirror backs, but Roman influence could lie behind its design.

Further north in Caledonia slender confronted trumpets in high relief adorn a series of heavy penannular armlets.[72] These status symbols for Caledonian chiefs sometimes bear inset glass settings in their round terminals. One from Castle Newe, Banff, was found near a coin of Nerva (AD 96–8), while another armlet was associated with Roman material of AD 150–200, suggesting a currency in the second century and later.

In a related tradition is the Deskford carnyx or boar's head war trumpet (of which only the mouthpiece survives), and a series of substantial spiral snake bracelets, which were perhaps inspired by Roman snake bracelets. Associated material suggests a currency in the later first century AD and beyond.[73]

CHAPTER EIGHT

THE POST-ROMAN PERIOD

Although the Roman occupation lasted a mere four centuries, its legacy even to the present day has been considerable. The end of Roman Britain has, until recently, been so devoid of historical and archaeological data that it became lost in the general term the 'Dark Ages'. However, as time passes and retrieval methods improve, it becomes clear that Roman-style life continued well into the fifth century, and very probably much later when it was increasingly diluted by Anglo-Saxon culture. With the loss of the Roman central administration in the early fifth century, such vital archaeological evidence as coinage and mass-produced pottery gradually waned in importance.

The system of towns, fortresses and villas was gradually replaced with Anglo-Saxon style tribal units. Wood replaced stone as a building material and local matters became of greater importance than Imperial or continental. Considerable evidence now exists for the survival of Roman-style life in towns; for the survival of Roman Christianity; and for the use of villa sites until well into the fifth century.

CONTINENTAL INCOMERS TO BRITAIN

In the fourth century barbarians made a number of raids on the frontiers and gradually, in the late fourth and fifth centuries the army was withdrawn from Britain in response to unrest elsewhere. In AD 409 Emperor Honorius sent his famous directive to the people of Britain to 'look to their own defences', and from then on Britannia was an independent area. None the less, it still saw itself as Roman.

Concurrent with these political developments were barbarian folk movements across Europe which eventually led to the establishment of Anglo-Saxon kingdoms in the former Britannia by the early seventh century. They were non-literate and pagan at the period of the Migrations, and the process of migration and settlement has been studied through archaeology and later records of varying reliability. Many scholarly arguments, debates and theories have accompanied the study of the process, but it seems that Anglo-Saxon settlement was as much a take-over at the top, and an acculturation of the surviving Romano-British population, as extensive replacement in depopulated areas. The incomers, though tribally organized under leaders, initially displayed little social stratification that can be discerned through archaeology; but a distinctive series of finds suggests the gradual emergence of a rich, Anglo-Saxon dominated élite during the sixth and seventh centuries. Certainly, larger kingdoms began to form out of smaller groupings.[1] Settlement began in East Anglia, with a spread from Kent and the south-east almost as early.[2]

The Anglo-Saxon settlements were confined, until the late sixth century, to areas which had formed part of Britannia. Beyond the frontiers of Roman Britain the native Celtic tribes maintained their traditional lifestyle through the early centuries AD, though there were various political changes perhaps partly stimulated by the presence of their Roman neighbours. In particular, there are signs that from the fourth century or even earlier there were new élites which developed into the kingdoms of the early medieval period.

The incomers did not build in stone, generally did not defend their settlements, did not live in towns and, despite keeping in contact with their continental cousins, were organized on a local rather than a large-regional basis. Culturally, the Anglo-Saxons spoke Germanic dialects, and had what at first appears to have been a very different lifestyle and material assemblage from the Romano-Britons. While it cannot be disputed that they belonged to a less complex society which was able to function on a more self-sufficient level without a centralized administration, the cultural gaps between the Anglo-Saxons and the average Romano-Briton were not huge by the fifth century. Once the central administration had withdrawn, the Romano-British were forced to adopt an alternative system which, not surprisingly, had much in common with that of the incoming barbarians.

THE SURVIVAL OF ROMANO-BRITISH CULTURE

There is growing evidence that the Romano-British lifestyle did not die out very rapidly,[3] and that the seeds for its demise lay not with the barbarian incomers but with the processes already at work in later Roman Britain and in the western provinces of the Roman Empire generally.[4] The populace retained elements of Roman culture through the fifth century and beyond. There is growing evidence for the survival of literacy through the fifth century – Latin inscriptions and an administration based on the Roman system survived, probably with elements of Roman law.[5] The secular centres of power remained towns, though some hillforts in south-west Britain seem to have been pressed back into service and refurbished as local centres, for example Cadbury Castle in Somerset.[6] The towns, however, did not function as they had done in the fourth century and earlier. Many were considerably depopulated and run-down – modern archaeological investigations have shown, however, that they did not cease to function completely. They seem to have served as the administrative centres of small areas. In some cases it appears that they controlled a surrounding territory (the equivalent of the old 'civitas') in which Anglo-Saxon settlement was slow to be established.

There is growing evidence that the fourth-century Roman town buildings were in many cases adequate to serve fifth-century needs, and that in a few places new building in wood was taking place. This process started before the withdrawal of the Roman army and is particularly well attested at Wroxeter in Shropshire.[7] The survival of Verulamium (St Albans) into the fifth century is attested both by archaeology and by documentary evidence – there is evidence for a wooden waterpipe being laid down in one of the buildings in Insula XXVII at some point after AD 460, and the Life of St Germanus records the fact that the saint visited the shrine of St Alban in 428, and met some of the civic fathers.[8] Gildas, a sixth-century historian of dubious reliability, records cities in Britain at the time of his writing.[9]

Most villa buildings were abandoned between the late fourth and the early fifth centuries, although there is no evidence that the lands around them were abandoned. On the contrary – there is incontrovertible evidence that some Romano-British villa estates were taken over directly by Anglo-Saxons. At Barton Court Farm (Oxon.) and Orton Hall Farm (Northants), timber structures were erected alongside the old villa buildings.[10]

The use of coinage was a vital part of Roman civilization, so the question of when it ceased to be in use is of some importance in this context. The last coins to come into Britain were silver issues of *c.* 420.[11] However, when regular circulation within Britain ceased is at present unknown – coinage could have remained in circulation for many decades but, owing to its scarcity, was not subject to casual loss.

Similarly, the commercial production of Roman wheel-made pottery came to an end, but old pots were still in use on some sites during the fifth century, for example in the British hillfort at Cadbury Congresbury, also in Somerset.[12] There is no reason to suppose that these could not have been kept in occasional use or as heirlooms over many decades, perhaps even centuries.

ROMAN INFLUENCES IN POST-ROMAN ART

In the area of artistic endeavour, the records are less ambivalent over cultural interaction than in either the domestic or political arenas. Much Roman influence can be seen in the fifth to seventh centuries, in both Anglo-Saxon art and, interestingly, in those areas that had never been subject to strong Roman influence. Since the Celts and the Anglo-Saxons shared an essentially barbarian background, there was also much interchange between the two. It is very significant to note that many Romano-British objects have been found in Anglo-Saxon graves, implying that the population was intermingling from the start.

Surviving Romano-British Technology

The decay of traditional Roman lifestyles was clearly connected closely with the loss of technological expertise which traditionally had been taught and fostered by the legions. Architecture in particular was affected by the loss of mass-produced bricks, and stone working. A number of the techniques used by Dark Age artists and craftsmen, however, did survive from Romano-British times. They include the use of niello and enamel. In the post-Roman period the Anglo-Saxons seem to have on occasions used enamel. Since it was not a part of the ornamental repertoire of their homelands, it seems logical to assume they learned the technique from Romano-British craftspeople. It appears for example on some disk brooches made in the Midlands, the Anglo-Saxon disk brooch itself being probably a derivative of the Romano-British series.[13]

Parcel gilding was another technique which probably survived from Roman Britain,[14] while the sophisticated use of different alloys, including brass, on the Celtic metalworking site of the Mote of Mark, Kirkcudbright, is likewise probably a technological survival. The widespread use in metalworking in post-Roman Dark Age Britain of small triangular lidded crucibles, might be a Roman survival, though these are also found in Migration Period contexts in Northern Europe.[15]

Millefiori glass-working similarly seems to have been a survival in the Celtic areas from Romano-British traditions. In Roman Britain millefiori was used for a variety of objects, including on 'votive stools', disk brooches and inkwells. It is far from certain whether any millefiori was made in Britain rather than imported – although claims have been made for a factory producing it at Namur in Gaul. It is, however, very likely that some millefiori was produced in Roman Britain, since the earliest millefiori work of the post-Roman period, which employs slices of millefiori in a sea of red enamel, seems to have been a Roman technique. Other types of millefiori working developed later in Ireland, and there is evidence for its production at the Anglo-Saxon monasteries of Monkwearmouth and Jarrow in Northumbria,[16] as well as at Dinas Powys in South Wales and possibly at Luce Sands in Wigtownshire. In England the Roman type of millefiori work is seen particularly in a small group of hanging bowls which may have been made in Lindsey or elsewhere in the East Midlands – they include the millefiori work on the Sutton Hoo hanging bowl. Where millefiori occurs in an early context in the areas settled by the Anglo-Saxons, it is usually assumed to have been imported ready-made from the Celtic regions.

ANGLO-SAXON ART

After the initial period of the settlements, Anglo-Saxon art developed regional features which reflected something of the Romano-British past. The matter is complicated because the art of the Anglo-Saxons in their homelands had already been profoundly influenced by Roman provincial art well before the time of their settlements in England,[17] and while it is possible to point to a Roman model for particular motifs or techniques, it is often far less easy to determine whether the survival is due to factors at work on the Continent or in Britain. This observation also holds true for Germanic culture of the post-Roman period in general, for which even less evidence survives.

ANIMALS

A feature of both Celtic and Anglo-Saxon art of the Dark Ages is a liking for semi-naturalistic animals. These seems to echo a Roman past. The animals are generally simplified, sometimes crouching or running, often looking back over their shoulders. The most common creatures encountered are horses, deer and dolphins, less often birds of prey, though fantastic beasts such as sea-horses or griffins also occur. The best-known series of such animals appears on some late Roman buckles which sometimes turn up in Anglo-Saxon graves.[18] These have loops (see below) in the form of confronted sea-horses or dolphins, less often horses. Of the many examples some are imported and others are British versions. Some are decorated with ring-and-dot ornament, and some have cheerful, open mouths reminiscent of the animals that adorn the hanging bowl escutcheon loops. Similar creatures have been found on bracelet terminals, and on a gold ring from the Thetford Treasure. Crouching animals can be found on such items as a bone knife handle from Corbridge,[19] on a silver ring from Wantage, Oxon., or on two of the silver rings from the Amesbury, Wilts., find.[20] They can also be seen on a buckle plate from Leicester and on a late Roman harness pendant from Margidunum, Notts.[21] Other semi-naturalistic animals appear in Roman Britain as enamelled brooches, on bronze folding knife handles (and a handle from Silchester, Hants, in the form of a horse), on a penannular brooch from Bath,[22] and on a bronze mount from Wroxeter, Shropshire, to give but a few examples. Some of the post-Roman creatures are almost identical to the Roman. The pairs of confronted animals remained a feature of Dark Age Celtic buckles, for example at the Mote of Mark, Kirkcudbright, or even on a buckle from Orkney.[23]

In Anglo-Saxon England the tradition of semi-naturalistic animals can be seen in Quoit Brooch style metalwork[24] dating from the earlier fifth century. There has been an active debate about its origins. The style is so called on account of the most diagnostic example which is on a silver quoit brooch from Sarre, Kent. This has a penannular brooch as a central element surrounded by a flat hoop or quoit, parcel gilt with zones of running quadrupeds with double outlines and hatched fur. The Sarre brooch has, additionally, three-dimensional doves on the plate and the pin which are reminiscent of the woodpeckers found on a ring from the Thetford Treasure and on other Roman pieces. Its beaded border recalls late Roman silver plate. The type of animal represented on this brooch is found not only on brooches but on a variety of other items of personal adornment, such as a buckle set from Mucking, Essex. The origins of the style has been much debated — it could be Romano-British, but an origin in Jutland, a Frankish ancestry and one elsewhere on the Continent have all been canvassed. The penannular element, however, is difficult to parallel outside Britain, and the likeliest ancestry for the style is probably within Romano-British art.

The highly stylized animal heads of the zoomorphic penannular brooches also contributed to Anglo-Saxon art. Anglo-Saxon cruciform brooches, though distinctively Germanic, have in England (though not in the Continental homelands) a footplate in the form of a stylized horse head.[25] A similar type of head can be seen on an Anglo-Saxon finger-ring from Guildford, Surrey, which seems to be a descendant of the snake rings found widely in Roman Britain.

Much of the material culture of the post-Roman Celtic world had its roots in Roman Britain. Wales, the south-west peninsula and much of northern Britain reverted to Celtic cultures. However, although some subsistence equipment belonged to an Iron Age past, much more was the result of gradual acculturation from their Romano-British neighbours or temporary overlords.[26] The range of personal adornment in particular, found in the fifth to seventh centuries, represents a continuation and development from types and styles of artefacts current in Britain in the fourth century – brooch and pin types, other types of dress fastener, beads, armlets and the like all were modifications of versions current either within Britannia or beyond its frontiers.[27]

In the Celtic areas semi-naturalistic animals are found in a variety of guises, for example in rock art or in the form of the mysterious Pictish symbols. The latter are incised on undressed stones, but seem to be ultimately derivative of Romano-British tombstones – claims that they are descendants of Iron Age animals are difficult to substantiate, and the starting date for the series, which may be as early as the fourth or fifth century, is in keeping with a Roman contribution to their development.[28]

The Celtic areas outside the former

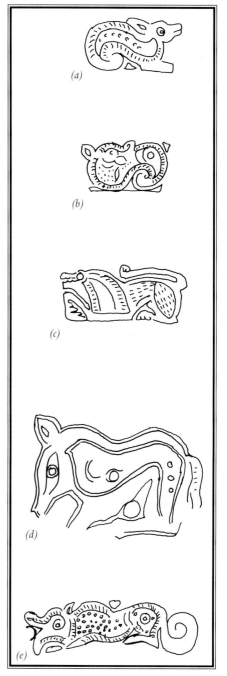

Quoit brooch style animals, fifth century AD:
(a) Faversham, Kent; (b) Howletts, Kent;
(c) Sarre, Kent; (d) Croydon, Surrey;
(e) Bifrons, Kent. (Jennifer Laing, after Evison)

Britannia seem to have enjoyed a developmental increase at about the same time as the Anglo-Saxon kingdoms evolved. The sudden prominence of Ireland in particular, as the producer of magnificent artistic endeavours from the seventh century onwards, has long been documented and discussed. This apparent renaissance of Iron Age traditions has long fascinated scholars, but is more apparent than real. It is more easily explicable in terms of a long period of incubation in which Celtic and Roman concepts merged, to be brilliantly reinterpreted by Irish artists of the period. The art of both Celtic Britain and Ireland at this period was remarkably simple, lacking the interlace and elaborate animal patterns that characterize such later seventh- and eighth-century masterpieces as the Book of Kells or the 'Tara' brooch. Although there is a limited amount of La Tène Celtic art in Ireland, there is little evidence for the kind of flourishing tradition that existed in Britain before the arrival of the Romans, and there are few pieces that can be dated with any confidence after the first century AD.[29] During the centuries of Roman occupation in Britain, however, Romano-British objects and influence crossed the Irish Sea both directly and indirectly through contacts with North Britain where the natives, as has been seen (page 153) had borrowed from Romano-British art.[30] During the Roman occupation the triskele was transmitted from Britain – it is well exemplified on a disc from Lambay, Dublin, which has a beaded border like Romano-British brooches. Other triskeles, including the 'broken-backed' types are to be found in Ireland, for example on a bronze box from Navan, Co. Armagh.[31] A series of Irish horsebits have designs which seem to have Romano-British affinities – one from Killevan, Anlore, Co. Monaghan, was found with a bronze disc with running scrolls which may have come from the Lower Rhine.[32] The development of a type of crested bird head found in Irish art may similarly have its origins in Roman Britain, perhaps being influenced by 'dragonesque' brooches.[33] Towards the end of the Roman occupation an increasing quantity of metalwork was taken from Roman Britain to Ireland, probably partly as a result of raids. A pendant from Feltrim Hill, Co. Dublin, appears to have been based on a Roman harness pendant, while a bronze strap-end from Rathgall, Co. Wicklow, probably has its origin in Roman military equipment.[34]

Among the objects that reached Ireland from Roman Britain were penannular brooches, pins and bracelets. In the fourth century a type of penannular brooch was developed out of earlier antecedents which had terminals in the form of very stylized animal heads. These were transmitted to Ireland where copies were produced which rapidly developed along native lines and gave rise to the famous series of brooches of which the 'Tara' is a classic example.[35] Various types of Romano-British pin also made the crossing, such as the proto-hand pin, which has a projecting head with a crescentic plate and a line of 'beads' or fingers, sometimes five, sometimes three.[36] Silver examples are found in late Roman Britain, and their heads are often inlaid with enamel and with simple ornament including peltas and scrolls with a central void like an eye, which makes them look a little like a dodo's head. Good examples have been found at Tripontium (Cave's Inn) in Warwickshire, and at Long Sutton in Somerset, while a simpler version was found with coins of the mid-fourth century at Oldcroft, Glos. A silver pin from Castletown, Kilberry, Co. Meath, is almost exactly the same as British examples from Traprain Law, East Lothian, and Moresby,

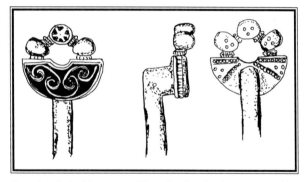

Proto-hand pin, Tripontium, Warwicks.; late fourth century. Width of head: 1.2 cm. (Drawing: L. Laing)

Cumbria.[37] It also seems likely that bracelets with ring-and-dot and linear ornament were being exported from later Roman Britain, perhaps the Bristol Channel region, where at Lydney Park a particularly fine series has come to light. A fragment of one of these bracelets was among the finds at the Dark Age fort of Clogher, Co. Tyrone, where metalworking was carried out, including the manufacture of brooches.[38]

The repertoire of motifs found on the brooches and pins of the fifth and sixth centuries in both Britain and Ireland is fairly basic, all of it derived from the traditions of late Roman Britain. It mostly comprises variations on the pelta and the dodo head, with ring-and-dot, running scrolls and other basic linear elements. By the sixth century penannular brooches in Ireland were being enamelled, and some have inlays of millefiori.

HANGING BOWLS

The most useful artefacts for studying the transition in art from Roman Britain to the Dark Age Celts are the hanging bowls which are found in both Anglo-Saxon and Celtic contexts. There are over ninety of these, and they comprise small vessels with three or four suspension hooks or escutcheons, and with a decorative base plate or 'print'. Because of their importance in tracing the development of art from the end of the Roman period into the Dark Ages, they have been intensively studied. For long believed to be Irish, it is now apparent that they were almost all produced in Britain, mostly by surviving Romano-British communities.[39] In the seventh century these bowls, or even the escutcheons from them, were used as status symbols in Anglo-Saxon graves, and had the same kind of function as imported Rhenish and 'Coptic' (East Mediterranean) bowls, perhaps in gift-exchange as well as in conspicuous display.[40] Some even seem to have been copied by the Anglo-Saxons, who on occasion repaired old bowls and sometimes even added a new escutcheon.

Hanging bowl from Lullingstone, Kent. (After Praetorius)

Hanging bowls are found in late Roman Britain. A bowl from a hoard at Water Newton, found in 1974, had two escutcheons bent outwards, and could be dated to the mid-fourth century by associated finds.[41] In late Roman Britain there was a tradition of beaten bronze vessels, well exemplified by a hoard from Irchester, and two hanging bowls from Finningley, N. Yorks., seem to be in the same tradition – they were found with two late Roman flanged bowls, and have plain escutcheons with hooks in the form of animals with knobbed manes. The Finningley bowls have features shared with Dark Age bowls such as slightly thickened in-turned rims, in-turned escutcheons, and a kicked-up or omphaloid base.[42]

The animals that appear on the escutcheon hooks of hanging-bowls seem to have a Romano-British ancestry. The commonest form is like a dolphin, with open mouth. Similar dolphins appear engraved on the plates of a pair of escutcheons from Faversham, Kent. Another type of escutcheon animal is bird-shaped – a datable Roman example is known from Naunheim-an-der-Lahn in Germany, and without association there is one from Barton, Cambs. Such bird-shaped escutcheons are possibly derived from the three-dimensional duck brooches found in Roman Britain.

The simplest of the decorated hanging bowl escutcheons have patterns based on the pelta, executed in openwork. This type of design was current in late Roman harness fittings, for example on one from Richborough, Kent. An escutcheon from Eastry in the same county is shaped like a pelta, while other escutcheons have patterns of Romano-British derivation such as marigolds, trellis, running scroll and ring-and-dot. The largest series of bowls have enamelled escutcheons with confronted trumpet pattern designs, sometimes with a concentric layout, sometimes based on the triskele. Other enamelled bowls have 'fine line' work, with a pattern in reserve against a red enamelled ground – such designs, seen for example on an escutcheon from Faversham, Kent, may employ dodo-head scrolls. There are echoes in the confronted trumpet pattern escutcheons of the triskeles of the Romano-British disc brooches, though the confronted trumpets come from another Roman source – Sir Thomas Kendrick demonstrated how all the elements slightly differently arranged were to be found on an enamelled patera handle from Roman Britain.[43]

REVERENCE FOR THE ROMAN PAST

Anglo-Saxon reverence for the Romano-British past persisted, and was reinforced by fresh contacts with Mediterranean culture attendant on the advent of Christianity to Anglo-Saxon England at the end of the sixth century.[44] It is particularly apparent in coinage. When they began issuing coins in the seventh century AD under the influence of their Merovingian Frankish neighbours, the Anglo-Saxons sometimes copied Roman types.[45] The most common design was borrowed from the reverse of Constantinian bronze coins showing a standard with an inscription relating to vows taken. A gold coin of Offa imitated the Romulus and Remus reverse of the 'Urbs Roma' commemorative coins of the House of Constantine. In the same way Celtic silver plate shows signs of having been inspired by some produced in the late Roman Empire. The silver spoon in the St Ninian's Isle Treasure, for example, seems to be modelled on a Roman one, while the silver pronged implement from the hoard is best matched in a series of similar implements of uncertain function from the Roman world.[46] Of course, it is not always possible to be certain whether the Dark Age artists were copying Romano-British objects, or whether the inspiration came from the Antique world, perhaps by way of the Franks or even Byzantium – the shape of the Dark Age Celtic chalices from Ardagh and Derrynaflan is more probably inspired by a Byzantine model than by a Roman chalice of the type represented in the Water Newton Hoard.

NOTES

INTRODUCTION

1. The philosopher R.G. Collingwood, the doyen of Romano-British studies in the inter-war years, dismissed Romano-British art trenchantly, saying that it hardly ever rose to the level of even third-rate artistic achievement, and noting that 'the empire was not an age of good taste' (Collingwood & Myres, 1937, p. 249).

2. The first scholar to make a detailed study of Romano-British art, Professor Jocelyn Toynbee, published her key studies in the 1960s when, thanks to a change in attitude towards Roman art, readers were able to appreciate the qualities she saw in particular works. But even Toynbee tended to regard any mainstream classical work found in Britain as probably an import, and to concentrate on the insularity of the bulk of the surviving remains.

Toynbee viewed Romano-British art in terms of its artistic achievement and, although she discussed the context in which it was produced, did not highlight the information it shed on Romano-British society and the mechanics of Romanization. More recently, Martin Henig has made a major contribution to the study in *The Art of Roman Britain* (1993).

3. Kendrick, 1950, p. 143.
4. Ibid., p. 147.
5. Munby, 1977, p. 415.
6. Ibid., p. 422.
7. Quoted in ibid., p. 422.
8. Birley, in his Introduction to the reprint of Horsley, 1975, p. iii.
9. Ibid., p. v.
10. Piggott, 1985.
11. Now known to be true. Piggott, 1985, p. 40.
12. Randall, 1933.
13. Piggott, 1985, pp. 53–5.
14. Piggott, 1976, p. 145.
15. Lepmann, 1970; Irwin, 1972.
16. Rhodes, 1990, for Roach Smith generally, but especially his contribution to Anglo-Saxon studies.
17. 1996, 9-11 and chapter 8.

CHAPTER ONE

1. Millett, 1977, p. 285.
2. Ibid., p. 287.
3. Frere, 1970.

4. Wheat, cattle, gold, silver, iron, slaves, hides and hunting dogs were the exports, with imports of bracelets, necklaces, amber and glassware, the latter perhaps being used ultimately in enamel making, or for making such glass playing pieces as those found in a chieftain's burial at Welwyn Garden City; Stead, 1967.
5. For example from Welwyn – Smith, 1907.
6. For example from Lexden, Colchester – Laver, 1927; Foster, 1986.
7. Foster, 1977; Green, 1986, p. 41.
8. Hawkes, 1951.
9. Piggott, 1971.
10. Not yet fully published, but see Henig, 1995, p. 35 and illus. 13.
11. Fox, 1958, pp. 105–6; Macgregor, 1976, pp. 156–9.
12. Gurney, 1990.
13. Macgregor, 1976, p. 158.
14. Kilbride-Jones, 1980, p. 79 and fig. 20.
15. Merrifield & Megaw, 1969.
16. Macgregor, 1976, p. 160.
17. Hattatt, 1985, fig. 60, nos 524–5.
18. Megaw, 1970, no. 268.
19. Brailsford, 1975.
20. Wild, 1970.
21. Gillam, 1958, p. 82: – 'When [the dress fastener] appears at Drumashie, beyond the farthest limits of permanent Roman penetration, it carries a sense of Rome; when it appears at the Roman chartered town of Colchester it carries a sense of the Celtic north . . .'.
22. Macgregor, 1976, no. 10.
23. Megaw, 1970, no. 296.
24. Corcoran, 1952.
25. Kilbride-Jones, 1980, fig. 48, no 2.
26. Macgregor, 1976, no. 150.
27. Ibid., no. 210.
28. Ibid., pp. 99–100.
29. Beswick *et al.* 1990.
30. Toynbee, 1962, no 1.
31. Strong, 1980, p. 137.
32. Toynbee, 1964, p. 58.
33. Cunliffe, 1971b, pl. 66.
34. Toynbee, 1964, p. 63.
35. Josef Stryzygowski, 1923, one of the first to discuss it, talked about late Roman and early Byzantine art (the Byzantine Empire was the successor to the Roman) as 'Hellas suffocating in the embrace of the Orient'.
36. Laing & Laing, 1994, pp. 212–13.

37. Henig, 1995, p. 147.
38. Strong, 1987, p. 171.
39. Phillips, 1977b, p. 44.
40. Ibid., p. 37.
41. Toynbee, 1962, no. 89.
42. Ibid., no. 35.
43. Phillips, 1977b, p. 43; general discussion of characteristics of Romano-British interpretation in Lindgren, 1980.
44. Toynbee, 1962, no. 8.
45. Phillips, 1977b, p. 47.

CHAPTER TWO

1. Wiedemann, T., 1988, discusses this issue in connection with gladiatorial games.
2. Several recent commentators have noted this, for example: 'By comparison [with Christianity] Celtic and Roman paganism differed only in superficial detail' (Potter & Johns, 1992, p. 158).
3. Millett, 1995, p. 107.
4. Henig, 1984, takes a classical view of the religion of Roman Britain. The provincial approach can be set in its wider perspective by consulting Ferguson, 1970.
5. The literature is by now extensive on Celtic cults in Roman Britain, starting with Ross, 1967, and Webster, 1986, and going through a series of books by Green, notably 1986.
6. Toynbee, 1964, p. 65.
7. Green, 1983, p. 30.
8. Examples are known from Woodeaton, Lypiatt Park, Bath and the Walbrook Mithraeum.
9. Lewis, 1965, discusses Romano-British temples generally.
10. de la Bedoyère, 1983, pp. 170–7 for possible reconstructions. Original excavation of the temple and baths in Cunliffe, 1984, and Cunliffe & Davenport, 1985.
11. Henig, 1995, p. 40; Cunliffe & Davenport, 1985.
12. Toynbee, 1962, no. 20.
13. Ibid., p. 127 (no. 1).
14. Toynbee, 1964, p. 49.
15. Webster, 1986, pp. 137–8.
16. Wedlake, 1982.
17. Toynbee, 1964, p. 68.
18. Ibid., pp. 66–7.
19. Ibid., pp. 67–8.
20. Ibid, p. 66.
21. Ibid., p. 84.
22. Ibid., p. 83.
23. de la Bedoyère, 1989, p. 148; Jenkins, 1958.
24. Toynbee, 1964, p. 83.
25. Toynbee, 1962, no. 21.
26. Ibid, no 20.
27. Woodward & Leach, 1992.
28. Hutchinson, 1986, for the cult of Bacchus in Britain.
29. Johns & Potter, 1983.

30. Toynbee, 1962, no. 62.
31. Toynbee, 1964, p. 76.
32. For these generally, Harris & Harris, 1963.
33. For Carrawburgh Mithraeum generally, Richmond & Gillam, 1951.
34. For Mithras generally, Vermaseren, 1963.
35. For the Walbrook sculptures generally, Toynbee, 1986.
36. Toynbee, 1962, no. 69.
37. Toynbee, 1964, p. 99.
38. Toynbee, 1962, no. 36.
39. For this suggestion, Salway, 1981, p. 712.
40. Richmond & Gillam, 1951.
41. Thomas, 1981; Watts, 1991.
42. Frere, 1975b, pp. 277–302; King, 1983.
43. Interim report by Crummy in Rodwell (ed.), 1980.
44. Brown, 1971.
45. West, 1976.
46. For the question of continuity of Roman Christian sites into the Anglo-Saxon period, recent summary in Laing & Laing, 1996, pp. 7, 89. Canterbury cathedral in Blockley, 1991.
47. The main discussions of Romano-British Christianity are in Thomas, 1981, and Watts, 1991.
48. As followed by Salway, 1981, p. 723.
49. Painter, 1977.
50. Johns & Potter, 1991.
51. Brailsford, 1955, nos 29–31.
52. Conveniently figured in de la Bedoyère, 1989, pl. 117.
53. Curle, 1923, pp. 13–15.
55. de la Bedoyère, 1989, p. 186.
56. Toynbee, 1964, pp. 7-14; Painter, 1966, pp. 49–54.
57. Goodburn, 1986, p. 28.
58. Meates, 1955, is a popular account, but see more recently Liversidge & Weatherhead in Meates, 1987, pp. 5–44.
59. Kent & Painter, 1977, p. 33: the pagan original owner, Eutherius, whose name is inscribed on some of the pieces in Greek, probably gave the treasure to Lupicinus, a Christian general in the Imperial entourage who was sent to Britain by Julian.
60. Davey & Ling, 1987, pp. 138–45.
61. Meates, 1955, p. 129.
62. Davey & Ling, 1981, Appendix, no. 7.
63. Henig, 1995, p. 141.
64. Thomas, 1981, pp. 221–5.
65. Henig, 1995, p. 141.
66. Henig, 1995, p. 126. Henig, who was the first to recognize the stylistic connection, places the Vatican Virgil in the fourth century but Dark has argued that the early fifth-century date usually ascribed to the book is more probable. Dark, 1994, pp. 185–6; for a discussion setting it in the fifth century, Kitzinger, 1977, p. 67.
67. Green, 1983, pp. 23–6.
68. For long the authenticity of this as an ancient find

was questioned, see *Wilts. Arch. and Nat. Hist. Magazine* L (1944), 99–100.

69. Toynbee, 1964, p. 95. Toynbee suggested that the finger to the mouth was to stress that the secrets of the cult were not to be divulged, a theory followed by other writers.

70. Green, 1983, p. 26.

71. Ibid.

72. Macdonald, 1934, pp. 415–17.

73. Toynbee, 1962, no. 70.

74. Toynbee, 1964, p. 140.

75. Green, 1983, pp. 20–3.

76. Toynbee, 1962, no. 39.

77. Ibid., no. 95.

78. Convenient illustration Potter & Johns, 1992, p. 168 and fig. 72. For Jupiter columns generally, Green, 1986, pp. 61f.

79. Webster, 1986, pp. 63–6.

80. Toynbee, 1964, p. 172. 'They recall a group of human mothers chatting together on a bench in a park or garden while watching their children at play.'

81. Quoted in Webster, 1986, p. 65.

82. Green, 1986, p. 174 and fig. 76.

83. Brunaux, 1988.

84. Stead & Turner, 1985.

85. Green, 1986, pp. 128–9.

86. Ashbee, 1963.

87. Ross, 1968.

88. Ross, 1974, p. 53.

89. Ibid., p. 54.

90. Piggott, 1968, pp. 58–9; Cunliffe, 1991, p. 570.

91. Alcock, 1972.

92. Various discussions of continuity, for example in Ross, 1974; Piggott, 1968; Green, 1986; Webster, 1986.

93. Ross, 1974, chaps 6–7; Green, 1986, chap. 6.

94. e.g. Green, 1978; Green, 1981b; Foster, 1977.

95. Toynbee, 1964, p. 127; Wheeler & Wheeler, 1932, pp. 88–9 & pl. 25.

96. Toynbee, 1962, no. 58.

97. Ibid., no. 59.

98. Hawkes, 1951.

99. Toynbee, 1964, p. 126.

100. Ross, 1974, p. 464.

101. Ibid., pp. 466–7.

102. Ibid., pp. 469–70.

103. Green, 1986, p. 80

104. Toynbee, 1962, no. 75.

105. Ibid., no. 80.

106. Ibid., no. 79.

107. Cunliffe, 1984, fig. 44.

108. Goodchild, 1947.

109. Toynbee, 1962, nos 2–5.

110. Wheeler & Wheeler, 1932, pl. 27.

111. Toynbee, 1962, no. 128.

112. de la Bedoyère, 1989, pp. 153–6.

113. Wheeler & Wheeler, 1932.

114. Toynbee, 1962, no. 87.

115. Ibid., no. 85.

116. Ibid., no. 89.

117. Ibid., p. 160.

118. Ibid., no. 86.

119. Toynbee, 1962, no. 47. A similar, but better sculpture of a lioness with a human head protruding from her mouth was unearthed in January 1997 at Cramond on the Firth of Forth, and presumably came from the tomb of an officer posted to the fort there (*The Times*, 21 January 1997).

120. Green, 1982.

CHAPTER THREE

1. Strong, 1966.

2. Sherlock, 1976, p. 11.

3. Kent & Painter, 1977, pp. 15–19.

4. Niblett, 1993.

5. Salway, 1980, p. 630.

6. Two lead pigs (bars) from near Southampton have inscriptions showing they were cast in AD 49, presumably from Mendip lead, and it is known that C Nipius Ascanius was deriving lead from Clwyd by AD 60. Salway, 1980, p. 634.

7. Boon, 1974, pp. 275–6.

8. Wheeler, 1956.

9. Hedeager, 1987.

10. Toynbee, 1964, pp. 301–2; the cups fully discussed after restoration by Johns, 1986, pp. 1–13.

11. Henig, 1995, p. 32.

12. Toynbee, 1962, no. 109.

13. Toynbee, 1964, pp. 304–6.

14. Henig, 1995, p. 93.

15. Bland & Johns, 1993.

16. Brailsford, 1955; Painter, 1977a; Kent & Painter, 1977, pp. 33–9; Toynbee, 1964, pp. 308–12.

17. Curle, 1923.

18. Breeze, 1982, p. 152.

19. Toynbee & Painter, 1986, pp. 15–65, esp. 32.

20. Toynbee, 1964, p. 317.

21. Ibid., p. 306; Rokewood, 1842.

22. Read, 1898, pp. 7–12.

23. Brown, 1973, pp. 184–206.

24. Munich Treasure, Kent & Painter, 1977, pp. 20–1.

25. Toynbee, 1964, p. 319.

26. Ibid.

27. Ibid., p. 320; Henig, 1995, p. 128 and illus. 130.

28. Toynbee, 1964, p. 322.

29. Ibid., p. 323.

30. Ibid, pp. 324–5.

31. The literature on samian is enormous. Useful discussions can be found in Collingwood & Richmond, 1969, pp. 235–50, but there are useful short introductions, for example de la Bedoyère, 1988, and Johns, 1977.

32. Hull, 1963.

33. For the range, see Oswald, 1920.

34. Toynbee, 1962, no. 148.

35. Toynbee, 1964, p. 390; May, 1909, pl. 4, no 1.

36. Toynbee, 1964, p. 391.

37. Ibid., p. 392.

38. Perring, 1977, discusses art in R–B pottery generally.

39. Swan, 1980, p. 20. More detailed account of the Nene Valley industry in Hartley, 1960, and Howe, Perrin, & Mackreth, 1980.

40. Toynbee, 1962, no. 155.

41. Webster, 1989, pp. 1–28; Webster,1991, pp. 129–62.

42. Toynbee, 1962, no. 158; Charleston,1955, pl. 65.

43. Toynbee, 1962, p. 157.

44. Toynbee, 1964, p. 417.

45. Ibid.

46. This name is a cautionary reminder to archaeologists that nicknames given to finds will with the passage of time become meaningless. Few will remember something of the Scottish comedian whom the figure was seen to resemble, just as few still remember Sir Mortimer Wheeler and can recognize an element of him in the features of the Celtic head from Msecke Zehrovice in Czechoslovakia that bears his name. Who will remember that the fossil hominid 'Lucy' is named after a Beatles song playing on the radio at the time of discovery, or that 'Balbus' in the Lullingstone Roman fresco is named after a character in a long disused Latin primer? Pete Marsh, the Iron Age/Romano-British burial from Cheshire, may retain his nickname longer.

47. Toynbee, 1964, p. 401; 1962, no. 161. The literature on these two figures is extensive, as they are seen as classic examples of Celtic deities – see Webster, 1986, pp. 90–1 or Green, 1986, pp. 66–7; on Taranis: Ross, 1974, p. 252.

48. Toynbee, 1962, no. 165.

49. Ibid., no. 164. Face pots generally, Braithwaite, 1984, pp. 99–131.

50. Henig, 1995, p. 137.

51. Toynbee, 1964, p. 429.

52. Ibid., p. 430.

53. Toynbee, 1962, p. 379.

54. Ibid., nos 140–2.

55. Ibid., p. 378.

56. The significance of coin types in the Ancient World first discussed at length by Macdonald, 1905 – Roman coin types pp. 177f.

57. Reece, 1987; Casey, 1980; recent accounts of Romano-British coinage. Laing, 1969 (especially chapter 8), and Sutherland, 1937, are older accounts.

58. de Jersey, 1996, and Haselgrove, 1993, provide useful summaries of Celtic British coinage. More detailed study in Van Arsdell, 1989.

59. For the complex symbolic language of Augustan coins, Zanker, 1990.

60. Laing & Laing, 1993, pp. 216–21.

61. Reece, 1987, p. 28.

62. Casey, 1980, pp. 27–8.

63. Reece, 1987, p. 6.

64. Casey, 1980, fig. 1.

65. Goodchild, 1941; Collingwood & Richmond, 1969, p. 299.

66. Toynbee, 1962, no. 166; Boon, 1974, p. 150 suggests the model may have been a commemorative medallion issued at Rome to celebrate Severus's victories in Scotland.

67. Toynbee, 1964, p. 334.

68. For this and other Roman coins commemorating events in Britain, Askew, 1951, reprint 1980; useful summary in de la Bedoyère, 1989, pp. 197f. For the arch and others also commemorating the conquest, Webster, 1965, pp. 80–5.

69. Reece, 1987, pp. 115–16. Original discussion in Todd, 1967.

70. C.H.V. Sutherland believed that the best copies were semi-official, produced by the Roman army, but subsequently it has been demonstrated that all were fakes, graded in quality from the excellent to the blatantly crude.

71. Boon, 1988, pp. 126-32.

72. Ibid., p. 128.

73. Ibid., pp. 130–1; Calverton by H.B. Mattingly in N. Staffs J. Field Studies, III (1961), 19–36.

74. Casey, 1977.

75. Perhaps as with Akhenaten in Egypt in the fourteenth century BC, it was deemed necessary not only to reproduce accurately the peculiarity of his features, but to exaggerate them in the interests of art.

CHAPTER FOUR

1. The best account of Romano-British women is Allason-Jones, 1989a.

2. Allason-Jones, 1989a, p. 21.

3. Ibid.

4. Ibid., p. 49.

5. Ibid., p. 137.

6. Ibid., p. 136.

7. Boon, 1974, p. 131.

8. Allason-Jones, 1989a, pp. 109–14.

9. Bland & Johns, 1993, p. 22.

10. Ibid.

11. Potter & Johns, 1992, p. 146.

12. Higgins, 1976, p. 60.

13. Wheeler & Wheeler, 1932, p. 82.

14. Stevenson, 1954–6.

15. Bland & Johns, 1993, pp. 19–20.

16. Johns & Potter, 1992, p. 167 and fig. 70.

17. Allason-Jones, 1989a, p. 122.

18. Ibid.

19. Guido, 1978.

20. Toynbee, 1964, p. 363.

21. Birley, 1977, pl. 46–7.

22. Toynbee, 1964, p. 367.

23. Ibid.
24. Ibid., p. 372.
25. Ibid.
26. Allason-Jones, 1989a, p. 127.
27. Ibid., p. 128.
28. Ibid.
29. Johns, 1996, p. 77.
30. Johns & Potter, p. 147; *Britannia*, 17 (1986), 403.
31. Kent & Painter, 1977, p. 61, no. 140.
32. Allason-Jones, 1989a, p. 125.
33. Charlesworth, 1961, p. 24.
34. Henig, 1995, p. 72, with refs.
35. de la Bedoyère, 1988, p. 124.
36. Henig, 1995, p. 169.
37. Carson & O'Kelly, 1977.
38. Kent & Painter, 1977, p. 72.
39. Henig, 1978, for a discussion of Romano-British examples.
40. Henig, 1993, p. 74.
41. Ibid., p. 134.
42. Cunliffe, 1984, p. 74.
43. Ibid., p. 75.
44. Johns, 1996, p. 127; Allason-Jones, 1989a.
45. Ibid.
46. Johns, 1996, p. 129.
47. Ibid., p. 130.
48. Ibid., p. 158.
49. For brooch types generally, Hattatt, 1985; Hattatt, 1987; Hattatt, 1989. A scheme for brooches can also be found in Collingwood & Richmond, 1969, chap. xv.
50. Boon & Savory, 1975.
51. Allason-Jones, 1989a, p. 126.
52. Johns, 1996, pp. 161–2.
53. Evans, 1896.
54. Feachem, 1968; Kilbride-Jones, 1980, pp. 170–83.
55. Megaw & Megaw, 1989, p. 229.
56. Goodchild, 1941.
57. de la Bedoyère, 1988, p.121; Collingwood & Richmond, 1969, p. 300.
58. Ibid., fig. 106, no. 106.
59. Stead & Rigby, 1986, fig. 49, no. 152.
60. Fowler, 1960; Kilbride-Jones, 1980, 1980a.
61. Curle, 1932, p. 338.
62. Kent & Painter, 1977, p. 28, no. 21.
63. Laing, 1996, p. 29.
64. Johns, 1996, p. 169.
65. For the types of pin encountered, Cool, 1990.
66. Toynbee, 1964, pp. 366–7.
67. Johns, 1996, p. 140.
68. Ibid., p. 141.
69. Ibid., p. 142.

CHAPTER FIVE

1. Frere, 1987, pp. 235–6.
2. Hingley, 1989, p. 4.
3. Salway, 1981, pp. 544–5; see also Cunliffe, 1978.
4. Potter & Johns, 1992, p. 68.
5. Taylor, 1984, p. 83.
6. Haselgrove, 1982.
7. Salway, 1981, p. 544–5.
8. The unit was the derbfine – the male descendants of a common great-grandfather, along with their wives and sons.
9. Charles-Edwards, 1972, pp. 3–33; Stevens,1966.
10. Hingley, 1989, p. 8 and *passim*. Smith, 1978, p. 149–56.
11. Collingwood & Richmond, 1969, pp. 183–4.
12. Hogg, 1966, p. 23.
13. Potter & Johns, 1991, p. 70.
14. *Current Archaeology*, 85 (1982), 43–8.
15. May, 1996.
16. Potter & Trow, 1988.
17. Meadows, 1996.
18. Leech, 1982.
19. Bowen & Fowler, 1966, p. 51.
20. Taylor, 1984.
21. Millett & Graham, 1986.
22. Hingley, 1989, p. 12.
23. Quoted from Ibid., p. 21.
24. Cunliffe, 1971a; Cunliffe, 1971b.
25. Detsicas, 1983, pp. 120–6.
26. Rodwell & Rodwell, 1986.
27. Ward-Perkins, 1938.
28. O'Neill, 1945.
29. Wacher, 1978, p. 113.
30. Ibid., p. 117.
31. Johnson, 1983, p. 13.
32. Millett, 1995, p. 71.
33. Walters, 1981.
34. Hayward, 1972.
35. Pollard, 1974.
36. Walters, 1986, p. 152.
37. de la Bedoyère, 1991, p. 158.
38. Mynard, 1987.
39. Johnson, 1972.
40. de la Bedoyère, 1991, p. 133.
41. Neal, 1996, p. 43.
42. Taylor, 1983, p. 8.
43. Ibid.
44. Gracie, 1970; Gracie & Price, 1979.
45. Taylor, 1983, p. 31.
46. Ibid., p. 32.
47. Johnston, 1983, p. 12.
48. Cunliffe, 1971b, chapter VII convenient summary.
49. Bidwell, 1996, p. 27.
50. King, 1996, pp. 67–8.
51. Keevil, 1996.
52. Cunliffe, 1971b, p. 109.
53. Four main styles were defined at Pompeii, the First Style occurring around the second century BC and employing *trompe l'oeil* effects to imitate expensive

marble and other veneers and architectural elements. The Second Style, which evolved around 100 BC, used architectural settings appropriate to a theatre set. The Third Style became current around 15 BC and combined delicate architectural elements with small pictures in panels, imitating an art gallery. The Fourth Style, current around the time of Nero, had false windows and architectural perspectives, executed in a light manner and populated with miniature figures as though on a stage. Ling, 1991; Picard, 1970.

54. Davey & Ling, 1982, 30.
55. Ibid., no. 18.
56. Ibid., no. 17.
57. Ibid., p. 33.
58. Ibid., no. 2, pp. 83–4.
59. Ibid., no. 26, pp. 136–8.
60. Ibid., no. 12.
61. Ibid., p. 37.
62. Allason-Jones,1989a, p. 89.
63. Davey & Ling, 1982, no. 30, pp. 147–8.
64. As implied by Allason-Jones, 1989a, p. 89.
65. Ling, 1985, chapter 6 on techniques in Britain; for techniques in the Empire, Pratt, 1976.
66. Ling, 1985, pp. 55–6.
67. Allason-Jones, 1989a, p. 89.
68. Cunliffe, 1971b, pp. 106–7.
69. Smith, 1969, p. 81.
70. Ibid., pp. 71–2.
71. Ibid., p. 72.
72. Henig, 1995, p. 32.
73. Smith, 1969, p. 75.
74. Ibid., p. 76.
75. Ibid., p. 78.
76. Henig, 1995, p. 122.
77. Smith, 1969, p. 80.
78. Smith, 1969, lists of subject matter, pp. 82–6.
79. Johnson, 1977, p. 195.
80. Smith, 1969, pp. 97–8.
81. Neal, 1976, esp. p. 238.
82. Johnson, 1995, p. 8.
83. Ibid., pp. 8-9.
84. Ibid., p. 11.
85. Cookson, 1984, pp. 120–1.
86. Ibid., p. 121.
87. Meates, 1955, etc.
88. Toynbee, 1962, p. 126.
89. Henig, 1995, p. 76; Luna in Potter & Johns, 1992, p. 121.
90. Henig, 1995, p. 76.
91. Liversidge, 1969, p. 154.
92. Ibid.
93. Ibid., p. 135.
94. Toynbee, 1964, p. 85.
95. Liversidge, 1955, pp. 29–30.
96. Ibid., p. 31.

97. Ibid., p. 34.
98. Ibid., p. 61.
99. Ibid., pp. 3–6.
100. Ibid., p. 16.
101. Henig, 1995, p. 70.
102. Liversidge, 1969, p. 167.
103. Millett, 1995, p. 72.
104. Neal, Wardle & Hunn, 1990.
105. Todd, 1978, p. 201.
106. Potter & Johns, 1991, p. 87.
107. Rivet, 1958, p. 30, for concise account of Roman geographical sources relating to Britain.
108. de la Bedoyère, 1991, p. 121.
109. Ibid., p. 240.
110. Black, 1994.
111. Smith, 1969, p. 91.
112. Henig, 1995, p. 120.
113. Smith, 1969, p. 94.
114. Ibid., p. 91.
115. Ibid., pp. 91–4.
116. Smith, 1977, on mythological subject matter.
117. Neal, 1981.
118. Toynbee, 1964.
119. Miles, 1986.

CHAPTER SIX

1. For example at Verulamium, Insula xxviii, 1, where a third-century building had an underground passage with possible apsidal shrine, later converted to a cellar. Frere, 1983.
2. Tacitus, Agricola xxi, quoted and discussed Salway, 1980, p. 142.
3. Potter & Johns, 1992, p. 75.
4. Cunliffe, 1991, chap. 14; Collis, 1984.
5. Dixon, 1994.
6. Salway, 1981, pp. 567, 574–5 discusses the status of London, pointing out that its fourth-century name (Augusta) suggests a high rank.
7. Wacher (ed.), 1966; Wacher, 1995, pp. 23–32.
8. Ibid., p. 378.
9. Burnham & Wacher, 1990.
10. Frere, 1987, pp. 252–3 – but population 'guesstimates' are notoriously unreliable.
11. Wacher, 1995, pp. 71–81.
12. Ibid., pp. 71–2.
13. Ibid., p. 97.
14. Frere, 1987, p. 242.
15. Ibid., p. 244.
16. Wacher, 1966, pp. 60–1; Frere, 1987, p. 241, where they are assigned to the second century.
17. Wacher, 1995, p. 223, where it is also suggested an Italian model might lie behind the plan.
18. Marsden, 1975.
19. de la Bedoyère, 1991, p.96.
20. de la Bedoyère, 1991, p. 112.
21. Hill, Millett, & Blagg, 1980.

22. de la Bedoyère, 1991, p. 114.
23. Toynbee, 1964, pp. 50–1.
24. Ibid., p. 51.
25. Ibid., pp. 46–7.
26. Ibid., p. 50.
27. Ibid.
28. Ibid., p. 56.
29. RIB 5; Ireland, 1986, p. 466.
30. Suetonius, Titus, 4.1.
31. Hurst, 1972, p. 52.
32. Toynbee, 1964, p. 52.
33. Wacher, 1995, p. 298.
34. Toynbee, 1964, p. 129.
35. RIB 311; Ireland no. 464.
36. de la Bedoyère, 1991, p. 102.
37. Crummy, 1982.
38. Kenyon, 1934.
39. Stead, 1975.
40. Potter & Johns, 1992, pl. 34.
41. Marsh, 1979.
42. Fulford, 1989.
43. Painter, 1970.
44. Toynbee, 1962, no. 53.
45. Toynbee, 1964, p. 118.
46. Burn, 1969, p. 46.
47. Perring & Roskans, 1991.
48. de la Bedoyère, 1991, pp. 146–7.
49. Philp, 1989.
50. Johnson, 1995, p. 15.
51. Wacher, 1995, p. 314.
52. Davey & Ling, 1982, no. 40.
53. Ibid., no. 41.
54. Ibid., no. 44.
55. Ibid., no. 43.
56. Ibid., no. 22.
57. Ibid., no. 23.
58. Toynbee, 1962, no. 15.
59. Ibid., no. 28.
60. Ibid., no. 7.
61. RIB 105, 151.
62. Bushe-Fox, 1913, p. 11; Bushe-Fox, 1914, p. 13; Bushe-Fox, 1916, p. 65.
63. Wright, 1872, p. 159.
64. Atkinson, 1942, pl. 52.
65. Devizes Museum Catalogue, II (1934), 202 and fig. 34.
66. Documented only by an inscription – RIB 712.
67. Frere, 1987, p. 251.
68. Wacher, 1995, p. 68.
69. Wacher, 1995, p. 67.
70. Marsden, 1975, pp. 100–2.
71. Bateson, 1981, pp. 105–6.
72. Bateson, 1981.
73. Hawkes & Hull, 1947, pp. 345–6.
74. Bateson, 1981, p. 102.
75. May, 1904, pp. 67–87.
76. Blockley, 1989.

CHAPTER SEVEN

1. Frere, 1987, p. 207.
2. Ibid., p. 143.
3. Ibid., p. 97.
4. Salway, 1981, pp. 322–3.
5. The walls in Britain have given rise to a considerable volume of literature from the eighteenth century onwards. Among recent works, mention may be made of Maxwell, 1989, and Breeze & Dobson, 1987.
6. Collingwood & Richmond, 1969, chap. 4.
7. Wacher, 1978, p. 31.
8. Salway, 1981, p. 511.
9. Bowman, 1994.
10. Ibid., p. 17.
11. Ibid., p. 93.
12. Ibid., p. 88.
13. Ibid., p. 97.
14. Most useful discussion de la Bedoyère, 1991, chapter 2.
15. Frere, 1987, pp. 207–8.
16. de la Bedoyère, 1991, p. 56.
17. Wacher, 1978, pp. 40–1.
18. RCHM, 1962.
19. Collingwood & Richmond, 1969, chap. III.
20. Strickland, 1996, p. 109.
21. The literature is considerable, but see Maxwell, 1989; Dobson & Breeze, 1987; Breeze, 1982.
22. Johnson, 1976; 1983.
23. Johnson, 1976; 1980; 1983, best discussions of the Saxon Shore forts and late Roman fortification methods.
24. Laing & Laing, 1996, p. 89.
25. Ibid., p. 90.
26. Cunliffe, 1968.
27. de la Bedoyère, 1991, p. 40.
28. Ibid., p. 46.
29. Ibid., p. 51.
30. Simpson & Richmond, 1941.
31. Wilson, 1975, p. 189.
32. Henig, 1993, p. 45.
33. Birley, 1977, p. 90.
34. Davey & Ling, 1982, pp. 45–6.
35. Ibid., no. 5.
36. Ibid., no. 53.
37. Bishop 1985.
38. Bishop & Coulston, 1989, p. 42.
39. Ibid., p. 40.
40. Ibid., p. 49.
41. Ibid., p. 69.
42. de la Bedoyère, 1989, pp. 32–4.
43. Bidwell, 1985, p. 132, no. 6.
44. Toynbee & Wilkins, 1982.
45. Williams in Philp, 1981, pp. 148–9.
46. Toynbee, 1964, p. 299.
47. Ibid., p. 300.
48. Ibid., p. 299.
49. Toynbee, 1964, p. 300.

50. Jackson, 1984, p. 246.
51. Toynbee, 1962, no. 101.
52. Toynbee, 1964, p. 291.
53. Just such a chamfrein was discovered at Newstead – Curle, 1911.
54. Curle, 1911, pp. 168–70.
55. Toynbee, 1962, p. 168.
56. Ibid., no. 103.
57. Ibid., pp. 167–8.
58. Toynbee, 1964, p. 298.
59. RIB 1912.
60. Toynbee, 1964, p. 149.
61. RIB 1341.
62. RIB 1428.
63. RIB 1284.
64. Toynbee, 1964, p. 185.
65. Ibid, p. 186.
66. *The Times*, 12 December 1996, p. 3.
67. Toynbee, 1962, no. 92.
68. Ibid., no. 82.
69. Macgregor, 1964, p. 113.
70. Macgregor, 1962.
71. Macgregor, 1976, p. 42.
72. Simpson, 1968; Macgregor, 1976, pp. 106–10.
73. Ibid., pp. 103–5.

CHAPTER EIGHT

1. The subject of early state formation has been much debated recently, see for example Bassett, 1989, p. 4, or Yorke, 1990. Archaeological evidence for growing social stratification in Welch, 1992.
2. Dickinson, 1983.
3. Cleary, 1989; Dark, 1994; Higham, 1992; Laing & Laing, 1996.
4. Jones, 1996.
5. Dark, 1994, chap. 6.
6. Alcock, 1995.
7. Cleary, 1989, pp. 152–3 summarizes.
8. Frere, 1975, p. 319; Johnson, 1979, p. 154.
9. 'But the cities of our land are not populated even now as they once were' – *Ruin of Britain*, p. 26.
10. Mackreth, 1978; Laing & Laing, 1990, p. 87.
11. Kent, 1961; Kent, 1979, p. 28.
12. Rahtz *et al.*, 1992, esp. p. 228.
13. Brown, 1981.
14. Oddy, 1979.
15. Lamm, 1978, p. 101.
16. Cramp, 1970.
17. Haseloff, 1974.
18. Hawkes & Dunning, 1961.
19. Kendrick, 1936, Pl. XV, 4.
20. Henig, 1995, pp. 172–3.
21. Laing & Laing, 1995, p. 85 and illus.
22. Ibid., p. 106.
23. Laing, 1993, p. 38.
24. Hawkes, 1961; Evison, 1965; Ager, 1984.
25. Laing & Laing, 1996, p. 30.
26. Laing, 1990.
27. For a general review of the origins of brooch and pin types, Fowler, 1963.
28. Laing & Laing, 1995, pp. 101–11.
29. Laing & Laing, 1990, pp. 179–91.
30. Warner, 1996.
31. Raftery, 1984, p. 284.
32. Lloyd-Morgan, 1976, pp. 217–22.
33. Laing & Laing, 1990, pp. 195–6.
34. Raftery, 1970.
35. Many discussions exist of the evolution of penannular brooches: see Fowler, 1963, for start of series and Laing, 1993, chapter II for their development.
36. Laing, 1990, discusses late Roman examples. See also Kilbride-Jones, 1980.
37. Kilbride-Jones, 1980, fig. 68.
38. Warner, 1979.
39. Bruce-Mitford, 1987.
40. Brenan, 1991, p. 137.
41. Johns & Carson, 1975, pp. 57-8.
42. Kennett, 1968.
43. Kendrick, 1932.
44. Higgitt, 1973.
45. Webster & Backhouse, 1991, p. 66; Kent, 1961.
46. Wilson, 1973, p. 115.

BIBLIOGRAPHY

Ager, B. 1984. 'The smaller variants of the Anglo-Saxon Quoit Brooch', *Anglo-Saxon Studies in Archaeology and History*, 4, Oxford, 1–58

Akerman, J.Y. 1844. *Coins of the Romans Relating to Britain*, London

Alcock, L. 1971. *Arthur's Britain*, London

——. 1972. *By South Cadbury is that Camelot . . .* London.

——. 1995. *Cadbury Castle Somerset, The Early Medieval Archaeology*, Cardiff

Allason-Jones, L. 1989a. *Women in Roman Britain*, London

——. 1989b. *Ear-Rings in Roman Britain*, Oxford (BAR)

Allen, J.R. & Fulford, M. 1987. 'Romano-British Settlement and Industry on the Wetlands of the Severn Estuary', *Antiquaries Journal*, 67, 237–89

Anderson, A.S. 1984. *Roman Military Tombstones*, Princes Risborough

Arnold, C.J. 1984. *From Roman Britain to Saxon England*, London

Ashbee, P. 1963. 'The Wilsford Shaft', *Antiquity*, XXXVII, 116–20

Askew, G. 1951. *Coinage of Roman Britain*, London

Atkinson, D. 1942. *Excavations at Wroxeter 1923–1927*, Oxford

Barber, A.J., Walker, G.T., Paddock, J. & Henig, M. 1992. 'A bust of Mars or a hero from Cirencester', *Britannia*, 23, 217–18

Barrett, A.A. 1978. 'Knowledge of the literary classics in Roman Britain', *Britannia*, 9, 307–13

Bassett, S. (ed.) 1989. *The Origins of the Anglo-Saxon Kingdoms*, Leicester

Bateson, J.D. 1981. *Enamel working in Iron Age, Roman and sub-Roman Britain*, Oxford (BAR 93)

Bedoyère, G. de la. 1988. *Samian Ware*, Aylesbury

——. 1989. *The Finds of Roman Britain*, London

——. 1991. *The Buildings of Roman Britain*, London

——. 1993. *Roman Villas and the Countryside*, London.

Beswick, P., Megaw, J.V.S. & Northover, P. 1990. 'A Decorated Iron Age Torc from Dinnington, Yorks', *Antiquaries Journal*, 71, 16–33

Bidwell, P. 1985. *The Roman Fort at Vindolanda*, London

——. 1996. 'The exterior decoration of Roman buildings in Britain', in Johnson, P. (ed.) *Architecture in Roman Britain*, 19–29

Birley, R. 1977. *Vindolanda, a Roman frontier post on Hadrian's Wall*, London

Bishop, M.C. (ed.) 1985. *The Production and Distribution of Roman Military Equipment*, Oxford (BAR 275)

—— & Coulston, J.C. 1989. *Roman Military Equipment*, Princes Risborough

Black, E.W. 1986. 'Christian and Pagan hopes of salvation in Romano-British mosaics', in Henig & King (eds), *Pagan Gods and Shrines of the Roman Empire*, Oxford, 147–58

——. 1994. 'Villa-Owners, Romano-British Gentlemen and Officers', *Britannia*, 25, 99–110

Blagg, T.F.C. 1977. 'Schools of Stonemasons in Roman Britain', in Munby & Henig (eds), 51–74

——. 1989. 'Art and Architecture', in Todd, M. (ed.) *Research on Roman Britain, 1960–1989*, London (*Britannia* Monograph 11), 203–17

——. 1990 'Architectural munificence in Britain: the evidence of inscriptions', *Britannia*, 21, 13–31

Bland, R. & Johns, C. 1993. *The Hoxne Treasure, an Illustrated Introduction*, London

Blockley, K. 1989. *Prestatyn 1984–5: an Iron Age farmstead and Romano-British industrial settlement in North Wales*, Oxford (BAR 210)

——. 1991. 'Canterbury Cathedral' *Current Archaeology*, 136, 124–30

Boon, G.C. 1974. *Silchester, the Roman Town of Calleva*, Newton Abbot

——. 1988. 'Counterfeit coins in Roman Britain' in Casey & Reece, (Eds), 102–188

—— & Savory, H.N. 1975. 'A silver trumpet brooch with relief decoration from Carmarthen', *Antiquaries Journal*, 55, 41–61

Bowen, H.C. & Fowler, P.J. 1966. 'Romano-British Rural Settlements in Dorset and Wiltshire' in Thomas, C. (ed.) *Rural Settlement in Roman Britain*, 43–67

Bowman, A.K. 1994. *Life and Letters on the Roman Frontier*, London

Brailsford, J. 1955. *The Mildenhall Treasure: a Provisional Handbook*, 2nd ed., London

——. 1975a. *Early Celtic Masterpieces from London in the British Museum*, London

——. 1975b. 'The Polden Hill hoard, Somerset', *Proceedings of the Prehistoric Society*, 41, 222–34

Braithwaite, G. 1984. 'Romano-British face pots and head pots', *Britannia*, 15, 99–131

Branigan, K. 1976. *The Roman Villa in South-West England*, Bradford-on-Avon

—— & Miles, D. 1988. *The Economies of Romano-British Villas*, London

Breeze, D. 1982. *The Northern Frontiers of Roman Britain*, London

—— & Dobson, B. 1987. *Hadrian's Wall,* 3rd ed., Harmondsworth

Brenan, J. 1991. *Hanging bowls and their Contexts*, Oxford (BAR 220)

Brown, D. 1973. 'A Roman pewter hoard from Appleford, Oxon', *Oxoniensia*, XXXVIII, 184–206

——. 1981. 'Swastika Patterns', in Evison, V. (ed.) *Angles, Saxons and Jutes*, Oxford, 227–40

Brown, P.D.C. 1971. 'The Church at Richborough', *Britannia*, 2, 225–31

Bruce-Mitford, R.L.S. 1987. 'Ireland and the hanging bowls: a review', in Ryan, M. (ed.) *Ireland and Insular Art*, AD 500–1200, Dublin, 30–9

Brunaux, J.L. 1988. *The Celtic Gauls: Gods, Rites and Sanctuaries*, London

Burn, A.R. 1969. *The Romans in Britain*, Oxford

Burnham, B. & Wacher, J.S. 1990. *The Small Towns of Roman Britain*, London

Bushe-Fox, J.P. 1913. *Excavations of the Site of the Roman Town of Wroxeter, Shropshire*, Oxford (Soc. Ant. Lond. Res. Rep. 1)

——. 1914. *Second Report on the Excavations of the Site of the Roman Town of Wroxeter, Shropshire*, 1913, Oxford (Soc. Ant. Lond. Res. Rep. 2)

——. 1916. *Third Report on the Excavations of the Site of the Roman Town at Wroxeter, Shropshire*, 1914, Oxford (Soc. Ant. Lond. Res. Rep. 10)

Carson, R.A.G. & O'Kelly, C. 1977. 'A Catalogue of the Roman coins from Newgrange, Co. Meath, and notes on the coins and related finds', *Proc. Royal Irish Academy*, 77C, 35–55

Casey, J. 1977. 'Tradition and Innovation in the Coinage of Carausius and Allectus', in Munby & Henig (eds), *Roman Life and Art in Britain*, 217-30

——. 1980 *Roman Coinage in Britain*, Princes Risborough

—— & Reece, R. (eds). 1988. *Coins and the Archaeologist*, London

Charles-Edwards, T.M. 1972. 'Kingship, status and the origins of the Hide', *Past and Present*, 56, 3–33

Charleston, R.J. 1955. *Roman Pottery*, London

Charlesworth, D. 1961. 'Roman jewellery in Northumberland and Durham', *Archaeologia Aeliana*, 4th ser., 39, 1–36

——. 1973 'The Aesica Hoard', *Archaeologia Aeliana*, 5th ser., 1, 225–34

Clay, P. 1984. 'A cheek-piece from a cavalry helmet found in Leicester', *Britannia*, 15, 235–8

Cleary, A.S.E. 1989. *The Ending of Roman Britain*, London

Collingwood, R.G. & Myres, J.N.L. 1937. *Roman Britain and the English Settlements*, Oxford

Collingwood, R.G. & Richmond I.A. 1969. *The Archaeology of Roman Britain*, 2nd ed., London

Collingwood, R.G. & Wright, R.P. 1965. *The Roman Inscriptions of Britain, I Inscriptions on Stone*, Oxford

Collis, J. 1984. *Oppida: Earliest Towns North of the Alps*, Sheffield

Cookson, N.A. 1984. *Romano-British Mosaics. A reassessment and critique of some notable stylistic affinities*, Oxford (BAR 135)

Cool, H.E.M. 1979. 'A newly discovered inscription on a pair of silver bracelets from Castlethorpe, Buckinghamshire', *Britannia*, 10, 165–8

——. 1986. 'A Romano-British gold workshop of the second century', *Britannia*, 17, 231–7

——. 1990 'Roman metal hairpins from southern Britain', *Archaeological Journal* 147, 148–82.

Corcoran, J.X.W.P. 1952. 'Tankards and tankard handles of the British Iron Age', *Proceedings of the Prehistoric Society,* 18, 85–102

Coulston, J.C. & Phillips, E.J. 1988. *Corpus Signorum Imperii Romani Great Britain 1*, 6 Hadrian's Wall West of of the North Tyne and Carlisle, London

Cramp, R. 1970. 'Decorated window-glass and millefiori from Monkwearmouth', *Antiquaries Journal*, 50, 327–35

Crummy, P. 1980, in Rodwell, W. (ed.) *Temples, Churches and Religion: recent research in Roman Britain*, Oxford (BAR 77), 243–83

——. 1982. 'The Roman theatre at Colchester', *Britannia*, 13, 299–302

——. 1993. 'Aristocratic graves at Colchester', *Current Archaeology*, 132, 492–7

Cunliffe, B.W. 1968. *Fifth report on the Excavations of the Roman fort of Richborough, Kent*, London (Soc. Ant. Res. Rep. 23)

——. 1971a. *Excavations at Fishbourne*, 2 vols, London (Soc. Ant. Res. Rep. 26–7)

——. 1971b. *Fishbourne, a Roman Palace and its Garden*, London

——. 1978. 'Settlement and population in the British Iron Age, some facts, figures and fantasies', in Cunliffe, B. & Rowley, T. (eds), *Lowland Iron Age Communities in Europe*, Oxford, 3–24

——. 1984. *Roman Bath Discovered*, 2nd ed., London

——. 1988. *The Temple of Sulis Minerva at Bath; vol. 2: the finds from the sacred spring*, Oxford, Committee for Archaeology, Monograph 16

——. 1991. *Iron Age Communities of the British Isles*, London, 3rd ed.

—— & Davenport, P. 1985. *The Temple of Sulis Minerva at Bath; vol. I: the site*, Oxford

—— & Fulford, M. 1982. *Corpus Signorum Imperii Romani, Great Britain*, vols 1 and 2: Bath and the rest of Wessex, London

Curle, A.O. 1923. *The Treasure of Traprain. A Scottish hoard of Roman silver plate*, Glasgow

Curle, J. 1911. *A Roman frontier post and its people. The fort of Newstead in the parish of Melrose*, Glasgow

——. 1932. 'Inventory of Roman objects . . . not definitely associated with Roman constructions', *Proceedings of the Society of Antiquaries of Scotland*, LXVI, 277–397

Dark, K.R. 1994. *Civitas to Kingdom, British political continuity, 300–800*, Leicester

Davey, N. & Ling, R. 1981. Wall-paintings in Roman Britain, London (Soc. Promotion Roman Studies Monograph 3)

De Jersey, P. 1996. *Celtic Coinage in Britain*, Princes Risborough

Detsicas, A. 1983. *The Cantiaci*, Gloucester

Dickinson, T. 1983. 'Anglo-Saxon Archaeology: Twenty-Five Years On', in Hinton, D. (ed.) *25 Years of Medieval Archaeology*, Sheffield, 38–43

Dixon, P. 1994. *Crickley Hill: The Hillfort Defences*, Nottingham, 1994

Ellison, A. & Henig, M. 1981. 'Head of Mercury from Uley, Gloucestershire', *Antiquity*, LV, 43–4

Eriksen, R.T. 1980. 'Syncretic symbolism and the Christian Roman mosaic at Hinton St Mary: a closer reading', *Proc. Dorset Natural History & Archaeological Society*, CII, 43–8

Evans, A. 1896. 'On two fibulae of Celtic fabric from Aesica', *Archaeologia*, 55, 179–98

Evison, V. 1965. *Fifth Century Invasions South of the Thames*, London

Feachem, R. 1968. 'Dragonesque fibulae', *Antiquaries Journal*, 48, 100–3

Ferguson, J. 1970. *The Religions of the Roman Empire*, London

Foster, J. 1977. *Bronze Boar Figurines in Iron Age and Roman Britain*, Oxford (BAR 39)

——. 1986. *The Lexden Tumulus*, Oxford (BAR 156)

Fowler, E. 1960. 'The origins and development of the penannular brooch in Europe', *Proceedings Prehistoric Society*, 26, 149–77

——. 1963. 'Celtic Metalwork of the Fifth and Sixth Centuries AD', *Archaeological Journal*, CXX, 98–160

Fox, C. 1958. *Pattern and Purpose: Early Celtic Art in Britain*, Cardiff

Frere, S.S. 1970. 'A mould for a bronze statuette from Gestingthorpe', *Britannia*, 1, 266–7

——. 1971. *Verulamium Excavations*, I, Oxford

——. 1975a. 'Verulamium and the towns of Britannia', *Aufstieg und Niedergang der Romischen Welt*, II, 290–327

——. 1975b. 'The Silchester Church: the excavation by Sir I. Richmond in 1961', *Archaeologia*, 105, 277–302

——. 1982. 'The Bignor Villa', *Britannia*, 13, 135–95

——. 1983. *Verulamium Excavations II*, (Soc. Ant. Lond. Res. Rep. 41), London

——. 1987. *Britannia: a history of Roman Britain*, 3rd ed., London

Frey, O.-H. & Megaw, J.V.S. 1976. 'Palmette and Circle: Early Celtic Art in Britain and its Continental Background', *Proceedings Prehistoric Society*, 42, 47–65

Fulford, M. 1989. *The Silchester Amphitheatre excavations of 1979–85*, London (Britannia Monograph no. 10)

Gage, J. 1836. 'A letter from John Gage . . . communicating the recent discovery of Roman sepulchral relics in one of the greater barrows at Bartlow, in the parish of Ashdon, Essex', *Archaeologia*, 26, 2, 300–17

Gillam, J.P. 1958. 'Roman and Native, AD 122–197', in Richmond, I.A. (ed.) *Roman and Native in North Britain*, Edinburgh, 60–90

Goodburn, R. 1986. *The Roman Villa: Chedworth*, London

Goodchild, R.G. 1938. 'A priest's sceptre from the Romano-Celtic temple at Farley Heath, Surrey', *Antiquaries Journal*, XVIII (1938), 391–6

——. 1941. 'Romano-British disc brooches derived from Hadrianic coin types', *Antiquaries Journal*, 21, 1–8

——. 1947. 'The Farley heath sceptre binding', *Antiquaries Journal*, 18, 83–5

Gracie, H.S. 1970. 'Frocester Court Roman Villa; First Report', *Trans Bristol & Gloucester Antiquarian Society*, 88, 15–86.

—— & Price, E.G. 1979. 'Frocester Court Roman Villa: Second Report', *Trans Bristol & Gloucester Antiquarian Society*, 97, 9–64

Green, C.J.S. 1982. 'The cemetery of a Romano-British Christian community at Poundbury, Dorchester, Dorset', in Pearce, S.M. (ed.) *The Early Church in Western Britain and Ireland*, Oxford (BAR 102), 61–76

Green, M. 1983. *The Gods of Roman Britain*, Princes Risborough

——. 1986. *The Gods of the Celts*, Gloucester

Guido, M. 1978. *The Glass Beads of the Prehistoric and Roman Periods in Britain*, London (Soc. Ant. Lond. Res. Rep. 35)

Gurney, D. 1986. *Settlement, Religion and Industry on the Fen Edge. Three Romano-British sites in Norfolk*, Hunstanton

——. 1990. 'Archaeological finds in Norfolk in 1990', *Norfolk Archaeology*, XLI, 96–106.

Hanson, W.S. & Maxwell, G. 1983. *Rome's North-West Frontier*, London

Harris, E. & Harris, J. 1963. *The Oriental Cults of Roman Britain*, London

Hartley, B. 1960. *Notes on the Roman Pottery Industry in the Nene Valley*, Peterborough

Haselgrove, C.C. 1982. 'Indigenous settlement patterns in the Tyne-Tees Lowlands', in Clack, P. & Haselgrove, C. (eds) *Rural Settlement in the Roman North*, Durham, 57–103

——. 1993. 'The Development of British Iron-Age Coinage', *Numismatic Chronicle*, 153, 31–64

Haseloff, G. 1974. 'Salin's Style I', *Medieval Archaeology*, 18, 1–13.

Hattatt, R. 1985. *Iron Age and Romano-British Brooches*, Oxford

——. 1987. *Brooches of Antiquity*, Oxford

——. 1989. *Ancient Brooches and other Artefacts*, Oxford

Hawkes, C. & Hull, M.R. 1947. *Camulodunum, First Report on Excavations at Colchester*, London (Soc. Ant. Res. Rep. 14)

Hawkes, C.F.C. 1951. 'Bronze-workers, cauldrons and bucket animals in Iron Age and Roman Britain', in Grimes, W.F. (ed.) *Aspects of Archaeology in Britain and Beyond*, London, 172–99

Hawkes, S.C. 1961. 'Jutish Style A: a study of Germanic art in southern England in the fifth century AD', *Archaeologia*, 98, 29–74

—— & Dunning, G.C. 1961. 'Soldiers and settlers in Britain, fourth to fifth century', *Medieval Archaeology*, 5, 1–50

Hayward, L.C. 1972. 'The Roman villa at Lufton, near Yeovil, Somerset', *Proc Somerset Archaeological Society*, 116, 59–77.

Hedeager, L. 1987. 'Empire, frontier and the barbarian hinterland: Rome and northern Europe from AD 1–400', in Rowland, S.M. & Kristiansen, K. (eds), *Centre and Periphery in the Ancient World*, Cambridge, 125–40

Henig, M. 1974. *A Corpus of Roman Engraved Gem-stones from British Sites*, Oxford, 2nd ed. (BAR 8)

——. (ed.) 1983. *A Handbook of Roman Art*, Oxford

——. 1984. *Religion in Roman Britain*, London

——. 1985. 'Graeco-Roman art and Romano-British imagination', *Journal British Archaeological Association*, CXXXVIII, 1–22

——. 1993. *Corpus Signorum Imperii Romani Great Britain*, 1, 7 The Cotswold region with Devon and Cornwall, London

——. 1995. *The Art of Roman Britain*, London

—— & King, A.1986. *Pagan gods and shrines of the Roman Empire*, Oxford (Univ. Committee for Arch. Monograph 8)

Higgins, R. 1976. 'Jewellery' in Strong & Brown (eds), 53–62

Higgitt, J.C. 1973. 'The Roman Background to medieval England', *Journal British Archaeological Association*, 3rd ser., XXVI, 1–15

Higham, N. 1992. *Rome, Britain and the Anglo-Saxons*, London

Hill, C., Millett, M. & Blagg, T. 1980. *The Roman Riverside Wall and Monumental Arch in London, Excavations at Baynard's Castle, Upper Thames Street, London, 1874–76*, London (LAMAS Special Paper 3)

Hingley, R. 1989. *Rural Settlement in Roman Britain*, London

Hogg, A.H.A.1966. 'Native Settlement in Wales' in Thomas, C. (ed.), 28–38

Hopkins, K. 1978. *Conquerors and Slaves*, Cambridge

Horsley, J. 1733. *Britannia Romana or the Roman Antiquities of Britain*, London (reprint 1975)

Howe, M.D., Perrin, J.R. & Mackreth, D.F. 1980. *Roman Pottery from the Nene Valley: a Guide*, Peterborough

Hull, M.R. 1963. *The Roman Potters' Kilns at Colchester*, London (Soc. Ant. Res. Rep.)

Hurst, H.R.1972. 'Excavations at Gloucester 1968–71', *Antiquaries Journal*, 52, 24–69

Hutchinson, V. 1986. *Bacchus in Roman Britain, the evidence for his cult*, Oxford (BAR 151)

Ireland, S. 1986. *Roman Britain. A Sourcebook*, London

Irwin, D. (ed.) 1972. *Winckelmann: Writings on Art*, London

Jackson, R. 1984. 'A Roman stamped shield boss from London', *Britannia*, 15, 246–50

——. 1989. 'A bronze mould from Dolland's Moor, Newington-next-Hythe, Kent', *Antiquaries Journal*, 69, 327–9

Jenkins, F. 1958. 'The Cult of the "Pseudo-Venus" in Kent' *Archaeologia Cantiana*, 72, 60–76

Johns, C. 1977. *Arretine and Samian Pottery*, London

——. 1986. 'The Roman silver cups from Hockwold, Norfolk,' *Archaeologia*, 108, 1–13

——. 1996. *The Jewellery of Roman Britain*, London

—— & Carson, R.A.G. 'The Waternewton Hoard', *Durobrivae, A Review of Nene Valley Archaeology*, 3, 10–12

—— & Potter, T.W. 1983. *The Thetford Treasure*, London

——. 1991. 'The "rediscovery" of the Risley Park Roman Lanx', *Minerva*, ii, no. 6, 6–13

Johnson, D. 1977. 'The Central Southern Group of Romano-British Mosaics', in Munby, J. & Henig, M. 195–215

Johnson, P. 1995. *Romano-British Mosaics*, 2nd ed., Princes Risborough

—— (ed.) 1996. *Architecture in Roman Britain*, London (CBA Res. Rep. 94)

Johnson, S. 1976. *The Roman Forts of the Saxon Shore*, London

——. 1979. *Later Roman Britain*, London

——. 1980. *Later Roman Britain*, London

——. 1983. *Late Roman Fortification*, London

Johnston, D.E. 1972. 'A Roman building at Chalk, near Gravesend', *Britannia*, 3, 112–48.

——. 1983. *Roman Villas*, Princes Risborough

Jones, M. 1996. 'Rebellion Remains the Decisive Factor', *British Archaeology* 20 (Dec.), 8–9

Keevill, G.D. 1996. 'The reconstruction of the Romano-British villa at Redlands Farm, Northamptonshire', in Johnson, P. (ed.) 44–55

Kendrick, T.D. 1932. 'British Hanging Bowls', *Antiquity*, VI, 161–84

——. 1936. *Anglo-Saxon Art to AD 800*, London

——. 1950. *British Antiquity*, London

Kennett, D.H. 1968. 'The Irchester Bowls', *Journal of the Northampton Museum & Art Gallery*, 4, 5–39

Kent, J.P.C. 1961. 'From Roman Britain to Saxon England', in Dolley, M. (ed.) *Anglo-Saxon Coins*, London, 1–22.

——. 1979. 'The End of Roman Britain, the literary and numismatic evidence reviewed', in Casey, P.J. (ed.), *The End of Roman Britain*, Oxford (BAR 71), 15–27

—— & Painter, K.S. 1977. *Wealth of the Roman World, AD 300–700*, London

Kenyon, K.M. 1934. 'The Roman theatre at Verulamium', *Archaeologia*, 84, 213–61

Kilbride-Jones, H.E. 1980. *Celtic Craftsmanship in Bronze*, London

——. 1980. *Zoomorphic Penannular Brooches*, London (Soc. Ant. Lond. Res. Rep. 39)

King, A. 1983. 'The Roman church at Silchester reconsidered', *Oxford Journal of Archaeology*, 2, 225–37

——. 1996. 'The south-east facade of Meonstoke aisled building', in Johnson, P. (ed.), 56–69

Kitzinger, E. 1977. *Byzantine Art in the Making*, London

Laing, L. 1969. *Coins and Archaeology*, London

——. 1990. 'The Beginnings of "Dark Age" Celtic art', in Bammesberger, A. & Wollmann, A. (eds) *Britain 400–600: Language and History*, Heidelberg, 37–50

——. 1993. 'A Catalogue of Celtic Ornamental Metalwork in the British Isles, *c.* AD 400–1200', *Nottingham Monographs in Archaeology*, 5, Oxford

——. 1996 'The Hoard of Pictish Silver from Norrie's Law, Fife', *Studia Celtica*, XXVIII, 11–38

—— & Laing, J. 1990. *Celtic Britain and Ireland, AD 200–800*, Dublin

——. 1992. *Art of the Celts*, London

——. 1993. *Ancient Art*, Dublin

——. 1995. *Britain's European Heritage*, Stroud

——. 1995b *The Picts and the Scots*, rev. ed. Stroud

——. 1995c *Celtic Britain and Ireland: Art and Society*, London

——. 1996 *Early English Art and Architecture*, Stroud

Lamm, K. 1978. 'Early Medieval metalworking on Helgö in Central Sweden' in Oddy, W.A. (ed.), *Aspects of Early Metallurgy*, London, 97–116

Laver, P.G. 1927. 'The Excavation of a Tumulus at Lexden, Colchester', *Archaeologia*, 76, 241–54

Lawson, A.K. 1986. 'A fragment of a life-size bronze equine statuary from Ashill, Norfolk', *Britannia*, 18, 333–9

Leech, R. 1982. *Excavations at Catsgore 1970–1973: a Romano-British Village*, Bristol

Lepmann, W. 1970. *Winckelmann*, London

Lewis, M.J.T. 1965. *Temples in Roman Britain*, Cambridge

Lindgren, C. 1980. *Classical Art Forms and Celtic Mutations. Figural Art in Roman Britain*, Park Ridge, NJ

Ling, R. 1983. 'The Seasons in Romano-British mosaic pavements', *Britannia*, 14, 13–22

——. 1985. *Romano-British Wall Painting*, Princes Risborough

——. 1991a. *Roman Painting*, Cambridge

——. 1991b. 'Brading, Brantingham and York. A new look at some fourth-century mosaics', *Britannia*, 22, 147–57

Liversidge, J. 1955. *Furniture in Roman Britain*, London

——. 1969. 'Furniture and Interior Decoration', in Rivet (ed.), 127–72

——. 1974. *Britain in the Roman Empire*, London

Lloyd-Morgan, G. 1976. 'A note on some Celtic discs from Ireland and the province of Lower Germany', *Proc. Royal Irish Academy* 76C, 217–22.

MacCormick, S.G. 1981. *Art and Ceremony in Late Antiquity*, Berkeley & Los Angeles

Macdonald, G. 1905. *Coin Types, their Origin and Development*, Glasgow

——. 1934. *The Roman Wall in Scotland*, Oxford

Macgregor, M. 1962. 'The Early Iron Age metalwork from Stanwick, N.R. Yorks. England', *Proc. Prehist. Soc. 28*, 17–57

——. 1976. *Early Celtic Art in North Britain*, Leicester

Mackreth, D. 1978. 'Orton Hall Farm, Peterborough: a Roman and Saxon Settlement', in Todd, M. (ed.) *Studies in the Romano-British Villa*, Leicester, 209–28.

Marsden, P. 1975. 'The excavation of the Roman palace site in London, 1961–1972', *Trans. London & Middlesex Archaeological Society*, XXVI, 1–102

Marsh, G. 1979. 'Three theatre masks from London', *Britannia*, 10, 263

Mason, D.J.P. 1986. 'An elliptical peristyle building in the fortress of Deva', in Johnson, D. (ed.), 77–92

Maxwell, G.S. 1989. *The Romans in Scotland*, London

Maxwell, V.A. 1989. *The Saxon Shore*, London

May, J. 1996. *Dragonby, Report on Excavations at an Iron Age and Romano-British Settlement in North Lincolnshire*, Oxford (Oxbow Monographs 61)

May, T. 1904. *Warrington's Roman Remains*, Warrington

——. 1909. *The Roman Pottery in the York Museum*, York

Meadows, I. 1996. 'Wollaston: The Nene Valley, a British Moselle?', *Current Archaeology*, 150, 212–15

Meates, G.W. 1955. *Lullingstone Roman Villa*, London

—— (ed.) 1987. *The Roman Villa at Lullingstone, II, the Wall Paintings and Finds*, Maidstone

Megaw, J.V.S. 1970. *The Elusive Image: Art of the European Iron Age*, Bath

Megaw, R. & Megaw, J.V.S. 1986. *Early Celtic Art in Britain and Ireland*, Princes Risborough

Merrifield, R. & Megaw, J.V.S. 1969. 'The Dowgate Plaque. A Bronze Mount of the British Iron Age from the City of London', *Archaeological Journal*, 126, 154–9

Miles, D. (ed.) 1986. *Archaeology at Barton Court Farm, Abingdon, Oxon*, London

—— & Palmer, S. 1983. 'Claydon Pike', *Current Archaeology*, 86, 88–92

Millett, M. 1977. 'Art in the "Small Towns", "Celtic" or "Classical"', in Munby & Henig (eds), 283–96

——. 1990. *Romanization of Britain*, Oxford

——. 1995. *Roman Britain*, London

—— & Graham, D. 1986. *Excavations on the Romano-British small town of Neatham, Hampshire, 1969–79*, Gloucester

Munby J. 1977. 'Art, Archaeology and Antiquaries', in Munby & Henig (eds), 415–36

—— & Henig, M. (eds) 1977. *Roman Life and Art in Britain*, Oxford (BAR 41)

Mynard, D.C. (ed.) 1987. *Roman Milton Keynes: excavations and fieldwork 1971–82*, Aylesbury (Bucks. Arch. Soc. Monographs 1)

Myres, J.N.L. 1969. *Anglo-Saxon Pottery and the Settlement of England*, Oxford

——. 1986. *The English Settlements*, Oxford

Neal, D. 1976. 'Floor Mosaics', in Strong, D. & Brown, D. (eds), *Roman Crafts*, London, 241–52

——. 1981. *Roman Mosaics in Britain: an Introduction to their Schemes and a Catalogue of Paintings*, London (Britannia monograph no. 1)

Neal, D.S. 1996. 'Upper Storeys in Romano-British villas', in Johnson, P. (ed.), 33–43

——, Wardle, A. & Hunn, J. 1990. *Excavations on the Iron Age, Roman and Medieval Settlement at Gorhambury, St Albans*, London

Niblett, R. 1993. 'A Royal Burial at St Albans', *Current Archaeology*, 132, 484–8

Oddy, W.A. 1979. 'Gilding and tinning in Anglo-Saxon England', in Oddy, W.A. (ed.) *Aspects of Early Metallurgy*, London, 129–34

O'Neil, H.E. 1945. 'The Roman villa at Park Street, near St Albans, Hertfordshire' *Archaeological Journal*, 102, 21–110

Oswald, F. 1920. *Index of Figure Types on Samian Ware*, London

Painter K.S. 1966. 'The design of the Roman mosaic pavement at Hinton St Mary', *Antiquaries Journal*, 56, 49–54

——. 1970. 'A Roman bronze helmet from Hawkedon', *Proc. Suffolk Institute Archaeology*, 31, Pt.1, 57–63

——. 1977a. *The Mildenhall Treasure, Roman silver from East Anglia*, London

——. 1977b. *The Water Newton Early Christian Silver*, London

Perring, D. 1977. 'Aspects of Art in Romano-British Pottery', in Munby & Henig (eds), 253–82

—— & Roskans, S.P. 1991. *The Archaeology of Roman London, 2: Early Development of Roman London East of the Walbrook*, London

Phillips, C.W. (ed.) 1970. *The Fenland in Roman Times*, London (Royal Geog. Soc. Memoir)

Phillips, E.J. 1975. 'The gravestone of M Favonius Facilis at Colchester', *Britannia*, 6, 102–5

——. 1977a. *Corpus Signorum Imperii Romani Great Britain*, 1, 1 Corbridge. Hadrian's Wall east of the North Tyne, London

——. 1977b. 'The Classical Tradition in the Popular Sculpture of Roman Britain', in Munby & Henig (eds), 35–50

Philp, B. 1981. *The Excavation of the Roman forts of the Classis Britannica at Dover, 1970–1977*, Dover (Kent Monograph Series 3)

——. 1989. *The Roman House with Bacchic Murals at Dover*, Dover (Kent Monograph Series, 5)

Picard, G. 1970. *Roman Painting*, London

Piggott, S. 1968. *The Druids*, London

——. 1971. 'Firedogs in Iron Age Britain and Beyond', in Boardman, J., Brown, M.A. & Powell, T.G.E. (eds) *The European Community on Later Prehistory*, London, 243–70.

——. 1976. *Ruins in a Landscape. Essays in Antiquarianism*, Edinburgh

——. 1985. *William Stukeley, an Eighteenth-Century Antiquary*, London

Pollard S. 1974. 'A late Iron Age and a Romano-British villa at Holcombe, near Uplyme, Devon', *Proc. Devon Arch. Soc.*, 32, 59–161

Potter, T. 1986. 'A Roman jeweller's hoard from Snettisham, Norfolk,' *Antiquity*, LX, 137–9

Potter, T.W. 1989. 'The Roman fenland, a review of recent work', in Todd, M. (ed.) *Research on Roman Britain, 1960–89*, London, 147–76

—— & Johns, C. 1992. *Roman Britain*, London

—— & Trow, S. 1988. *Puckeridge-Braughing, Hertfordshire. The Ermine Street excavations, 1971–2* (Hertfordshire Archaeology 10)

Pratt, T.P. 1976. 'Wall Painting', in Strong, D. & Brown, D. (eds) *Roman Crafts*, London, 223–30

Raftery, B. 1970. 'A Decorated Strap End from Rathgall, Co. Wicklow', *Journal Royal Society Antiquaries Ireland*, 100, 200–11

——. 1984. *La Tène in Ireland*, Marburg

Rahtz, P., *et al.* 1992. *Cadbury Congresbury 1968–73, a late/post-Roman hilltop settlement in Somerset*, Oxford (BAR 223)

Randall, H.J. 1933. 'Splendide Mendax', *Antiquity* vii, 49–60

RCHM (Royal Commission for Historic Monuments). 1962. *Eburacum*, York

Read, C.H. 1898. 'List of pewter dishes and vessels found at Appleshaw and now in the British Museum', *Archaeologia*, LVI, 7–12

Reece, R. 1987. *Coinage in Roman Britain*, London

Rhodes, M. 1990. 'Faussett Rediscovered: Charles Roach Smith, Joseph Mayer, and the Publication of Inventorium Sepulchrale', in Southworth, E. (ed.) *Anglo-Saxon Cemeteries: A Reappraisal*, Stroud, 25–64

RIB (Roman Inscriptions of Britain), see Collingwood & Wright, 1965

Richmond, I.A. 1944. 'Three fragments of Roman official statues', *Antiquaries Journal*, XXIV, 1–8

—— & Gillam, J.P. 1951. *The Temple of Mithras at Carrawburgh*, Newcastle

Rivet, A.L.F. 1958. *Town and Country in Roman Britain*, London

—— (ed.) 1969. *The Roman Villa in Britain*, London

Rodwell, W.J. & Rodwell, K.A. 1986. *Rivenhall: Investigations of a villa, church and village, 1950–1977*, London (CBA Res. Rep. 55)

Rokewood, ?. 1842. 'Silver dish and other vessels found in Suffolk', *Archaeologia* XXIX, 389–90

Ross, A. 1974. *Pagan Celtic Britain*, 2nd edn, London

——. 1968. 'Shafts, Pits, Wells – Sanctuaries of the Belgic Britons?' in Coles, J.M. & Simpson, D.D.A. (eds) *Studies in Ancient Europe*, Leicester, 255–85

Salway, P. 1981. *Roman Britain*, Oxford

Selkirk, A. 1981. 'Stonea', *Current Archaeology*, 81, 298–301

Sherlock, D. 1976. 'Silver and silversmithing', in Strong, D. & Brown, D. (eds) *Roman Crafts*, London, 11–24

Simpson, F.G. & Richmond, I.A. 1941. 'The Roman fort at on Hadrian's Wall at Benwell', *Archaeologia Aeliana*, 4th ser., 19, 37–43

Simpson, M. 1968. 'Massive Armlets in the North British Iron Age', in Coles, J. & Simpson, D.D.A. (eds) *Studies in Ancient Europe*, Leicester, 233–54

Smith, C.R. 1840. 'On some Roman bronzes discovered in the bed of the Thames in January, 1837, Communicated by Charles Roach Smith', *Archaeologia* 28,1 38–46

Smith, D.J. 1969. 'The Mosaic Pavements', in Rivet, A.L.F. (ed.), 71–126

——. 1977. 'Mythological figures and Scenes in Romano-British Mosaics', in Munby & Henig (eds), 105–94

Smith, J.T. 1978. 'Villas as a key to social structure' in Todd, M. (ed.) 1978, 149–86

Smith, R.A. 1907. 'On Late-Celtic Antiquities discovered at Welwyn, Herts', *Archaeologia* LXIII (1911–12), 1–30

Spratling, M. 1970. 'Bronze shield mount', in Alcock, L. 'Excavations at South Cadbury Castle, 1969: A Summary Report', *Antiquaries Journal*, 50, 21–2

Stead, I.M. 1967. 'A La Tène III burial at Welwyn Garden City', *Archaeologia*, 101, 1–62

——. 1975 'A Roman pottery theatrical face-mask and a bronze brooch blank from Baldock, Herts,' *Antiquaries Journal*, 55, 397–8

——. 1985a. *The Battersea Shield*, London

——. 1985b. *Celtic Art*, London

——. 1991. 'The Snettisham Treasure: excavations in 1990', *Antiquity*, LXV, 447–65

—— & Rigby, V. 1986. *Baldock: the excavation of a Roman and pre-Roman settlement*, London

——. & Turner, R. 1985. 'Lindow Man', *Antiquity*, LIX, 25–9

Stevens, C.E. 1966. 'Social and economic aspects of rural settlement', in Thomas, A.C. (ed.) *Rural Settlement in Roman Britain*, 108–28

Stevenson, R.B.K. 1954-6. 'Native bangles and Roman glass', *Proc. Society Antiquaries Scotland*, LXXXVIII, 208–21

Strickland, T.J. 1996. 'Recent Research at the Chester legionary fortress: the curtain wall and the barrack veranda colonnades', in Johnson, D. (ed.) *Architecture in Roman Britain*, 104–19

Strong, D.E. 1966. *Greek and Roman Silver Plate*, London

Strong, D. 1982. *Roman Art*, Harmondsworth

—— & Brown, D. (eds) 1976. *Roman Crafts*, London

Stryzygowski, J. 1923. *The Origins of Christian Church Art*, Oxford

Stupperich, R. 1980. 'A reconsideration of some fourth-century British mosaics', *Britannia*, 11, 289–301

Sutherland, C.H.V. 1937. *Coinage and Currency in Roman Britain*, Oxford

Swan, V. 1980. *Pottery in Roman Britain*, Aylesbury

Taylor, C. 1983. *The Archaeology of Gardens*, Princes Risborough

Taylor, C.C. 1984. *Village to Farmstead*, London

Taylor, H.M. & Taylor, J. 1965. *Anglo-Saxon Architecture*, 2 vols, Cambridge

Thomas, A.C. (ed.) 1966. *Rural Settlement in Roman Britain*, London

——. 1981. *Christianity in Roman Britain to AD 500*, London

Thompson, F.H. 1965. *Roman Cheshire*, Chester

Todd, M. 1967. 'Romano-British Mintages of Antoninus Pius', *Numismatic Chronicle*, 7th ser., VI, 147–53

—— (ed.) 1978. *Studies in the Romano-British Villa*, London

Toynbee, J.M.C. 1962. *Art in Roman Britain*, London

——. 1964a. *Art in Britain under the Romans*, Oxford

——. 1964b. 'A new Roman mosaic pavement found in Dorset', *Journal Roman Studies*, LIV, 7–14

——. 1986. *The Roman Art Treasures from the Temple of Mithras*, London (London & Middlesex Arch. Soc. Special Paper no. 7)

—— & Painter, K.S. 1986. 'Silver picture plates of late Antiquity', *Archaeologia*, CVIII, 15–65

—— & Wilkins, A. 1982. 'The Vindolanda horse', *Britannia*, 13, 245–51

Tufi, S.R. 1983. *Corpus Signorum Imperii Romani Great Britain*, 1, 3 Yorkshire, London

Van Arsdell, R.D. 1989. *Celtic Coinage of Britain*, London

Vermaseren, M.J. 1963. *Mithras, the Secret God*, London

Wacher, J.S. (ed.) 1966. *The Civitas Capitals of Roman Britain*, Leicester

——. 1966. 'Earthwork defences of the second century', in Wacher (ed.), 60–9

——. 1978. *Roman Britain*, London

——. 1995. *The Towns of Roman Britain*, 2nd ed., London

Walters, B. 1981. 'Littlecote', *Current Archaeology*, 80, 264–8

——. 1986. 'Exotic Structures in 4th-century Britain', in Johnson, D. (ed.) *Architecture in Roman Britain*, London, 152–62

Ward-Perkins, J.B. 1938. 'The Roman villa at Lockleys, Welwyn', *Antiquaries Journal*, 18, 339–76.

Warner, R. 1979. 'The Clogher Yellow Layer', *Medieval Ceramics*, 3, 37–40

——. 1996. 'Yes, the Romans did Invade Ireland', *British Archaeology*, 14 (May), 6–7

Watts, D. 1991. *Christians and Pagans in Roman Britain*, London

Webster, G. 1965. *The Roman Conquest of Britain*, London

——. 1986. *Celtic Religion in Roman Britain*, Totowa, N J.

——. 1989. 'Deities and religious scenes on Romano-British pottery', *Journal of Roman Pottery Studies*, ii, 1–28

——. 1991. 'Romano-British scenes and figures on pottery', in Webster, G. *Archaeologist at Large*, London, 129–62

Webster, L. & Backhouse, J. 1991. *The Making of England, Anglo-Saxon Art and Culture AD 600–900*, London

Wedlake, W. 1982. *The Excavation of the Shrine of Apollo at Nettleton, Wiltshire, 1956–1971*, London (Soc. Ant. Lond. Res. Rep. 40)

Welch, M. 1992. *Anglo-Saxon England*, London

West, S. 1976. 'The Roman site at Icklingham', *East Anglian Archaeology*, 3, 63–126

Wheeler, R.E.M. 1956. *Rome Beyond the Imperial Frontiers*, Harmondsworth

—— & Wheeler, T.V. 1932. *Report on the Excavation of the Prehistoric, Roman and post-Roman site in Lydney Park, Gloucestershire*, London (Soc. Ant. Lond. Res. Rep. 9)

Wiedemann, T. 1992. *Emperors and Gladiators*, London

Wild, J.P. 1970. 'Button-and-loop fasteners in the Roman provinces', *Britannia*, 1, 137–55

Wilson, D.M. 1973. 'The Treasure', in Small, A., Thomas, C. & Wilson, D., *St Ninian's Isle and its Treasure*, Oxford, 45–148

Wilson, R. 1975. *Guide to the Roman Remains in Britain*, London

Woodward, A. & Leach, P. 1992. *The Uley Shrines. Excavation of a ritual complex on West Hill, Uley, Gloucestershire, 1977–9*, London

Wright, R.P. 1872. *Uriconium*, London

Yorke, B. 1990. *Kings and Kingdoms of Anglo-Saxon England*, London

Zanker, P. 1990. *The Power of Images in the Age of Augustus*, Ann Arbor

INDEX

Page numbers in italics refer to illustrations